THE GUITARIST'S GUIDE TO SONAR™

Craig Anderton

Course Technology PTR
A part of Cengage Learning

COURSE TECHNOLOGY
CENGAGE Learning®

Australia, Brazil, Japan, Korea, Mexico, Singapore, Spain, United Kingdom, United States

COURSE TECHNOLOGY
CENGAGE Learning®

The Guitarist's Guide to SONAR™
Craig Anderton

Publisher and General Manager,
Course Technology PTR:
Stacy L. Hiquet

Associate Director of Marketing:
Sarah Panella

Manager of Editorial Services:
Heather Talbot

Marketing Manager:
Mark Hughes

Acquisitions Editor:
Orren Merton

Project and Copy Editor:
Catheen D. Small

Interior Layout:
Shawn Morningstar

Cover Designer:
Mike Tanamachi

Indexer:
Kelly Talbot Editing Services

Proofreader:
Kelly Talbot Editing Services

For product information and technology assistance, contact us at
Cengage Learning Customer & Sales Support, 1-800-354-9706

For permission to use material from this text or product,
submit all requests online at **cengage.com/permissions**
Further permissions questions can be emailed to
permissionrequest@cengage.com

SONAR is a trademark of Cakewalk, Inc. All other trademarks are the property of their respective owners.

All images © Cengage Learning unless otherwise noted.

Library of Congress Control Number: 2011926535

ISBN-13: 978-1-4354-5768-3

ISBN-10: 1-4354-5768-4

Course Technology, a part of Cengage Learning
20 Channel Center Street
Boston, MA 02210
USA
Cengage Learning is a leading provider of customized learning solutions with office locations around the globe, including Singapore, the United Kingdom, Australia, Mexico, Brazil, and Japan. Locate your local office at:
international.cengage.com/region

Cengage Learning products are represented in Canada by Nelson Education, Ltd.

For your lifelong learning solutions, visit **courseptr.com.**

Visit our corporate Web site at **cengage.com.**

Printed in the United States of America
1 2 3 4 5 6 7 13 12 11

This book is dedicated to the engineers who create music software. They're the first to get blamed if there's a bug and the last to get props when people record some great piece of music using the tools they create— but their dedication and smarts have made it possible for more musicians than ever to enjoy the art of recording.

Acknowledgments

I'd like to thank . . .

Orren Merton at Course Technology PTR, who thought the world needed a series of books dedicated to helping guitar players get the most out of computer-based recording and who thought I was the guy to write them. Next stop: *The Guitarist's Guide to Pro Tools.*

Cathleen Small, the editor for this book. She's not only extraordinarily competent at what she does (sadly, she has no plans to run for president), but she makes sure the publication process runs as smoothly as possible—not an easy task.

Steve Thomas of Cakewalk. Despite having a zillion things to do at any given moment, he took a personal interest in this project and made sure I had what was needed to make this book a reality.

About the Author

Craig Anderton is an internationally recognized author, musician, and lecturer. He has played on, produced, or engineered more than 20 major-label releases, mastered more than a hundred tracks, and written more than 20 books, as well as given seminars on technology and the arts in 38 states, 10 countries, and 3 languages. In addition to maintaining an active musical career, he is currently editor-in-chief of www.harmonycentral.com and executive editor of *Electronic Musician* magazine.

Contents

Part II
Using and Managing Effects   45

Part III
Recording Techniques 99

Chapter 24 SONAR's Miscellaneous FX   189

Part V
MIDI and Guitar   195

Chapter 25 Guitar Tablature with SONAR   197

Chapter 26 MIDI Guitar with SONAR   201

Chapter 27 The "Virtual" MIDI Guitar   209

Part VI
Advanced Techniques
213

Introduction

WHEN COMPUTER-BASED MIDI SEQUENCING PROGRAMS first appeared, they were aimed squarely at keyboard players. Audio generated too much data, and MIDI's compact data format was a good match for the computer equivalents of the Model T.

Over time, computers became faster, and storage systems delivered higher capacity at lower cost, but only in the past few years have computers provided a truly affordable recording solution for guitar players. Part of this is because computers simply weren't fast enough to let you play guitar through a computer running plug-in effects, unless you were willing to put up with distracting delays. And while amp simulation software has been around for a while, the art of accurate simulation—which also benefits from faster computers—has improved dramatically in the past few years.

So the time is right to talk about computer-based recording and processing from a guitar player's standpoint. This book covers some of the considerations unique to recording guitar with any computer-based system and then progresses into guitar-specific techniques for Cakewalk SONAR. Although based around SONAR X1 Producer, much of the material applies to SONAR X1 Studio, as well as pre-X1 versions, such as SONAR 8.5.

The first eight chapters are designed to flow in order, but after that, the book is more about a collection of tools and tips that you can dip into as needed. Are you having problems nailing a solo? Then check out Chapter 15, "Perfect Takes with Composite Recording." Miss the sound of that ancient phase shifter you sold on eBay? Then read Chapter 30, "How to Emulate Vintage Effects." Not happy with the sound of amp sims? There are plenty of ways to sweeten their sound, as described in Chapter 13, "How to Improve Amp Sim Tone." Think of this book as a reference that can help you solve problems, but also, there's a lot of material intended to inspire you to try new and different techniques and get your creative juices flowing.

But always keep in mind that music is about expression, not technological sophistication. Make music that's as unique as your fingerprint and be true to yourself. You have your own contribution to make, so make it!

I've said it before, and I'll say it again: No one cares what guitar you play, what software you use, or your favorite brand of computer; no one cares whether your song was recorded in two hours or two years. *All that matters is the emotional impact of the music itself.*

Happy recording, and I hope this book helps bring you that much closer to realizing your musical dreams.

—Craig Anderton

Part I

Setting Up Your SONAR System

Recording with a Computer

THE GUITAR IS A WONDERFUL INSTRUMENT, with the versatility to move effortlessly from classical Bach pieces to heavy metal—and anything in between. So perhaps it's not surprising that combining computers and guitars is a match made in heaven, as computers can perform so many different types of tasks.

Whether you want to tune up your guitar, record it, create a virtual pedalboard for live performance, extend an existing amplifier setup, or create entirely new tones, the computer is the gateway to all of these options. What's more, thanks to advances in technology, today's computers can handle the data-intensive, timing-critical tasks demanded by the music-making process.

The SONAR family of products differs in several ways, but they all have one thing in common: They need to run on a computer (and the more powerful the computer, the better). Although there are plenty of ways to record, from portable solid-state recorders to stand-alone, self-contained recording studios, computer-based recording offers several advantages compared to traditional recording methods.

Advantages of Computer-Based Recording

The advantages to computer-based recording are many.

▷ **Low cost.** If you already have a computer, SONAR software is relatively inexpensive. Even if you don't have a suitable computer, buying a new system is less expensive—even without adjusting for inflation—than the four-track tape recorders that were popular back in the '70s.

▷ **High quality.** The audio interfaces that translate "outside world" audio into a data stream the computer can understand have benefited from advances in technology and offer extremely high quality. Even budget models can produce professional results.

▷ **Perfect backups.** The data on hard drives can be "cloned" to another hard drive, creating an identical backup copy.

▷ **Easy expandability.** You can upgrade computers over their useful life (more memory, various peripherals, a better audio interface, and so on) to increase the speed, quality, or ease of use.

▷ **No theoretical limit to the number of tracks.** Today's computers can easily handle dozens (if not hundreds) of tracks and are limited only by the limitations of current technology—which aren't very limiting!

▷ **Editing.** Whether you want to delete just one bad note or swap an entire verse with another, it's easy with computer-based editing. You can even alter timing: If a solo was perfect except that the first note came in a bit late, no problem—just slide it a little bit early.

▷ **Reliability.** No mechanical device is perfect, but overall, today's computers are workhorses that frequently go for years without any serious hiccups.

▷ **Software updates.** Software is often updated for free or for a nominal cost to increase functionality, reliability, or (more likely) both.

▷ **Small size.** A computer-based recording studio can fit easily in a corner of a bedroom or almost anywhere you have space. And, using amp simulation software means you can get the sound of a stack of amps cranked to 10, but at levels that won't cause the neighbors to call the police.

▷ **Easy collaboration with other SONAR users.** It's not a big deal to send files back and forth via email or by using "cloud" storage—or, for really big projects, by sending CD- or DVD-ROMs to a songwriting partner. In some cases, you can even collaborate with musicians who don't use SONAR by saving your files in a more universal format.

Disadvantages of Computer-Based Recording

And to be fair, let's also cover the disadvantages.

▷ **Software can be temperamental.** Software bugs, operating system upgrades, and occasional hardware problems can bring a project to a screeching halt. Many musicians buy a separate computer and dedicate it to recording, because the more "stuff" you have on your computer, the greater the odds that some pieces of software won't get along with each other. One word of warning: Don't use "cracked" software.

It's not just that stealing is wrong, but "warez" sites can contain spyware and viruses, and because the cracks are by definition modified from legitimate copies, they can wreak havoc on your computer.

▷ **You'll need to do maintenance.** Those who grew up on tape were thrilled by the idea of a recording medium that wouldn't need maintenance—but computers do indeed need maintenance. Companies are constantly updating their software, offering security patches for Internet browsers, altering operating systems, and the like; operating system updates can sometimes "break" a piece of software until that software is updated to work under the new system. Most importantly, you need to maintain good backups of your data. If all your precious music is stored on a hard drive, and that hard drive fails, recovering that data will be a long and expensive process—assuming that it can be recovered at all.

▷ **Potential for obsolescence.** Technology changes rapidly, and sometimes you'll find that an older computer just won't work in the real world any more. For example, when Apple changed from one microprocessor technology to another (Motorola PowerPC to Intel), their operating system updates continued to support both families up to a certain point, after which the PowerPC was no longer supported.

▷ **You need a relatively powerful computer.** Audio is a demanding application that stresses out a computer much more than surfing the Internet, using a word processor, or running spreadsheets. Fortunately, even relatively inexpensive desktop and laptop computers are up to the task. Basically, you want a system with at least a dual-core processor, a couple gigabytes of RAM, and fast internal hardware that's at least 500 GB. (Audio files take up a significant amount of space.)

Mac versus PC

With SONAR, this seems like a non-issue because SONAR is written for Windows. However, it's also possible to run Windows software on Intel-based Macs using Apple's Boot Camp option, where the computer boots up as a Windows machine. Although almost all SONAR users use Windows, several people have reported excellent results using Boot Camp.

As to whether Macs or PCs are better, Mac owners will tell you the Mac is superior, while PC owners will tell you the PC is superior. I use both, and they both have advantages and disadvantages; but really, they have more commonalities than differences. As mentioned earlier, a lot of musicians dedicate a computer to recording, so if you're a Mac fan, consider getting a PC for music—the price is right, and you'll have a flexible setup that can run almost anything.

As for laptops, Windows laptops are easier to replace or repair on the road, but Macs are easier to configure for audio. I've used both, but if you go for Windows, seek out a company that specializes in integrating laptops for audio. It's well worth a few extra bucks.

32-bit versus 64-bit Windows

Since Windows XP, Microsoft has offered both 32-bit and 64-bit versions of their operating systems. The XP version was iffy, Vista-64 was a step up, but with Windows 7, the 64-bit operating system has truly come of age. SONAR is available for both 32-bit and 64-bit versions, so you'll need to make a choice.

A 64-bit operating system is somewhat faster, as it can process data faster. But, that's far less important to musicians than the fact that it can address huge amounts of RAM. A 32-bit system is limited to about 3.5 GB of RAM, but there are already some virtual instruments that require 6 GB of RAM to run properly—so the handwriting is on the wall.

If you're looking toward the future, then go with 64 bits, because at some point, all computers will be running 64 bits (see Figure 1.1).

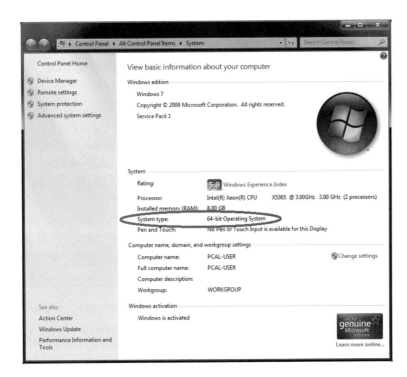

Figure 1.1
Not sure whether your system is 32- or 64-bit? With Windows 7, right-click on My Computer and look under System.

The tradeoff is that some older hardware may not be compatible, and it may never be compatible if the drivers aren't updating for 64-bit operations. Also, some programs are not available in 64-bit versions. This usually is not a problem, as Windows 7 lets you run 32-bit programs in a 64-bit environment. Still, occasional incompatibilities may crop up. Fortunately, you can install both 32-bit and 64-bit versions of SONAR in a 64-bit system, so you do have an option if some programs work properly only with a 32-bit version of SONAR.

If you have a lot of older hardware and programs for 32-bit operating systems, then you might want to stick with 32 bits for as long as you can. However, be aware that you can't update a 32-bit system to 64 bits without starting all over—reinstalling the system and then reinstalling 64-bit versions of your programs.

Desktop versus Laptop

Laptops used to be less powerful and upgradeable than desktops, but with today's technology, it's possible to run a serious music studio on a laptop. Here's a rundown of some of the advantages and disadvantages of each.

▷ **Expense.** Desktops deliver better value, because they don't need to use proprietary, miniature components. They'll also deliver better performance for an equivalent amount of money.

▷ **Expandability.** Expanding a laptop's internals is very difficult. You can probably put in a bigger hard drive or a wireless card, but any serious expansion requires using external devices that connect via USB or FireWire. With desktops, you can add internal hard drives, cards to increase the number of USB or FireWire ports, graphics cards to provide multi-monitor support (which is highly recommended for music programs), and the like.

▷ **Portability.** For live performance, a laptop is way more convenient—you don't need a monitor, keyboard, or mouse, as they're all built in. And thanks to battery power, if there's a brownout or power interruption, your laptop will keep humming along.

▷ **Reliability.** Score one for desktops. Because laptops need to be light, they tend to be more fragile. The smaller hard drives run hotter, and they usually don't last as long as bigger drives. It's tough to have enough ventilation to dissipate the heat generated by various components, which can shorten component life—while desktops have plenty of ventilation and fans.

Although many musicians are nervous about using laptops live, I've been using them since the late 1990s for live performance and have never had a problem. However, I'm also hyper-careful about putting them in harm's way. Here are some tips designed to help you get the most out of a live-performance laptop.

• **Avoid the onboard audio.** A separate USB or FireWire audio interface offers better audio quality and more durable connectors. With Windows, disable the onboard audio so it doesn't interfere with whatever audio interface you add.

• **Physically secure your laptop.** If someone trips over the power chord, expect a crash to the floor. I mounted the laptop that handles my stage setup in a pedalboard (see Figure 1.2) that sits on the stage (see Figure 1.3); if that seems too hazardous, I'll put it on a table. Once this is set up, I don't need to adjust much.

Figure 1.2
It's a good idea to protect your laptop in some kind of hard case, such as the kind designed for use with pedalboards.

Figure 1.3
The live laptop in action, during setup at a festival gig.

▷ **Don't run on battery power.** When using batteries, laptops often reduce performance automatically to extend battery life—and you need the highest possible performance for real-time guitar playing. With Windows, go into the power management options and choose the highest-performance one.

▷ **Redundancy = good.** If you can't carry a backup laptop, have backups of your data and programs.

▷ **With Windows, turn off unneeded services.** Run the msconfig utility to disable unneeded startup programs—the Internet contains a wealth of information on optimizing computers for better performance. And with all computers, disable any network or internal wireless card, as these can interfere with audio performance.

Usually a laptop will have an option to turn off wireless, but if not, here's the process for turning off internal wireless capabilities in Windows 7 or Vista.

1. Right-click on My Computer and select Properties.
2. Click on Device Manager. Open up Network Adapters by double-clicking on the heading or single-clicking on the arrow to the heading's left.
3. Locate the wireless driver, right-click on it, and select Disable (see Figure 1.4). You can always re-enable it when needed.

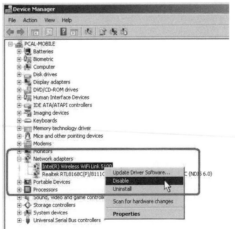

Figure 1.4
You can disable a laptop's internal wireless card using Windows Device Manager.

▷ **Avoid on-the-job training.** Never use new hardware or software (including updates) onstage or in the studio before testing *everything* under real-world conditions.

▷ **Carry a spare hard drive.** Laptop hard drives are more delicate than larger desktop drives. Fortunately, they're usually easy to replace; so if you don't have a second computer, carry a second hard drive that "mirrors" the one you use (Norton Ghost is good for mirroring), along with any tools needed to install it.

▷ **Don't plug USB memory sticks or copy-protection dongles directly into the computer.** Use a USB extension cord (see Figure 1.5) to prevent the USB device from breaking off at the base if pressure's put on it—this might also damage your motherboard, meaning an expensive repair.

▷ **Laptops are easy to steal.** Bring a backpack to the gig, and as soon as you're finished, stash the laptop in the backpack and wear it.

Figure 1.5
Using a short USB extension cable between a dongle and your laptop could potentially save the dongle, the computer, or both.

Interfacing Guitar with Computers

A GUITAR DOESN'T JUST PLUG INTO a computer the way it plugs into an amp. The guitar's audio must be converted into data before the computer can use it and then be converted back into audio so we can hear it.

The Computerized Signal Chain

The computerized signal chain consists of several stages, which go in the following order from input to output.

Guitar

If you don't know what this is, you are in the wrong place. But never forget that the guitar has a profound influence on the ultimate sound, no matter what follows it— sometimes the quickest, easiest fix for improving guitar tone is a new set of strings.

Analog-to-Digital Converter

This is built within a device called an *audio interface*. (We'll cover audio interfaces in the next chapter.) The audio interface accepts an analog input, such as from a guitar, and converts it to a data format the computer can understand. Its input will be audio connectors, and its output will be a digital signal cable or another connection that hooks into the computer.

Within the interface, a preamp usually precedes the analog-to-digital converter. This is because a guitar or bass with standard, non-active pickups puts out a low-level signal, so a preamp amplifies the signal before it works its way down the signal chain.

Computer

This runs the software that processes the data. You can think of SONAR not just as a virtual multitrack recorder, but as a "virtual rack" into which you "plug in" processors—except that these are virtual processors that exist only in the software world of ones and zeroes. Amp modeling software processes the guitar sound the same way that amps, cabinets, and effects would, but by virtual methods, such as mathematical models, instead of using physical components.

Digital-to-Analog Converter

This converts the processed data back to analog so you can feed it into a monitoring system and hear it. It's often built into the same audio interface that sends the signal into the computer. Note: Sometimes the audio interface is referred to as *I/O*, because it provides the input to the computer and takes the computer's output.

Monitoring System

A monitoring system could be headphones plugged into a jack in your audio interface, an amplifier with a set of speakers, a PA system, a guitar amp, or anything that lets you hear the results of what the computer does.

The Guitar's Special Requirements

Many computers include soundcards, or an onboard audio system, and offer audio input and output jacks (typically line and mic in, and line and headphones or speaker outs). All A/D and D/A conversion occurs inside the computer. While onboard soundcards are acceptable for consumer applications, such as playing games, they rarely provide studio-quality sound. Furthermore, most soundcard inputs aren't compatible with guitar.

Pro musicians use high-quality audio interfaces that perform the A/D and D/A conversion and communicate with the computer via a digital signal. These interfaces will have various inputs, though not all are suited for guitar; a guitar's signal is a much higher level than a mic, yet not as strong as a line-level signal.

There's also the potential for an impedance mismatch. A standard guitar with stock pickups has a relatively high output impedance, which tends to inhibit an efficient signal transfer to the next in a chain of electronic devices. This transfer is more efficient if the guitar feeds a high-impedance input (for example, more than 220k ohms) to avoid being loaded down; it's the electronic equivalent of having less "friction." Any significant loading leads to reduced high-frequency response and lower levels.

The majority of guitars use standard, passive pickups. Active pickups (ones that include preamps) have low impedances and do not need to feed a high-impedance input.

There are several ways to avoid loading from mismatched impedances.

> ▷ Use an interface designed specifically for guitar (see Figure 2.1). For example, Roland's VS-20 is more than just a USB interface, as it also includes guitar/voice-specific onboard hardware processing based on Boss multi-effects and a control surface for controlling SONAR (and all SONAR variants). However, the interface is an important element of the VS-20.

Figure 2.1

Native Instruments' Rig Kontrol is designed specifically for their Guitar Rig Pro software, but it works with other amp sims. It may just look like a pedalboard control, but it also includes a USB audio interface with dual inputs and even a headphone jack.

▷ Use a buffer designed specifically for guitar, such as the Waves Studio Guitar Interface. Designed in conjunction with Paul Reed Smith, it's designed to provide the absolute minimum coloration to your guitar and match its impedance to any subsequent interface.

▷ Use an active direct box, such as those made by Radial Engineering and others.

▷ Use an audio interface with an instrument input (for example, from Roland, MOTU, PreSonus, Yamaha, etc.). These inputs have a high impedance and are suitable for guitar or bass (see Figure 2.2).

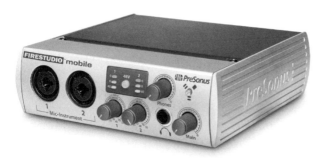

Figure 2.2

Designed as a general-purpose mobile interface, the PreSonus FireStudio Mobile features two instrument inputs that can handle guitar and bass.

About Latency (Computer-Based Delays)

Guitar players expect an instant response: Hit a string, hear a sound. Unfortunately, your computer will introduce delay—called *latency*—between the time you hit a note on your guitar and when you hear it come out of the speakers. Of course, you want to minimize latency as much as possible (hopefully to the point where you don't notice it, but at least low enough so that it's not an annoyance).

Latency occurs in the conversion process from analog to digital and digital to analog, as well as in the computer itself—even the most powerful processors can do only so many millions of calculations per second. As a result, the computer sticks some of the incoming audio in a buffer, which is like a savings account for your guitar signal. When the computer is so busy elsewhere that it can't deal with audio, it makes a "withdrawal" from the buffer instead. The larger the buffer, the less likely the computer will run out of audio data when it needs it. But a larger buffer also means that the guitar signal is being diverted for a longer period of time before hitting the computer, which increases latency.

Some latency is unavoidable. But to put matters in perspective, sound takes about 1 millisecond to travel 1 foot. So, 3ms of delay is about the same as moving 1 meter (or 1 yard) farther away from your speakers. I think most guitarists would agree that latencies below 10ms or so are acceptable, but anything much over that can be annoying. Nonetheless, because you want the best possible "feel" when playing guitar, let's investigate how to obtain the lowest possible latency.

How to Minimize Latency

There are several ways to reduce latency to acceptable levels, ranging from upgrading your hardware to using some software "tricks." Here are some common options.

Upgrade Your Hardware

Unfortunately, upgrading to a new computer or processor is the most expensive option, but it has benefits that go beyond simply reducing latency. With today's multicore processors and a quality audio interface, it's possible to obtain essentially negligible latencies.

Choose the Right Drivers

Software drivers provide communications between your computer and your audio interface—specifically, between SONAR and the audio interface's inputs and outputs. You can think of drivers as "software connectors" between the physical world of the interface and the computer's virtual world. They are the data gatekeepers, so how efficiently they do their task affects latency.

Steinberg (the company that created Cubase) devised the first universal low-latency protocol for audio interfaces based on ASIO (*Advanced Streaming Input Output*) drivers. These tie in closely with the computer's processor, bypassing various layers of both Mac and Windows operating systems. Since then, Microsoft has introduced the WDM/KS protocol (this replaces their far slower DirectSound and MME protocols) and the WaveRT protocol for Vista and Windows 7. However, ASIO remains extremely popular, particularly with pro audio programs designed for Windows (see Figure 2.3).

One caution: If you see "Emulated ASIO" among the driver choices, don't use it. This is not the same as ASIO, and it delivers vastly inferior performance compared to standard ASIO.

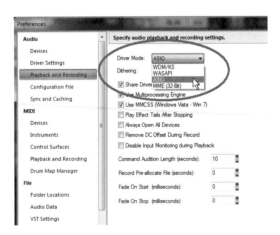

Figure 2.3

SONAR is shown choosing among ASIO, WDM/KS, WASAPI, and MME (32-bit) drivers, all of which are available when using Roland's VS-700R audio interface.

As to which driver protocol is best, it depends mostly on how the drivers are written. Although not all interfaces support all driver protocols, if multiple options are available, experiment to determine which gives the best performance with your system. One significant difference between ASIO and WDM/KS is that with few exceptions, ASIO can address only one ASIO interface at a time, regardless of whether several are connected to your computer. WDM/KS can address multiple interfaces, which is handy if you run out of I/O and you need more inputs or outputs than a single interface can provide.

Note that there are two "flavors" of WDM: standard, and WDM/KS (KS stands for kernel streaming). The KS version is far superior for pro audio; in fact, standard WDM may simply be an MME variant, and therefore can give the same consumer-level performance.

Drivers are very important and are frequently updated to improve performance or ensure compatibility with changes in operating systems. It's always a good idea to check an interface manufacturer's website for updated drivers, even if you bought a product the day it hit the stores.

Avid (the maker of Pro Tools) has its own audio engine, DAE (*Digidesign Audio Engine*). Pro Tools used to work only with Avid hardware, using its audio engine and driver protocol. However, in 2010, Avid "opened up" its audio interfaces so they could be used by other programs (and Pro Tools can now work with non-Avid interfaces). For example, if you're running SONAR, it can communicate with Avid's Eleven Rack guitar-oriented audio interface via ASIO.

Latency Reduction Tips and Tricks

One easy way to reduce latency is to wear headphones instead of listening to speakers, as there's no delay from the headphones to your ears—whereas listening on speakers will add at least a couple of milliseconds of latency.

Another method is to change latency during the course of working with a project. Even if your computer can do low latencies in theory, in practice lower latencies require more computer power. So, most audio interfaces provide a choice of latency settings, allowing a tradeoff between lowest latency and best computer performance. If all your computer has to do is run an amp simulator in stand-alone mode, then you can probably adjust your system for really low latency. But if you're running a complex project in SONAR and playing back lots of tracks, you may need to set the latency higher. The symptoms of running out of computer power include pops and crackles in the audio, unintended distortion, and rarely, a program freeze where it simply won't respond.

As a result of this "dynamic" nature of latency, if possible record your guitar parts early in the recording process as you can often set the latency to a lower value than you can later on.

But what if you want to add the guitar last? Simple: Export a rough mix of all your tracks. Open a new project, insert the mix, and then play along with it from the beginning of the song. Because all you have is a guitar and a stereo mix track, you'll be able to set a very low latency value. After you've completed your guitar track, export it, close the project, open your original project, and insert the guitar part starting from the beginning of the song.

Latency Spec Details

Soundcards are supposed to report their latency back to the host program. So, you might assume that a soundcard with a latency of 5.8 milliseconds is outperforming one with a listed latency of 11.6ms. But that's not necessarily true, because one card might list the latency a signal endures going into the computer ("one-way" latency), while another might give the "round-trip" latency—the input and output latency, which includes latencies introduced by the hardware as well as the sample buffers in the computer. Or it might give both readings (see Figure 2.4).

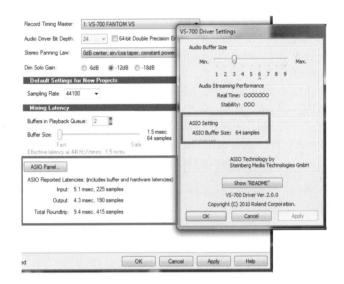

Figure 2.4

The SONAR/VS-700R combination reports complete latency specs. Note that although the ASIO buffer size is only 64 samples, when you also take hardware input and output latencies into account (225 and 190 samples, respectively), the total roundtrip latency is 415 samples, yielding 9.4ms of delay. I find this definitely acceptable for guitar.

Incidentally, these readings are not always accurate. Some audio interfaces do not report latency correctly and might be off by several milliseconds. There's no need to get paranoid about this, but do understand that if an audio interface claims that its latency is lower than another model's, but you sense more of a delay with the "lower latency" audio interface, it very well might not be lower.

SONAR offers several ways to trade off various system settings to arrive at the "sweet spot" of low latency and computer performance. Most of these adjustments happen in the Preferences menu, as covered in Chapter 4, "Setting Preferences in SONAR."

Guitarist's Guide to Audio Interfaces

As mentioned in the previous chapter, the audio interface's job is to convert your guitar signal into data for the computer's benefit and then convert that data back into an analog signal we can hear.

Audio Interface Types

There are many types of audio interfaces; let's start with a few broad categories and list their main advantages and disadvantages. As always, read the fine print; some may or may not have instrument inputs that are suitable for guitar. Also, not all audio interfaces have MIDI in and out, so if you plan to use MIDI footswitches or footpedals, check for this feature as well.

External Box

The simplest type of interface to install and use is a box that's external to your computer with at least one or two audio inputs, audio outputs, possibly MIDI in and out (we'll discuss MIDI later on), and a digital connection to your computer (see Figure 3.1).

The interface converts your signal to digital and then sends it to the computer via a digital connection. Although there are many connection protocols, the most popular ones for audio interfaces are USB 1.1, USB 2.0 (which is faster than USB 1.1), and FireWire. Unlike a standard audio connection, this single connection is bidirectional. It can send your input signals to the computer and receive output data from your computer (for example, the mixed output of a DAW or similar host program).

Figure 3.1
This top view of Native Instruments' Mobile I/O, a USB interface designed specifically for guitar and bass, is as simple and small as it gets: Input, output, two level controls, and a USB connection. It's targeted at guitar players who use laptops for live performance or recording.

Advantages:

▷ You don't need to open up the computer.

▷ It's easily transportable to other machines.

▷ Sensitive circuitry is kept outside of the electrically "dirty" computer environment.

Disadvantages:

▷ Possible performance penalty compared to internal cards (see next).

▷ USB and FireWire connections are inherently noisy, which requires quality filtering at the interface.

▷ Having too many devices on the USB or FireWire connection can cause problems. For example, you generally don't want to use a FireWire hard drive on the same port as a FireWire interface.

Internal PCI or PCIe Card

Like a graphics card, Ethernet card, and so on, the PCI or PCIe card inserts into a slot in a desktop computer's motherboard. Because the card hooks directly into your computer, it gives slightly better performance than an external USB or FireWire box (although practically speaking, differences are relatively minor). The card's backplate (the side that faces out from the computer) will typically have several jacks for analog audio and possibly some digital I/O (for example, S/PDIF) as well to accommodate digital gear—see Figure 3.2.

Figure 3.2
E-MU's 1212M PCIe Digital Audio System inserts in a PCIe slot on your computer's motherboard. (The second card takes up a card space but doesn't need to plug into anything—it links to the main card.) However, there's no high-impedance input for guitar, so you could need a separate preamp or buffer.

Some cards don't have jacks on the back but instead have a multi-pin connector and a "breakout" cable with various audio and/or MIDI connections.

Note that while PCI and PCIe cards are still in use, they are fading in popularity due to the convenience and prevalence of USB 2.0 and FireWire audio interfaces.

Advantages:

▷ Higher performance than external interfaces.

▷ No FireWire- or USB-related issues.

Disadvantages:

▷ You need to open up the computer and install the card, and then remove and reinstall it if you want to use the card with a different computer.

▷ If the card has analog audio on the card itself, extensive shielding and proper circuit-board layout is necessary to keep out computer noise.

▷ The card may conflict with previously installed cards (although with modern computers, this is unlikely).

Internal Card + External Box

In this case, the internal card still does most of the work. But instead of mounting connectors on the backplate or using a breakout cable, a multi-conductor cable runs from the card to the external box, which contains the various connectors, controls, and so on (see Figure 3.3).

Figure 3.3
MOTU offers two "external box" interfaces that are compatible with their PCI-424 card: the 2408mk3 and 24I/O. Both are designed for industrial-strength studio applications.

This type of approach has the same advantages and disadvantages as listed for PCI cards, with one exception: The disadvantage about requiring shielding isn't an issue, as the audio connections are kept far away from the computer, in the breakout box.

Guitar Processors with Built-In Interfaces

Some multi-effects guitar processors now include computer-interfacing capabilities. Roland's VS-20 (see Figure 3.4) is a fine example of this, but other devices from companies such as DigiTech, Zoom, and others offer USB interfacing.

Figure 3.4
Roland VS-20.

Some guitar processors have a USB interface built in, but the VS-20 is more like a USB audio interface/control surface with Boss COSM hardware effects built inside. You can record through these effects or re-amp through them to process dry tracks, as covered in Chapter 17, "Control Surfaces and the Roland VS-20 Interface for Guitarists."

Sometimes these units require that you record the processed sound, but with other devices (such as the VS-20), you can record the guitar "dry" and send audio from your computer into the processor and then route it back into the computer to get a processed sound even if the guitar was recorded without processing. This is similar to the re-amping process described in Chapter 12, "Re-Amping with SONAR."

Advantages:

▷ Combines effects and interface, thus saving money compared to buying two separate units.

▷ Generally usable for studio or stage.

▷ External hardware lets you record processed guitar with no latency, unlike processing it through computer software plug-ins.

Disadvantages:

▷ May not allow for re-amping.

▷ You're limited by the hardware, whereas with amp sims, you have no such limitations.

ExpressCard or PCMCIA (CardBus) Interface

These are designed for laptops and are the laptop equivalent of inserting a PCI or PCIe card in a motherboard (see Figure 3.5).

Figure 3.5
Echo Digital Audio's Indigo IOx provides audio in and out from an ExpressCard slot, but the company also makes PCMCIA slot–compatible interfaces, as well as companion interfaces designed specifically for laptop-oriented DJs.

Advantages:

▷ Extremely compact.

▷ High performance due to hooking directly into the computer.

▷ More portable for mobile applications than a separate interface box.

Disadvantages:

▷ Will likely not have guitar-friendly inputs, thus necessitating a preamp or buffer, which mitigates the portability and compactness of a card-based interface.

▷ Ins and outs are typically limited unless the design uses a breakout cable or has an external breakout box that connects to the card via a cable.

▷ For many users, USB and FireWire interfaces are more attractive options because they're more universal.

Digital Connections for External Boxes

We've touched on USB and FireWire, but let's dig further into the three main ways to hook an external box up to your computer. These options all provide a bidirectional data path and power (except for the four-pin FireWire connectors discussed later, which don't provide power). The box's power requirements can sometimes be low enough that USB and FireWire busses provide sufficient power, and the devices don't require an external power supply. In this case, the external device is called *bus-powered.* However, most devices also allow for external power in case the bus can't provide enough power or the bus is powering other devices as well.

▷ **USB 1.1.** Many inexpensive audio interfaces use USB 1.1 (see Figure 3.6). It's inexpensive but slower than the next two options. This places a limit on how many signals can go to your computer, their sample rate, and bit resolution. A typical maximum is six tracks of record or playback (or any combination thereof) with 24-bit, 44.1-kHz signals. Higher sample rates may cut that down to four or even two tracks.

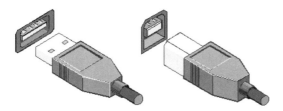

Figure 3.6
The connector on the left is the Type A USB connector, which typically plugs into your computer. The connector on the right is a Type B USB connector, which plugs into your USB interface.

▷ **USB 2.0.** This is the next-generation version of USB 1.1 and is much faster. Yet the connections are physically compatible, so USB 1.1 devices can work with a USB 2.0 port, and vice versa. However, a USB 1.1 device will remain slow even when plugged into a USB 2.0 port, and a USB 2.0 device will be slowed down if plugged into a USB 1.1 port.

▷ **USB 3.0.** So far, this higher-speed version of USB 2.0 is being used mostly for hard drives, video, and other applications that require extremely high transfer speeds. As of this writing, there are no USB 3.0 audio interfaces, partly because of compatibility concerns and partly because USB 2.0 is adequate for all but the most demanding audio applications.

▷ **FireWire (also called IEEE-1394).** This is a common, but arguably fading, connection protocol for high-speed devices. Although intended originally for use with peripherals such as camcorders, FireWire also works well for communicating digital audio between a computer and an external interface. If your computer lacks FireWire, it's not too difficult to add a FireWire PCI card that provides multiple FireWire ports. If you don't feel confident enough to do this, any computer store with a tech department will be able to take care of you.

There are two different types of FireWire connectors: 4-pin and 6-pin. The 6-pin types (see Figure 3.7) send/receive data as well as provide power.

Figure 3.7
This shows a 6-pin FireWire connector and its corresponding jack.

The 4-pin types (see Figure 3.8) do not provide power from the bus, so you must use an external adapter if a peripheral device uses a 4-pin connector.

Figure 3.8
This is a 4-pin FireWire connector, as typically used with laptop computers.

There are 6-pin to 4-pin adapters, but these only carry signal—they don't magically provide power to 4-pin devices.

There's an important caution involving FireWire (and sometimes even USB) interfaces. Although FireWire and USB devices are considered "hot swappable"—in other words, you should be able to plug and unplug them from a computer while the power to either or both is turned on—there have been reports of motherboards failing from having FireWire peripherals plugged into them. As a result, although the odds of encountering problems are remote, it's prudent to make connections while the computer and peripheral are powered down.

Audio Interface Zero-Latency Monitoring

An audio interface feature called *zero-latency* or *direct* monitoring supposedly reduces latency to virtually nothing, so what you hear as you monitor is essentially in real time. However, it does this by monitoring the signal going into the computer, thus bypassing the computer. That's useless if you use amp simulation software, because amp sim plug-ins work inside the computer: If you don't listen to what's coming out of your computer, you won't hear what the plug-in is doing. As a result, if you use an audio interface with the option to enable zero-latency or direct monitoring, turn it off for guitar (although you may find it useful for recording vocals or other sources that don't rely on plug-ins for their characteristic "sound").

Another option is to get your sound in an external effects box and feed that into your interface. If you monitor the output of the effects box, either at the effects box itself or using your interface's direct monitoring option, you'll hear your processed sound with no latency. This is one reason why effects boxes with computer interfacing can be a good choice for recording—you can use either plug-ins or the hardware effects inside the box.

Audio Interface Checklist for Guitarists

Is your head swimming yet with all these options? Then let's present a summary of the top 10 points to consider if you're in the market for an audio interface.

▷ **Run, don't walk, away from consumer-level components.** A computer's internal sound chip or a consumer soundcard (for example, Sound Blaster) isn't designed for guitar. If you try to use these, you will not be happy with the resulting sound.

▷ **Check for a Guitar, Instrument, DI, or High-Impedance 1/4-inch input.** You can always patch a preamp or a signal processor like a compressor to condition your guitar signal to work with standard interface inputs, but you might as well get an interface with this option built in.

▷ **Decide between FireWire, USB, or a PCI card to connect the computer and interface.** USB is rising; FireWire is fading. However, when you need *mucho* bandwidth (such as for high sample rates or when you're using lots of mics and direct inputs to record an entire rock band simultaneously), FireWire has a slight edge—and PCI cards have an additional edge over FireWire.

▷ **Consider adding a FireWire or USB card to your computer.** You'll often get better audio performance by inserting a PCI card with FireWire or USB ports into your computer (avoid combo USB/FireWire cards) and dedicating it to audio applications. Use the motherboard connectors for mice, keyboards, printers, hard drives, and so on. With FireWire, check the interface manufacturer's website for approved FireWire chip sets and ensure that the card uses those chips.

▷ **Determine your other needs.** Recording vocals? Look for at least one quality mic preamp. Think you'll need more mic inputs eventually? Check for what's called an *ADAT optical input.* This accepts eight digital audio streams through an optical cable; there are several devices on the market (for example, PreSonus DigiMax D8) that have eight mic pres and send their outputs to an ADAT output. Patch this output to the interface ADAT input, and there you have it—eight more mic preamps.

▷ **Bus-powered or not?** For portable recording or onstage laptops, a bus-powered interface is more convenient. However, a bus can supply only so much power, so this tends to apply only to simpler interfaces.

▷ **Are your sample rates of choice covered?** Not all interfaces (especially USB) can handle high sample rates, such as 96 kHz. A rate of 44.1 or 48 kHz is fine for most applications, but if you need high sample rates, check the specs to avoid disappointment.

▷ **Evaluate the freebies.** Interfaces often bundle software—"lite" versions of DAWs, loops and samples, free plug-ins, and so on. Some of this may just be "bloatware" you'll never use, but sometimes bundles add serious value (especially if there are some amp sim programs in there!).

▷ **Direct monitoring can be helpful.** Direct monitoring is particularly useful for drums, acoustic guitar, and vocals, as they generally don't require processing in the computer until mixdown. Most modern interfaces include a small software mixer you can load into your computer to control the interface's direct monitoring options.

▷ **Check for desirable "secret sauces."** Various interfaces have special, unique features that might tilt you toward selecting a particular interface. For example, Roland's VS-20 includes an onboard hardware multi-effects, Line 6's TonePort series comes bundled with POD Farm amp sim software, Native Instruments' Mobile I/O is ultra-portable, Zoom's G2.1Nu is basically an effects pedal that has an interface for talking to your computer, and so on. All other factors being equal, some of these special features might be important to you.

Setting Preferences in SONAR

T HE PREFERENCES MENU IS WHERE YOU CAN optimize SONAR's performance for use with guitar. To call it up in SONAR X1, choose Edit > Preferences or
press P. When the Preferences window appears, click on the Basic button in the
lower left, as the Advanced parameters aren't needed for basic audio setup.

Here's how to choose the correct settings for the various options.

Audio Devices

This shows the drivers available on your system and the hardware inputs and outputs
to which they correlate (see Figure 4.1).

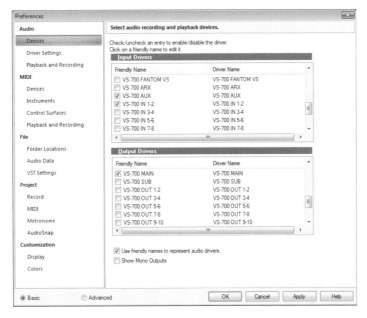

Figure 4.1
The Preferences menu's
Audio Devices options
shows what interface
devices are available
to SONAR.

This example shows the driver options for the VS-700 system—a sophisticated interface and control surface designed specifically for SONAR. For recording guitar, the AUX input (which is checked) offers a high-impedance input for guitar, so that's the input we want to use. Similarly, VS-700 MAIN (output) is checked, so we can plug in headphones or a monitor speaker and listen to the main stereo output.

The other inputs correlate to other physical inputs on the back of the interface. For example, if you had a stereo synthesizer connected to analog inputs 1 and 2, and you wanted to record it at the same time, you would also check VS-700 IN 1-2, as shown.

So why not just check all the inputs and outputs? You can, and that might even be a good idea if you're new to this and can't figure out which driver connects to which physical inputs and outputs. But, each checked driver draws a little more power from the CPU, so it generally makes sense to check no more inputs and outputs than needed.

Note that if multiple ASIO interfaces connect to your system, with a few exceptions choosing any input or output from one interface will gray out all the others as unavailable. One exception is that Roland's Octa-Capture interface is designed specifically to expand the VS-700 systems, so in "expand" mode, the ins and outs from both interfaces will be available.

Creating "Friendly" Driver Names

The VS-700 was designed to fit SONAR like a glove, so the driver names are pretty obvious. However, other interfaces might be more general-purpose, and not be very descriptive. For example, with an E-MU 1820 interface, one of two mic inputs—which is also a high-impedance input that accommodates guitars—shows up as E-Mu ASIO ASIO In 2. Fortunately, SONAR has a feature called "friendly names" (see Figure 4.2) that lets you rename these.

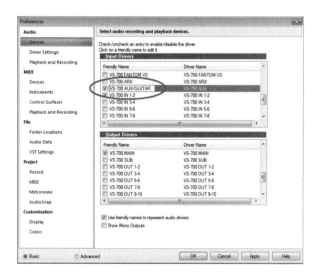

Figure 4.2

It's possible to rename drivers that appear in SONAR. For example, the AUX driver is being given a friendly name of AUX/GUITAR.

To give friendly names:

1. On the Audio Devices page, check Use Friendly Names to Represent Audio Drivers.
2. Under the Friendly Name column, double-click on the driver you want to rename.

3. Type the new name in the driver name field.

4. Click on Apply, and if you're finished setting Preferences, click on Close.

If you use an interface and can't make sense out of the driver names, don't panic—we'll cover how to deal with this, as well as how to select inputs in SONAR tracks, in Chapter 6, "Setting Up to Record in SONAR."

Audio Playback and Recording

Although this page comes after the Driver Settings in the Preferences menu, Audio Playback and Recording (see Figure 4.3) is where you choose the driver protocol, which changes the options in the Driver Settings section. So, let's investigate further before going to Driver Settings.

▷ **Driver Mode.** Here is where you choose the driver protocol. You may be able to select an option your interface doesn't have, in which case when you close the menu and reopen it, you'll see a valid driver option. In most cases you can choose from ASIO and WDM, and as mentioned previously, it's a good idea to try both and see which works best with your system. Note that this may have more to do with the drivers written for your interface than with SONAR or the interface hardware itself. Try WDM/KS, as it's a modern driver that gives performance. Don't bother with MME, because the latency will be intolerable. With SONAR, ASAPI isn't relevant. (Geek alert: WASAPI is a particular way of interacting with the WaveRT protocol that SONAR doesn't support, as it communicates with WaveRT via kernel streaming.)

▷ **Dithering.** This doesn't really relate to latency, so use the default. To learn more about dithering, check out SONAR's Help.

Figure 4.3

The most important parameter on this page is Driver Mode, where you can select among WDM/KS, WASAPI, ASIO, and MME.

Of the remaining options, it's probably best to leave them alone, and as with dithering, if you're curious about what they do, just click on the window's Help button. However, two settings are important for obtaining minimum latency, and a third setting can influence hard disk efficiency, thus increasing track count.

▷ **Use Multiprocessing Engine.** If you have a multicore processor (for example, a Core 2 Duo, Xeon, i7, and so on), this option will be available; otherwise, it will be grayed out. Make sure it's checked so SONAR can use all available processing power. However, note that even if unchecked, SONAR will still use the other available cores for some tasks.

▷ **Use MMCSS.** If your computer runs Vista or Windows 7, this will be available and should be checked.

▷ **Record Pre-Allocate File (Seconds).** This doesn't relate to latency, but I recommend a setting of 600 to 1,000 seconds, as this allows for more possible tracks and reduces hard-disk activity. I use 800.

After making any edits, click on Apply. Now let's return to the Audio Driver Settings parameters.

Audio Driver Settings

For many preferences, the defaults work fine but Audio Driver Settings is where you can tweak your system for minimum latency. There are slightly different windows for ASIO and WDM. Refer to Figure 4.4 to see the various ASIO options.

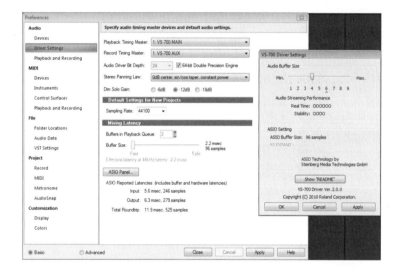

Figure 4.4
This window is the key to obtaining low latencies with ASIO interfaces.

▷ **Playback Timing Master and Record Timing Master.** You can just accept the defaults for these 99.9 percent of the time. If either one shows "None," then select an option (it doesn't really seem to matter which one) from the drop-down menu. If there are no options, then input and output drivers haven't been selected yet. Refer to the previous section on audio devices.

▷ **Audio Driver Bit Depth.** Your drivers may or may not have a choice of bit depths. If not, this option will be grayed out and will show the default bit depth. If choices are available, this is where you make your selection. Sixteen bits is the same resolution used for CDs, and it takes up less memory than using 24 bits, which gives higher resolution. Given the ever-decreasing price of hard-disk storage, most pros use 24 bits, but 16 is acceptable.

▷ **64-Bit Double Precision Engine.** Checking this gives the ultimate in dynamic range for SONAR's audio engine. You can usually just leave this checked, but if you encounter performance issues or plug-ins that operate unreliably with SONAR, try unchecking it to see whether that helps.

▷ **Stereo Panning Law.** This is graduate-level material that doesn't relate to latency. Just go for the default.

▷ **Dim Solo Gain.** Again, this doesn't relate to latency, but we might as well cover this useful feature anyway. Normally, soloing a track mutes all other tracks; Dim Solo lowers their level instead of muting them completely, and this parameter determines how much they're muted.

Default Settings for New Projects Section

And now, a complex answer to a simple question...brace yourself.

Sample rate is the rate at which audio is converted to digital data. The faster the rate, the more accurate the conversion—like how videos that show more frames per second give smoother visual motion. With most audio sources, 44.1 kHz is an adequate sample rate. But some overdriven/high-gain amp sims generate harmonics that can extend beyond the highest audio frequency a digital system was designed to handle. This causes aliasing or foldover distortion, terms that describe a particular type of distortion. The audible results are noise, atonal harmonics, and a "blurred," often "harsh" sound.

With some amp sims, you may be able to improve tone by increasing the sample rate at which it operates, and one option is to raise the project's sample rate to 88.2 or 96 kHz. (Both rates are supported by SONAR if the audio interface supports them. SONAR also supports 192 kHz—but personally, I feel this adds no audible benefit, bogs down your system, and generates huge amounts of data.) Now, I should mention I'm not some "golden ears" guy who insists that recordings done at 96 kHz sound *so* much better than a CD's standard 44.1-kHz sample rate, but some amp sims are a special case—especially at high gain settings.

However, you don't get something for nothing. Higher sample rates stress your computer more, so you may have to increase the system latency to avoid audio dropouts. Another issue is that it may not be possible to run at higher sample rates with complex projects. For example, some other plug-ins might not work properly at 96 kHz, and the demands on your computer might be excessive. One solution employed by Native Instruments, IK Multimedia, and Waves in their amp sims is to include an oversampling option (see Figure 4.5).

Figure 4.5
Native Instruments' Guitar Rig 4 LE, included with SONAR X1 Producer Edition, includes a "hi-resolution" mode that lets it run at double the internal sample rate compared to the project.

This runs the amp sim at a higher internal sampling rate than the project itself, giving many of the benefits of a higher sample rate in projects running at 44.1 or 48 kHz. Oversampling places more of a load on your CPU, but far less than doubling the sample rate of an entire project.

Mixing Latency Section

This section is different depending on whether you're using ASIO or WDM/KS drivers. We'll cover ASIO first.

ASIO Mixing Latency Settings

The biggest difference between WDM/KS and ASIO is that with ASIO, this section is pretty much read-only, as the interface itself will have some kind of control panel for adjusting latency-oriented parameters. You access this by clicking on the ASIO panel button.

In Figure 4.4, you can see the ASIO control panel toward the right (the window that says VS-700 Driver Settings). Here you can adjust the Audio Buffer Size, which as you'll recall, has a major effect on latency. This setting (96 samples) trades off less stability for faster real-time operation. In the Mixing Latency section, you can see that the total system latency (input and output, because there's latency when the signal goes into the computer and latency on the way out) is 11.9ms.

When you first start recording with SONAR, 512 samples is a conservative value that almost any computer and interface can handle. The latency will be annoying, but the reason for using 512 samples is just to make sure that the audio path is working as expected. Once you know all is well, you can try ever lower latencies until you find the "sweet spot."

WDM/KS Mixing Latency Settings

When you choose WDM/KS as your driver model, the first thing SONAR does is ask whether you want to test the characteristics of your Windows audio hardware. It takes only a few seconds; after testing, you'll see a list of supported operating modes and buffer sizes, at which point you can close the window. The testing process also allows SONAR to make some advanced adjustments automatically so you don't have to go into the Advanced Preferences. Unlike ASIO, you can make latency adjustments directly in the Driver Settings window (see Figure 4.6); you don't need to open a separate control panel.

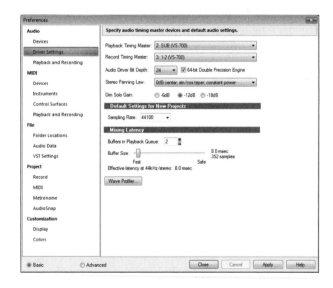

Figure 4.6
This window is similar to the one for ASIO, but it lets you adjust Mixing Latency within SONAR.

▷ **Buffers in Playback Queue.** You will not be able to set this lower than 2, which is the setting for lowest latency. If you experience dropouts or other indications of overly low latency, you can increase the number of buffers.

▷ **Buffer Size.** This slider varies from the lowest possible buffer size (Fast) to the largest (Safe) and will be your main control for latency.

It's hard to predict whether raising buffers in the playback queue or increasing buffer size will be the best way to improve latency characteristics, so try both. Generally, you'll use Buffer Size as the preferred control and, as with ASIO, 512 samples is a safe place to start.

The Two Different Ways to Express Latency: Samples and Milliseconds

Some manufacturers specify latency in milliseconds, some in samples, and some use both. Sample values aren't as intuitive as milliseconds, but it's not hard to translate samples to milliseconds. This involves math, but if the following makes your head explode, don't worry—skip ahead and just remember the golden rule of latency: Use the lowest setting that gives reliable audio operation. In other words, if the latency is expressed in milliseconds, use the lowest setting that works. If it's specified in samples, you still use the lowest setting that works. Now, the math.

With a 44.1-kHz sampling rate, the signal level is measured 44,100 times per second, and each of these creates a sample. So each sample is 1/44,100th of a second long, or about 0.023 ms.

If a soundcard's latency is 256 samples, at 44.1 kHz that means a delay of 256×0.023 ms—about 5.8 ms. One hundred twenty-eight samples of delay would be about 2.9 ms. At a sample rate of 88.2 kHz, each sample lasts half as long as a sample at 44.1 kHz, so each sample would be about 0.0125 ms. This means a delay of 256 samples at 88.2 kHz would be around 2.9 ms.

There! All done. Let's go back to nuts and bolts.

MIDI, File, Project, and Customization Preferences

These settings don't relate to latency, so we'll skip them for now. However, we'll revisit them as appropriate in other sections.

Audio Profiles

If you have selected the WDM/KS driver mode, are having problems with a WDM interface, and are using higher than 16-bit resolution, you may need to click on the Advanced button in the Preferences window, and under the Audio heading, select Audio Profiles. (This doesn't appear if you're using the ASIO driver mode.) You'll now see options for Stream > 16 Bit Data As. Most of the time, this will be preset to your interface's optimum setting. But if problems persist, contact the interface's manufacturer, ask what the preferred data format is when streaming data with resolutions above 16 bits, and choose the recommended format from the drop-down menu. Alternatively, you can just try each setting to determine which works best and use that.

Guitar Recording Options with SONAR

YOU HAVE SONAR, YOU HAVE A COMPUTER, and there's an interface you can plug into. But what do you plug into the interface? The answer is not as simple as just "a guitar"; let's investigate.

Miking a Physical Amp

Yes, this is the old-school way, but it's worked well for decades—and even if you want to use virtual amp sims, they emulate many traditional techniques, so you need to know at least some theory behind the process of miking an amp. At its most basic, you plug your guitar into an amp, get the sound you want, then stick a microphone in front of the amplifier. The microphone then plugs into the mic input on your audio interface, and you record the mic's output into SONAR.

The type of mic you use, where you place it, and the amp's placement in the room are the main influences on the sound.

Microphone Types

There are three mic types commonly used for miking guitar amps: dynamic, condenser, and ribbon. Dynamic mics tend to have a somewhat "darker" or "warmer" quality, but because amps can be loud, dynamic mics are also a popular choice because they can handle the levels and they have sonic characteristics that match guitar amps well. Shure's SM57 (see Figure 5.1) is often cited as one of the best dynamic mics for guitar amps, and it's pretty inexpensive compared to other mics. Almost all amp sims include a model of this venerable mic. Electro-Voice's RE20 is another popular choice, as is Sennheiser's MD 421.

Figure 5.1
Shure's SM57 is a classic guitar amp mic—you've heard it on plenty of hits.

Condenser mics tend to give a more "open" response. I like using them as secondary mics, a bit farther back from the amp, to add definition to the dynamic mic, which serves as the primary mic. AKG's C 414 B-ULS is a great choice, but it is pricey. However, their C 214 costs substantially less while offering many of the same benefits. Many famous producers like Neumann's U 87—but then again, they can afford it. Audio-Technica's AT4051 has a similar kind of character and is somewhat more affordable.

Although ribbon mics used to be hampered by fragility, newer models are much more rugged. They tend to have a warm kind of sound and an unusual pickup pattern that picks up sound from the front and back but rejects sounds coming in from the sides. As a result, in guitar setups with more than one cabinet, ribbon mics let you do interesting tricks by choosing which sounds are accepted and which are rejected. Beyer's M 160 is a classic ribbon mic; among newer mics, Royer's R-121 (and its less expensive sibling, the R-101) are very popular choices for miking guitar amps (see Figure 5.2).

Figure 5.2
Although not cheap, the R-121 has become a very popular ribbon mic for recording guitar amps.

Fortunately, although *great* mics are expensive, *good* mics are now relatively inexpensive. At any price point, experiment with what you have; it's possible to coax wonderful sounds using budget mics. Also note that many mics have switchable attenuators (called *pads*) to lower the sound level by a certain amount, such as −10 dB. With loud amps, engage this to avoid distortion.

Microphone Placement

Here the main variables are the distance from the speaker and whether the mic is pointed at the center of the speaker or off more to the side. Every engineer has his own view of what's best, but a good starting point is an inch or two back from the cone and about half to two-thirds of the way toward the speaker's edge. However, some engineers prefer moving the mic away from the speaker somewhat to capture more of the cabinet's influence on the sound, not just the speaker; this also allows picking up some room sound, although the disadvantage is you might get more bleed-through from other loud instruments.

Moving the mic closer to the speaker's center tends to give a brighter sound, while angling the mic toward the speaker or moving it farther away can give a tighter, warmer sound. Also, don't forget that the amp interacts with the room. Placing the amp in a corner or against a wall can increase the amount of bass; raising it off the floor can also change the sound considerably.

Miking Variations

While the one-mic/one-amp approach is common, there are many other possibilities. Some engineers like to use a second mic, often farther back from the amp and mixed at a lower level, to give more room "ambience." Others like to split the guitar signal to different amps, mike both amps, and mix them together to get a stereo image. As with other aspects of recording, the only rule is that there are no rules—if hanging an amp from the ceiling while recording it with a mic from an old RadioShack cassette deck gives the sound you want, then that's the sound to use.

One very cool aspect of amp sim plug-ins is that by going into a virtual world, you can create setups that would be difficult to do in the physical world—such as feed one amp into four different cabinets, each with a different mic type, and place them all in stereo.

Some amps even include direct outputs for recording straight into an interface or mixer, with tonal shaping to emulate a cabinet sound. You can record this direct output as well as the miked speaker output. However, note that the miked sound will be delayed slightly compared to the direct sound, as the mic will be a certain distance from the speaker, and sound takes a while to travel through air. You may need to "nudge" the miked sound ahead a little bit within SONAR so that the peaks of the two tracks line up (see Figure 5.3).

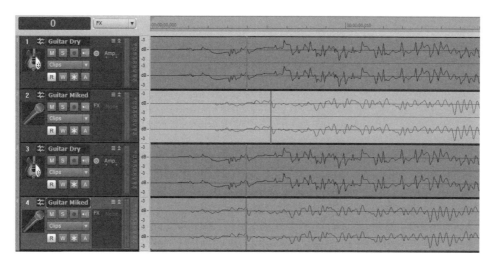

Figure 5.3
Track 1 shows the direct waveform, while Track 2 shows the miked waveform. The vertical lines indicate the same signal peak; note how the miked signal is delayed by a little over a millisecond, indicating that the mic was about a foot away from the speaker. Track 3 shows a clone of Track 1, while Track 4 shows a clone of Track 2 but with the track nudged ahead so that the peaks line up (as shown by the vertical lines).

Recording from an Effects Box or Multi-Effects

Instead of an amp, you might use an effects device, such as a Line 6 POD, Zoom G2.1Nu, Boss GT-10, Roland VS-20, DigiTech RP-series processor, and so on. These produce a hotter output than a mic and typically plug directly into an interface's line input. If the device has a computer interface, you may be able to monitor the effect output with no latency while listening to playback from SONAR; in any event, you can always monitor the sound within SONAR.

A variation on this is if you use an amp sim as a stand-alone processor in a laptop or other computer. You might, for example, use a laptop-based setup for live performance, in which case you'll have some sort of audio interface for feeding an amp, PA system, and so on. You can take this output and feed it into your computer's audio interface, as if you were using a hardware effects system such as those mentioned earlier.

Recording Direct and Using Plug-Ins

This technique requires that your audio interface have an instrument input, as discussed in Chapter 2, or that you're using a preamp or other device to provide a proper match between the guitar and audio interface. Recording direct produces a very clean sound, which is fine for some applications; but in general, guitarists tend to prefer more of an "amp sound," or at least add effects. This is where plug-ins come into play.

If you think of a computer as a rack, then plug-ins are like rack-mount effects that "plug in" to a track. The most important point to understand is that *plug-ins process whatever is recorded in the track.* This is why you want to record direct: That way, the plug-in can work with the dry, unprocessed guitar sound and process it as desired. You can change the sound at any time simply by changing the plug-in settings, right up to the final mixdown. For example, you may start off recording with an AC30-type bright sound, but as a song progresses, you find that it's becoming "heavier" as you add drums and bass. No problem: Change the plug-in to, for example, more of a Marshall Plexi sound.

However, this also means that if you want to monitor the processed sound while you're recording your guitar, the dry guitar needs to be processed by the plug-in, and you listen to the computer's output. This is why there's latency—the computer has to process the sound before you can hear it. With a fast computer, decent interface drivers, and headphones, you probably won't find this latency objectionable. If you do, you'll instead need to get your sound before it goes into the computer (for example, with an effects box, as described earlier) and monitor that instead of the computer output. This is a situation where effects boxes with a built-in inter-face can be fabulous, because while you're monitoring the effects, you can also be feeding in the computer's output to the effects box/interface via USB. If the interface has a headphone jack—which is very likely—you can then monitor other tracks you've recorded (drums, vocals, and so on).

Plug-In Technologies

There are two main types of plug-in technology: host-based (also called *native*) and hardware-based. Hardware-based plug-ins run only with certain specialized hardware computer cards or outboard FireWire boxes designed for digital signal processing, such as the UAD-2 series from Universal Audio. Host-based plug-ins, as provided with SONAR, use the computer's microprocessor to do any needed digital signal processing and therefore require no additional, specialized hardware.

Native plug-ins require a certain amount of CPU power, so the more plug-ins you run (especially virtual instruments, which are also considered plug-ins), the harder the CPU has to work. As a result, there are limits to how many plug-ins you can use with a software program. If you want to run more plug-ins, the two main solutions are to use a faster CPU or to increase the system latency.

Plug-In Formats

To make sure that plug-ins can load reliably into "host" programs, such as SONAR, specifications have been drawn up for various plug-in formats. Plug-ins need to follow these specifications to work with hosts that support particular formats. Although different formats aren't compatible with each other, most plug-in manufacturers recognize marketplace reality and produce their plug-ins in multiple formats to accommodate the greatest number of users. The main formats are:

▷ **DirectX.** This is an older Windows format. Although some programs have dropped DirectX support, SONAR continues to support this format.

▷ **VST.** Steinberg created the VST (*Virtual Studio Technology*) format for Mac and Windows, and it remains the most popular Windows plug-in format. SONAR supports VST. (Note: The Mac and Windows versions of a VST plug-in are functionally the same but are not compatible. For example, if a company produces a Windows plug-in but not a Mac version, you can't run the Windows plug-in on a Mac.)

▷ **AU.** Introduced with OS X, Apple created this plug-in format specifically for the Mac. As AU plug-ins are Mac-only, they aren't relevant to SONAR.

▷ **RTAS.** This plug-in format from Avid is used exclusively for Pro Tools and is not supported by SONAR.

With SONAR, there is no obvious difference between using DirectX or VST plug-ins, and SONAR includes a mix of both kinds; for example, the Sonitus effects are DirectX, but the PX-64 Percussion Strip is VST. They load into a track identically (see Figure 5.4) and function pretty much identically as well.

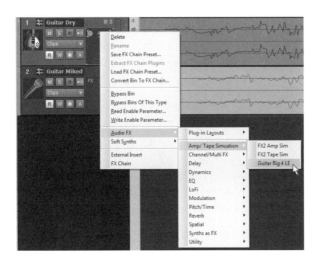

Figure 5.4

SONAR's plug-ins are arranged in a convenient menu, where you can choose the plug-in (or multiple plug-ins) you want to insert into a track. Here, Guitar Rig 4 is being selected.

So far we've talked about signal processors, but virtual instruments (including virtual "analog" synthesizers, sampled pianos, drum synthesizers, and so on) are also plug-ins. SONAR supports two virtual instrument protocols, DXi (*DirectX Instrument*) and VSTi (*Virtual Studio Technology Instrument*). Like DirectX, DXi is fading but remains supported by SONAR.

How to Combine Physical and Virtual Worlds

No law says you're limited to using only virtual amps or physical amps; you can get some great sounds by mixing and matching the two technologies.

Use a Real Cabinet

Some guitarists love the concept of amp sims but want to feel an actual speaker pushing air rather than going direct into a mixer or PA. Fair enough, but the problem here probably isn't the virtual amp, but rather the virtual cabinet. Fortunately, one of the cool aspects of using an amp sim is you can choose from multiple amp types and feed them into your favorite physical cab, which you can then mike.

In this application, bypass the cabinet in Guitar Rig 4 LE (see Figure 5.5) or your amp sim software of choice.

Figure 5.5
In Guitar Rig 4 LE and most other amp sims, it's possible to bypass the cabinet or preamp/amp if you want to combine, for example, an amp sim's effects with a physical amp and cabinet. With Guitar Rig, the speaker cabinet has a "power" button you can click on or off.

Of course you'll still need a physical power amp to drive the speaker(s). If you're using a standard guitar amp, you may be able to patch into an effects loop return and bypass the preamp stage completely. However, odds are the amp will still influence the sound, which may or may not be a good thing. It might be better to choose a simple, accurate power amp, such as the kind used to drive non-powered speakers (for example, QSC, Peavey, Phonic, Crown, Yamaha, Lab Gruppen, Mackie, Alto, and so on). This will reproduce the characteristics of whatever amp you've chosen in your amp sim as faithfully as possible.

Use a Physical Preamp

Similarly, if you like the sound of your amp's preamp but want the flexibility of using your sim's amp and cabinet, you can take a post-preamp effects loop output (send), feed it into your computer's audio interface, and run the signal through your sim's amp and cabinet. If you want to use hardware effects, you can insert them between the effects loop output and the audio interface input.

Doubling Up

Yet another option is to split your guitar into two paths (for example, with a Y-cord). One drives a guitar amp (which you can mike), while the other goes "dry" into the computer. This has two big advantages. First, you're playing through your amp, so you're getting the "feel" of the amp and no latency as you play. Second, you can process the dry track through amp sims to get entirely different sounds. If you like these better than the miked sound, you can use them instead—or combine them with the miked sound.

Setting Up to Record in SONAR

NOW THAT WE'VE COVERED THE VARIOUS WAYS to record a guitar track in SONAR, let's start tracking. Here are the main steps you need to take.

Insert an Audio Track

You need a track into which you can record. There are several ways to do this:

▷ Choose Insert > Audio Track.

▷ In the Track view, right-click in a blank space in the Track view's header area (where you see track names and numbers) and then select Insert Audio Track.

▷ In the Console view, in the Track drop-down menu, select Insert Audio Track.

▷ In the Inspector's left (track) module, you can right-click in most places and choose Insert Audio Track.

Select a Track Input Driver

To tell a track which input to record from, select the appropriate input driver in the track's input field. To do this in the Console, Inspector, or a track in the Track view, click on the Input field. You'll see a list of all drivers that were checked under Preferences > Audio Devices. (Note: If you don't see the Input field button, click on Modules in the Console's upper left or Display underneath the Inspector; make sure In/Out is checked. In the Track view, click on the Track Control list above the track strips, just to the left of the time ruler, and make sure I/O is selected.)

If the input is stereo, then you'll see individual entries for the left channel, right channel, and both channels (stereo); see Figure 6.1.

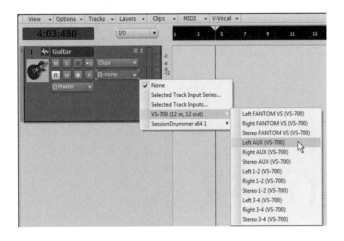

Figure 6.1

Input selection for the Console view, Track view, and Inspector is pretty similar. In this example, the VS-700 interface's Left Aux input is being selected as the input.

Associating Software Drivers with Physical Inputs

If you use an interface and can't make sense out of the driver names, don't panic—just check all the drivers in Preferences > Devices and then assign a track to any interface input. Plug your sound source (such as a guitar) into each input until you hear it—that's the input that correlates to the input driver you selected in the track. Now select a different input driver for the track and plug the sound source into other jacks until you find out which input correlates to the newly selected input driver.

Note that you can test outputs similarly, but if you're plugging outputs into speakers or headphones, remember to turn down the volume before making any changes.

Mono versus Stereo Inputs

Many interface inputs are shown as a stereo pair, but suppose you're not recording the guitar's output—instead, it's going through an amp with a line-level, mono direct output designed for recording. Let's also suppose you have a device like the VS-700, whose line-level input drivers are presented as a stereo pair—but also include each channel as an individual input. For example, Inputs 1 and 2 would appear as something like Left 1-2 (VS-700), Right 1-2 (VS-700), and Stereo 1-2 (VS-700). But the amp output is mono—what do you do?

In this case, if you had plugged the amp output into Input 1, you would select Left 1-2 (VS-700), because the *lower* number of a stereo pair is always considered to be the left channel, while the *higher* number of the pair is always considered the right channel. As you're plugged into Input 1, Left 1-2 (VS-700) is the correct choice. Had you plugged into Input 2, then you'd choose Right 1-2 (VS-700).

Select a Track Output Driver

Just as the track needs to receive a signal for recording, it also needs to feed an output for monitoring. The implementation is similar to assigning an input—use the Output drop-down menu to choose the desired track destination. In most cases, this will be the Master channel, which sets the overall level of the outputs from all the individual tracks and busses. However, this is still a software channel, so you need to send this to one of the hardware output drivers selected under Preferences > Devices (see Figure 6.2).

Figure 6.2
This shows SONAR's Console view. The leftmost channel is the track that's accepting the guitar signal at its input. The output is assigned to the Master channel (second from the left). The three channels on the right are hardware output devices that were enabled under Preferences. The Master channel is feeding the Main VS-700 hardware output. This is what drives the monitor speakers and headphones. However, it could also be assigned to the Sub hardware output or individual analog Outputs 1 and 2.

Record-Enable the Track

The following applies to the Console view, Track view, and the Inspector. Click on the track's Record Enable button; it will turn red (see Figure 6.3).

Figure 6.3
The Record Enable button turns red when enabled.

If you play your guitar, you should see activity in the associated track meter. Set the input level control on your audio interface (which will be either a hardware control or a software control within the audio interface's main routing and mixing application) so that the meter's lights are never red. In general, the optimum setting is for the meter's green lights to be lit, with the strongest peaks making occasional forays into the lower part of the meter's orange zone. However, note that you probably won't hear your guitar yet.

Monitoring through the Computer

We won't insert any plug-ins yet—we'll keep things simple at first and just record the straight guitar sound. (Chapter 8, "How to Use Plug-In Effects," covers how to add plug-ins to the signal path.) However, monitoring through the computer is essential if you're using plug-ins to obtain your particular sound, as you'll need to monitor the plug-in output, hence the computer's output. So we'll practice with monitoring through the computer anyway, just to get in the habit of doing so, and also to check out what latency does to the signal.

To monitor through the computer, click on the Input Echo button (to the right of the Record button; see Figure 6.4).

Figure 6.4
Turning on Input Echo allows you to monitor your guitar
through plug-ins by listening to the output of the computer.

Input Echo will turn blue to indicate that it's enabled. Now you should be able to hear your guitar. If not, make sure the outputs are assigned correctly, as described previously.

Sometimes for reasons known only to the laws of chance, you'll lose the ability to monitor through particular plug-ins. If this happens, don't panic; disable the Record and Input Echo buttons and then re-enable them. Most of the time, this restores monitoring through the plug-ins.

Monitoring the Input

If you have a slower computer and the latency is intolerable when monitoring through the computer, or you're getting your sound via external hardware effects plugged into the audio interface input, you can monitor the input signal coming *in* to the computer.

Most audio interfaces come with some kind of mixing and routing application that allows you to send interface inputs to interface outputs, or to ins and outs within SONAR (see Figure 6.5).

These applications vary from extremely basic to very sophisticated, possibly even including routing through processors inside the interface (as is the case with the VS-20 interface—see Figure 6.6).

Figure 6.5
The VS-700 includes a software application that controls all aspects of direct monitoring.
The guitar is feeding the Aux input, which is being routed directly to the Main hardware output.
This bypasses the computer altogether, so there's no latency.

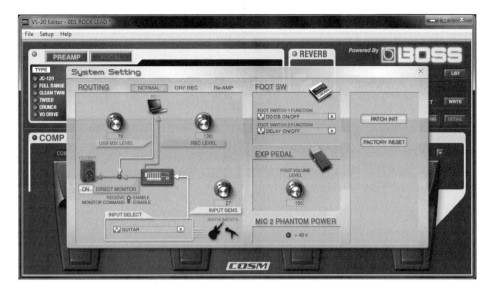

Figure 6.6
With the VS-20, your guitar goes through a hardware processor to get your guitar tone; you can then monitor that output directly, rather than going through your computer. Note that this interface application is a program unto itself where you can not only do routing and interfacing, but also edit the hardware processor.

With input direct monitoring, make sure that Input Echo is off. You won't hurt anything if it's left on, but as there will be latency through the computer and no latency with direct monitoring, if these two signals are happening at the same time, you'll hear a delay between them. Conversely, if Input Echo is on, you want to make sure that any direct monitoring faders are turned down.

How to Add a Metronome

We're almost ready to record, but it's a lot easier to record with a metronome, so let's find out how to do that. (Granted, a metronome isn't the most exciting rhythm section in the world, which is why we'll cover how to put together backing drum tracks in Chapter 35, "Create Drum Backing Tracks with Session Drummer 3.") You can choose a variety of Metronome characteristics, such as count-in length, the sounds used for the metronome, and where the sound is assigned.

If you open a project using the Normal template, the Metronome comes pre-assigned to its own bus, which feeds the Master out. You set the Metronome characteristics by going Preferences > Project > Metronome. (This is visible in both the Basic and Advanced Preferences views—see Figure 6.7.) If the Metronome bus takes up too much space in the Console view for your liking, right-click in a blank space in the Metronome bus and choose Narrow Strip.

I think the defaults Cakewalk has chosen for the Metronome are fine as is; however, the Preferences let you adjust several pertinent parameters—count-in for recording (in measures or beats); whether you want it during playback, recording, or both; and the levels of the Metronome clicks (the downbeat can have a different level compared to the other beats).

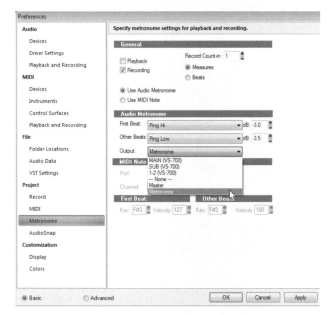

Figure 6.7

The Metronome is being assigned to the Metronome bus so it can have a dedicated volume control.

However, note that you also enable/disable the Metronome for recording or playback from the Control Bar, in the Control Bar's Transport module (see Figure 6.8). This is very convenient for adjusting the Metronome on the fly, without having to open the Preferences.

Figure 6.8

You can enable/disable the Metronome sound from within the Control Bar. Here, it's being enabled for recording but not playback.

Time to Record!

Okay—the guitar is feeding SONAR, we can monitor what we're playing, and the Metronome is set up. So, click the Transport's Record button (or type R) and start playing. When you're finished, click on the Transport's Stop button (or hit the QWERTY keyboard's spacebar).

Part II

Using and Managing Effects

About Busses

NOW THAT WE'VE HAD A CLOSE ENCOUNTER with tracks, let's up the ante and take a look at another structural element in SONAR: the bus. We need to know about this for when we discuss effects, but there are many other uses for busses as well.

Bus Basics

A bus is like a mixer in that it combines a number of signals and sends them somewhere. For example, the master bus is where all your track outputs terminate. This master bus then feeds a stereo hardware output so you can monitor the results over a speaker system or headphones.

Subgroup Busses

Another common bus type is the subgroup bus. As an example of how this works, consider a complex guitar-miking situation where you recorded five channels of guitar: one miked amp, a second miked amp, a direct out from one of the amps, and two room mics to add ambience. Suppose that while mixing you get a perfect balance of all these signals, but then decide you want the entire guitar sound to be just a teeny bit louder. You now have to adjust each fader, and there's no guarantee you'll get the balance exactly right. (In fact, I pretty much guarantee you won't!)

The solution is to feed each track's output into a subgroup bus that mixes together all the tracks and then sends that combined output to the master bus. Now, you can change the level of all mics simultaneously with the bus level control.

With most busses, there will be a separate send level control that's independent of the track's main fader and sets the level going to the bus. You can feed a signal into the bus either before or after the track's main fader (called pre- or post-fader, respectively).

If the send is post-fader, then the level going to the bus will be raised or lowered according to the track fader. If the send is pre-fader, then the send level to the bus is constant, regardless of the track fader setting. In the example of using multiple mics, if the guitar signals feed the subgroup bus pre-fader, then you can turn down the main track faders so they don't influence the mix at all and create the proper balance solely with the send level controls.

Another example of why you would choose pre- or post-fader involves reverb. Suppose you have reverb set up in a bus (we'll talk about effects busses next), so you can send different amounts of signal from various tracks into the reverb to create the effect of being in a concert hall. If the send is post-fader, then pulling down the track fader will also pull down the reverb's "tail," which will sound unnatural. If the send is pre-fader, then you can pull down the track fader, but the reverb's tail will decay naturally.

Effects Busses

An effects bus can add an effect to multiple tracks. The classic example is adding the same reverb ambience to several tracks so that they all sound as if they're playing in a common acoustic space.

A bus send level control picks off signals from each track and then sends them to the effects bus. Effects busses are typically stereo, so the effects sends section also includes a pan control so you can "weight" the effect sound toward one channel or the other (see Figure 7.1).

Figure 7.1

The Guitar track and Drums track each have sends enabled, and both sends are assigned to the Reverb bus. The Reverb bus (to the left of the Master bus) has the PerfectSpace reverb inserted.

Like any track, a bus has an FX Bin. Suppose you insert a reverb in the bus FX Bin. If you send a lot of signal into the bus from the vocal track and a little from the drums, the vocal will have heavy reverb, and the drums will have a little reverb. The reverb output is then assigned to the master bus so you can hear the reverb effect in the overall mix.

Another important point is that a send bus that contains effects (which generally add to the track output) is usually set for processed (wet) sound only. This is because the channel fader provides the unprocessed signal to the master bus, while the send bus effect contributes only the effect sound, adding it to the unprocessed signal. In fact, it's often recommended that you not include any straight sound in an aux bus effect. For example, a reverb effect would be set to reverb sound only, and the bus master level for the reverb would adjust the blend of the reverb added to the "dry" mix.

Because effects can work as track inserts or in a send bus, here is why you'd choose one option over the other. Every plug-in requires some amount of computing power, so the fewer plug-ins you use, the more processing "headroom" is available. Therefore, if you want to process several channels with the same effect, you're better off loading a single effect in an aux bus than you are inserting the same effect multiple times as track insert effects. For instance, when adding reverb, it makes more sense to use it as a send bus effect, synthesize the desired acoustic space, and mix in varying amounts of signal from each channel's send level control. This is particularly true with the PerfectSpace convolution reverb, which tends to draw a fair amount of CPU power.

One final consideration involving sends relates to trimming the overall level of all sends simultaneously. For example, suppose you start turning up more and more sends, to the point where they overload the input of the effect they're feeding. The solution is simple (see Figure 7.2): Reduce the bus return channel's input Gain control, which affects the signal coming into the bus channel. (The bus volume fader affects the bus return channel's output level, which typically dumps into the master output bus.)

Figure 7.2
Just like any other input channel, the bus return channel has an input Gain control for trimming the incoming signal.

Note that to see the Gain control in the Console view, select Input/Trim under Modules; in the Inspector, select Input/Trim under Display; and in Track view, select All or Mix from the View drop-down menu on the top right of the track strips.

However, this is just the short-form version of trimming bus levels; see the section "Gain-Staging with Busses" for more details.

Creating a Bus

With hardware mixers, there are a limited number of busses, and they typically have specific uses. However, SONAR treats busses as "objects" that have no dedicated purpose. Any bus you create can be an aux bus for effects, a master output bus, a bus for sending a separate mix to headphones, or whatever.

In the Console view, either one or two busses are already "sketched in" for the audio channels (they're grayed out until you actually assign a track to a bus) if Sends/Bank/Patch is selected under Modules. You select one or two sends by going Options > Sends and choosing Send Display: 1 or Send Display: 2 (see Figure 7.3).

Figure 7.3

The Console view is showing two sends for each channel. The sends in the left and right channels are grayed out, because no sends have been assigned yet. The middle channel has one send assigned to reverb and another to delay, so they're active and not grayed out.

To create a bus in Track view, right-click on a blank space inside the track where you want to add the send. In the context menu, select Insert > Send and either select a destination from busses that already exist, create a new stereo or surround bus, or invoke the Insert Send Assistant. (More on this later.) In the Console/Inspector views, click on the little + sign in the send section's upper right. This brings up the same basic bus context menu as in Track view.

If there are more than two sends in the Console/Inspector, there are scroll arrows like the ones used for FX Bins in these views. In Track view, you can either extend the track strip to the right to create more space for the sends to show on a single line or extend the bottom of the track to show the sends (see Figure 7.4).

Figure 7.4

In the upper layout, the track strip has been extended to the right, and the sends (outlined) are all in a line. In the lower layout, the track height has been adjusted so that the sends are stacked on top of each other.

Note that for sends to function, they must be enabled; to do this in Track view, click on the small rectangle/arrow to the left of the send bus name. (It's blue when enabled and gray when disabled.) In the Console/Inspector views, it's the small "power" button to the right of the send Post button. (Again, blue is enabled, and gray is disabled.) Disable unused sends to save CPU loading, or just delete the send altogether in any view by clicking on the drop-down menu that chooses the send destination and choosing Delete Send.

The Insert Send Assistant

There's a certain amount of housekeeping involved in creating a new bus; you need to name it, insert the desired effect, decide whether the send should be pre- or post-fader, and the like. Invoking the Insert Send Assistant simplifies this process by presenting a single window where you can define the bus characteristics (see Figure 7.5).

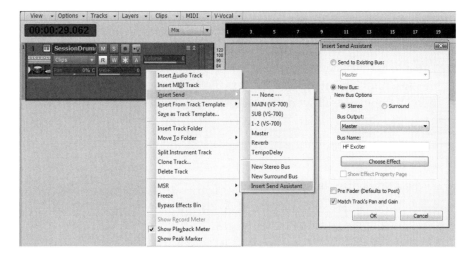

Figure 7.5

The Insert Send Assistant simplifies the process of creating a new send bus.

If you use the Insert Send Assistant to create a new stereo bus, you have the option to choose a post- or pre-fader send, name the bus, choose an effect for the bus FX Bin, choose a bus output, and more.

Busses That Feed Busses That Feed Busses That...

Note that you can create busses that feed into busses, which can in turn feed other busses. Although you'll seldom need to reach this level of complexity, here's one example of where you might need a bus feeding a bus.

Suppose you've recorded multiple guitar tracks, as described earlier, and assigned them to a subgroup for easy level changes. You've also recorded backup singers into three different mics and sent those tracks to their own subgroup.

Now you want to add a reverb send effect to the guitar and vocals. In this case, the subgroup busses would go to a reverb bus, so we have busses feeding another bus.

Multiple busses also provide far more flexibility for effects. For example, suppose you want several instruments to go through tempo-synched delay, but you also want them to go through a reverb. Furthermore, you want other tracks to go through the reverb but not the delay. You can create a delay bus and assign that to a separate reverb bus; tracks that need reverb and no delay can have sends that go directly to the reverb bus.

Gain-Staging with Busses

When working with effects placed in aux busses, there are potentially four places to alter levels:

▷ The channel's send control that feeds the bus

▷ The channel's main fader, if the send control is set to post-fader

▷ The bus input Gain control

▷ The bus output Volume fader

Furthermore, a signal processor inserted in the bus may have input and/or output level controls, and the processor's sound may depend on the incoming level. (For example, with distortion, more input signal generally increases the amount of distortion.) If these controls aren't set correctly, an overly "hot" level may cause distortion, while too low a level can degrade the sound. Here's the general procedure for proper level setting:

1. If the effect has input or output level controls, set them to unity gain (in other words, the signal is neither amplified nor attenuated).

2. Set the aux bus gain and output level controls to unity gain.

3. Adjust the individual send controls for the desired amount of effect. The higher you turn the individual send controls, the more that channel will contribute to the processed sound.

4. As the sends from the individual channels start to add up, they may overload the effect's input. Leave the effect input at unity gain and use the bus Gain control to reduce the level going to the effect.

5. If the signal going to the effect is too low, use the bus Gain control to bring it up. If there still isn't enough level to drive the effect, increase the processor's input control (if available) as needed.

Fine Points about Busses

When you have busses feeding busses that feed busses, the bus solo function needs to set some rules.

▷ When you solo a bus, all busses are muted except for any busses into which the soloed bus feeds, as well as any busses that feed into the soloed bus. Were these busses muted, there would be no point in soloing a bus, as you wouldn't hear anything.

▷ MIDI tracks assigned to external MIDI ports won't be muted, as the external MIDI device's audio output might return to SONAR via an audio track input.

The bus fader is always post-effect. However, you might want an effect that continues even after the bus output level fader has been turned down (for example, a long, repeating echo or a long reverb "tail" that fades into silence). In that case, use the bus Gain control to set the bus level, and leave the master fader set to 0.

8

How to Use Plug-In Effects

EFFECTS, ALSO CALLED *signal processors*, are a key element of great guitar sounds—but they're also vital for other instruments, vocals, mixes, and mastering. With guitar, effects are often part of the guitar's essential character; try to imagine hard rock without distortion (or surf music without spring reverb, for that matter!). When mixing, effects allow tweaking sounds so that they blend in better, stand out more, add interest to parts that could use a little spice, or do whatever is needed to create the ultimate mix.

SONAR uses *plug-ins*—virtual, software-based signal processors—for adding most effects (Chapters 19 through 24 describe the plug-ins provided with SONAR), although you can also integrate external hardware effects.

The Four Places to Insert Effects

Unlike a traditional hardware mixer that has a fixed way to insert effects, SONAR is much more flexible. It allows you to use effects in four basic ways: as insert effects within individual tracks, as effects within individual clips, as bus (send) effects that process all signals feeding the bus, and as master effects that affect the entire mixed output. Let's look further into each option. First we'll cover them from a conceptual standpoint and then we'll get practical.

Track (Channel) Insert Effects

Insert effects are named after the insert jacks found in hardware mixers, which are part of individual mixer channels. These channel inserts are located between the input pre-amp and the fader/pan pot circuitry, as this allows for proper gain staging—few effects are designed for mic-level signals, so the channel's preamp can bring the incoming signal up to a consistent level for feeding the effect. Also, if the effect generates any noise, pulling down the fader reduces both the channel audio and any noise generated by an insert effect.

SONAR follows the same concept. Insert effects appear within a specific track, affect only the track into which they are inserted, and affect the entire track unless you're using automation to, for example, bypass the effect in certain places. A few popular insert effects include dynamics control, distortion, delay, and chorusing, but of course there are many more.

Technically speaking, EQ is also an insert effect. However, because of EQ's importance, SONAR X1 Producer Edition "hardwires" the ProChannel channel strip, which includes EQ, into each channel so it needn't be inserted—just like almost all hardware mixers. ProChannel also includes dynamics control and saturation; these effects, along with EQ, can be in any order. (The Studio Edition also hardwires EQ into individual channels, but it uses the Sonitus EQ rather than the ProChannel.)

Clip Effects

In SONAR, it's possible to insert effects in individual clips within a track. In this case, the effect alters only that particular clip, and no other clips in the track.

Send Effects

Also called *bus effects* or *aux effects*, these effects are different from insert effects because they affect multiple tracks simultaneously (as described in Chapter 7).

Master Effects

This is a variation on the insert effect for individual tracks, but it involves inserting effects into the master output bus. These alter the entire mixed signal, not just individual tracks; for example, you might use EQ to brighten up the entire mix a bit or compression to make the mix seem a little louder overall. In SONAR, master effects are handled the same way as track insert effects—they insert into your master channel.

You may have heard of a process called *mastering*, where a mastering engineer adds processing to a finished stereo mix to sweeten the sound—think of it as a final "buffing." Although adding master effects as you mix can be handy if you want to get a sense of how mastering might affect the sound, if you intend to take your mix to a mastering engineer, do not insert any master effects when you export the mix as a file—a good mastering engineer will likely want to use a familiar set of high-quality mastering tools or plug-ins.

FX Bins

As we've covered plug-in basics, let's look at how to integrate them into a project.

Tracks, busses, the Inspector, and clips have FX Bins, which you can think of as empty racks where you screw in your effects boxes—but with virtual screws, of course! Right-click within an FX Bin, choose Audio FX, and you'll see your available plug-ins (see Figure 8.1).

There are two alternative ways to add effects:

    ▷ In the Inspector and Console views, click on the small + sign to the upper right of the FX Bin, and a menu will appear for accessing plug-ins.

    ▷ Open the Browser and click on the PlugIns tab. Click on the Audio FX button, and you'll see all available system plug-ins (see Figure 8.2). You can drag and drop these into any FX Bin. To replace—not just supplement—any existing effects, hold down the Alt key while dragging in an effect.

Figure 8.1

Here's how to access the plug-ins included with SONAR X1. Note that you can customize how these are organized and displayed with SONAR's Plug-In Manager utility (see Chapter 14, "The Care and Feeding of Plug-Ins"). Note that, for example, the Cakewalk DirectX and Sonitus effects are in their own folders. But you could also group plug-ins by function, manufacturer, how often you use them (a "favorites" folder), and so on.

Figure 8.2

The Browser shows all effects available on your system; you can then just drag and drop an effect (or FX chains, described later) into an FX Bin.

Viewing Effects in the FX Bin

To open an effect's graphic interface, double-click on the effect name. If there are more FX than you can see in the Bin at one time, SONAR has two ways of handling this. In the Inspector and Console view, up/down buttons just above the FX Bin's upper left let you scroll through the inserted effects. In Track view, small arrows to the right of the FX Bin scroll up or down through the list of effects.

Other FX Bin Options

To bypass an individual effect in a Bin, click on the Power on/off button to the left of the effect name. Blue indicates the effect is active, while gray indicates the effect is bypassed.

You can bypass all effects in all Bins by typing E. You can also do this from the Control Bar Mix section by clicking on the FX button. This is useful for two main reasons:

▷ Bypassing all effects reduces CPU consumption, which may allow you to reduce latency when recording guitar in real time.

▷ SONAR includes a feature called Path Delay Compensation. Some effects require so much processing power that they add their own latency; SONAR compensates for these by delaying all other effects/tracks by an equivalent amount so there's no perceived timing differences among the various tracks with their various effects. Bypassing all effects removes any added latency, which again can be helpful when recording guitar in real time.

In addition to working with individual effects, SONAR X1 lets you create "virtual racks" of effects plug-ins, called *FX chains*, so you can save and load groups of effects as a single entity. You manage effects and effects chains by right-clicking in the FX Bin and opening up a context menu (see Figure 8.3). Here are the context menu options.

Figure 8.3
The FX Bin context menu provides additional ways to manage effects and the FX Bin.

▷ **Delete** removes the effect or effect chain on which you right-clicked. You can also delete an effect by clicking on its name and hitting the QWERTY keyboard's Delete key.

▷ **Rename** applies only to effects chains—specifically, the one on which you right-clicked.

▷ **Save FX Chain Preset** saves the current group of FX in the FX Bin as an FX chain. When you save, this navigates to the FX Chain Presets folder. These files have a .fxc filename extension.

▷ **Extract FX Chain Plugins** deconstructs the FX chain on which you right-clicked to the individual effects that make up the chain. Use this command if you want to edit one of the effects in the FX chain. Note: You can also extract FX chain plug-ins automatically by holding down the Shift key as you drag an FX chain from the Browser into an FX Bin.

▷ **Load FX Chain Preset** navigates to the FX Chain Presets folder so you can load an FX chain.

▷ **Convert Bin to FX Chain** consolidates all the effects in the Bin into an FX chain. Note that if an FX Bin has a mix of individual effects and effects chains, you cannot save this as an FX chain unless you use the Convert Bin to FX Chain option to consolidate all these effects into a single FX chain.

If an FX chain is consolidated with individual effects into an FX chain, and you later extract the effects, the FX chain effects will be extracted in the order in which they appear in the FX chain and inserted in the chain of effects wherever the FX chain was located.

▷ **Bypass Bin** bypasses all effects in that particular FX Bin. In the Track view, all labels in the FX Bin will be dimmed. In the Console view and the Inspector, the effect names are grayed out.

▷ **Bypass Bins of This Type** bypasses all effects in all Bins of the same type in which you right-clicked. For example, if you clicked in a clip's FX Bin, then all effects in all clip FX Bins are bypassed, but not effects in tracks, busses, or master FX Bins.

▷ **Read Enable Parameter** and **Write Enable Parameter** relate to automation, which is covered in Chapter 16, "Mixing and Effects Automation."

▷ **Audio FX** is where you choose the effects you want to add.

▷ **Soft Synths** lets you insert a soft synth into an FX Bin. Generally, you'll use the Insert > Soft Synth command to place the synth in its own dedicated track, but this option is useful if the synth has an audio input that lets you process signals through the synthesizer, in which case it basically acts like a standard effect.

▷ **External Insert** creates a plug-in "shell" that lets you treat an external hardware processor (such as a cool vacuum-tube guitar effect!) as if it was a plug-in. We'll get into the details later in this chapter.

▷ **FX Chain** relates to constructing FX chains, as described later.

Clip FX Bins

Clip FX Bins act like Track view FX Bins, with a few small changes. One is that a clip does not have a designated FX Bin, but it creates one as soon as you drag in an effect or FX chain. The look is very much like an FX chain container, and it contains individual effects and FX chains. Closing the container window (by clicking on the large X in the upper left) leaves a small FX box; clicking on this reopens the container window.

FX Chains

You can think of an FX chain as "virtual multi-effects," with all effects connected in series. You can have several FX chains in a Bin, but you can't insert an FX chain within an FX chain. As with standard effects, you can see FX chains in the Browser. Simply drag and drop the FX chain into an FX Bin as you would with standard effects, and also as with standard effects, hold down the Alt key to replace all existing effects in the FX Bin. Chapter 10, "Build a Virtual Amp Channel with Effects Chains," includes detailed information on FX chains and how to apply them.

Drag-and-Drop Behavior with FX Chains

When using the Browser, drag-and-drop behavior for FX chains differs slightly depending on where you drag them. When dragged into a clip, track FX Bin (Track view, Inspector, or Console), or bus (Inspector or Console), the chain opens up a window that shows which effects are contained in the FX chain (see Figure 8.4). Also, if you close this window, double-clicking on the FX chain's name reopens it.

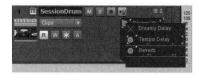

Figure 8.4
Dragging an FX chain usually opens up a window to show which effects are contained in the chain. To close this window, click on the X next to the chain's name.

> **Note**

When an FX chain is dragged and dropped into a track (in other words, in a space next to a waveform in that track), only the FX chain name shows up in the FX Bin, and the other effects are not shown upon dragging.

Constructing FX Chains from Scratch

The FX Bin offers a way to "construct" FX chains from scratch, without having to convert an FX Bin to an FX chain. This is handy if, for example, you already have a few effects in a Track view FX Bin that you don't want included in an FX chain. The following works for all FX Bins.

▷ Right-click in the FX Bin and select FX chain. A blank window will open. You can right-click on this and choose an audio effect from the Audio FX menu. The effect GUI will open; as soon as you close or move it, the FX chain's container window will close.

▷ You can also just drag an effect from the Browser on top the FX chain name. As soon as your mouse hovers over the FX chain name, its container window will open, and you can drop the effect wherever you want in the FX chain.

▷ You can close the container window at any time by clicking on the large X next to the FX chain name.

▷ Once you have the chain exactly as desired, you can right-click on it and choose Rename to give it a more descriptive name and then save it.

Integrating External Hardware Effects with SONAR

Plug-ins are wonderful, but they aren't all there is to effects. What about that cool fuzz pedal you have, the ancient Electro-Harmonix Memory Man you scored on eBay, or your favorite vintage tube compressor? Fortunately, you can make external hardware devices look like plug-ins to SONAR—with only a bit more effort than staying totally in the virtual world. However, note that you'll need an audio interface with at least one unused analog output and one unused analog input (or two of each for stereo effects). Here's how to insert external hardware in an FX Bin (see Figure 8.5).

1. Right-click in an FX Bin and choose External Insert.

2. The External Insert window will appear. Assign the send output to an unused interface output. In this example, it's going to the VS-700 Output 1 (the left channel of the input 1-2 stereo pair). Patch this output to your effect's input.

3. The slider above the Send meter adjusts the output level. It's set to −11.98 dB to accommodate the effect, which is designed for low-level inputs.

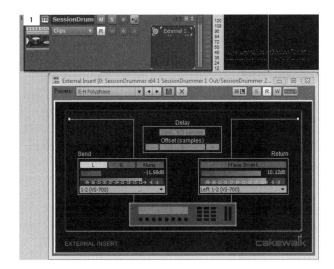

Figure 8.5

The External Insert plug-in allows you to treat physical hardware like a virtual plug-in, as far as SONAR is concerned.

4. Assign the Return section to an unused interface input. Patch the effect output to this input.

5. The Return section also has a slider for adjusting the gain. We need to increase the low-level output to be compatible with SONAR, which is why it shows +10.12 dB of gain. Note that you can also invert the phase in the Return section if needed.

6. Using external hardware introduces additional latency because the output has to go through a D/A converter, through the effect, and then come back into the system through an A/D converter. To compensate for this, click in the Delay field. SONAR will measure the degree of latency and then compensate automatically. In this example, the delay is about 20ms.

However, note that this compensation isn't always perfect. For example, if the external effect has a varying time delay, SONAR won't know which is the "real" delay. One possible solution is to bypass the external effect when you click on the Delay field, but this won't help if the effect introduces a delay when enabled. Fortunately, if necessary you can trim the offset manually in the Offset (Samples) field if you need really tight timing.

There are some other really useful External Insert features. Several of these parameters are automatable (Send Gain, Return Gain, Phase Invert, Left Mute, Right Mute, and Mono, which sums the right and left signals together so the same signal appears at the left and right hardware interface outputs). So, as one example, you can vary the output coming back from the effect, just as if it was a software plug-in being automated within SONAR.

Another really useful feature is that you can save the External Insert settings as a preset. If there's some piece of hardware you use a lot, saving the settings as a preset saves time.

Series, Parallel, and Series-Parallel Effects

WITH MOST GUITAR PEDALBOARDS, effects connect in *series.* This means the output of one effect feeds the input of the next effect. (SONAR's FX Bins work the same way.) Another somewhat less common way to connect effects is in *parallel.* In SONAR, this requires splitting the guitar into two (or more) separate paths; you can do this by duplicating tracks or by bussing, which allows you to process each signal path independently. You can then mix the outputs back together to create a mono signal or maintain the two separate paths and create a stereo output.

Parallel effects combinations can provide more sophisticated processing than series combinations. For example, putting bass through a wah gives a thin sound because the wah removes the bass "bottom." Placing the wah in parallel with the dry bass signal adds the filtered effect to the dry bass sound (which doesn't remove the low end).

Parallel effects chains are also a good way to create a stereo image, as one of the chain's paths can provide one channel, with the other path providing the other channel. For example, suppose you feed a guitar into two different amp simulations. You can pan one signal to the right and the other to the left to create a stereo spread from your two virtual cabinets.

You can take this even further with *series-parallel* effects chains. As with a parallel effects setup, this splits the signal path, but it also includes series effects within each split.

Creating Series and Series-Parallel Effects Chains

There are two ways to create parallel effects in SONAR. You can use SONAR's aux send busses (see Chapter 7 on sends and busses) to feed a signal into two effects, or you can clone a track and use different plug-ins on different tracks to create parallel effects.

To clone a track, right-click on a track number in Track view and then select Clone Track from the context menu. You have several available options when invoking the Clone function, such as the number of repetitions, the clone's starting track number, whether you also want to clone the effects, and so on (see Figure 9.1).

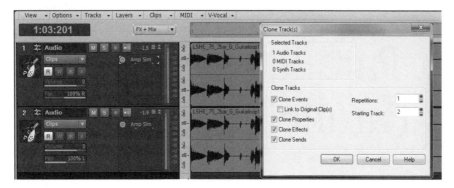

Figure 9.1

Track 1 has been cloned to Track 2, in accordance with the parameters set in the Clone Track dialog. Note that amp sims have been inserted as effects in both tracks, but as they use different cabinets, one sim is panned left, and the other is panned to the right.

Because these parallel, cloned tracks can also have series plug-ins within each track, it's possible to do parallel chains of series effects to create a series-parallel effects chain (see Figure 9.2).

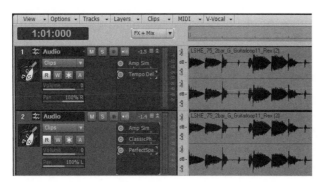

Figure 9.2

The cloned, parallel tracks from the previous example now have series effects inserted in the FX Bins, thus creating a series-parallel effects chain.

Series and Parallel Effects in Guitar Rig 4 LE

Guitar Rig 4 LE, included in SONAR X1 Producer Edition, allows for not only series effects but also parallel effects via its Split component (found under Tools). Inserting Guitar Rig 4 LE in a track's FX Bin makes it possible to create a parallel effects setup within a single track, so it's not necessary to do any cloning or bussing.

The Split component actually has three sub-modules; see Figure 9.3.

Figure 9.3
The Split module in Guitar Rig 4 LE allows
you to create parallel effects paths.

Split A creates the first split and is followed by a chorus to create one signal path. Note that you could also have multiple effects in series, not just chorus, to create a series-parallel path. Split B creates the second split and includes a phaser to create a second parallel signal path. The Split Mix sub-module mixes the two paths back again into a single output. It also includes a crossfade parameter for adjusting the proportion of the two splits, as well as a pan control for each split. The switch in the upper right can reverse Split B's phase, which produces some novel effects in some situations.

A split can either separate a stereo signal into its individual channels, with each channel becoming a separate signal path, or split a mono input signal into two paths. Furthermore, a unique feature of Guitar Rig is that you can have splits within splits (see Figure 9.4).

Figure 9.4
Guitar Rig 4 LE allows you to create splits within splits,
or even splits within splits within splits within splits....

Let's analyze the signal path. This setup uses two splits, which we'll call 1 and 2. Split 1A goes through a chorus, whose output goes into Split 2. This provides two paths, Split 2A and Split 2B, each of which goes through a separate delay. The Split 2 splits are then mixed back together, providing the final A path for Split 1A.

Split 1B goes through a phaser and reverb, therefore providing the B path for Split 1. Finally, Split 1A and 1B are mixed together in the final Split Mix module. This may seem a little confusing, but note that Guitar Rig 4 LE helps out by using different colors for splits when you have more than one split.

Effects Chains 2.0

I N CHAPTER 8, WE COVERED FX CHAINS as originally introduced in SONAR X1. However, with SONAR X1 Expanded, FX chains graduated to version 2.0 and added several functional and cosmetic improvements (including the ability to nest FX chains within FX chains). To check out these new features, we'll construct a virtual amp channel using FX Chains 2.0.

SONAR X1 Producer has two amp sims. Native Instruments' Guitar Rig 4 LE is a "lite" version of Guitar Rig 4; you'll find the manual in C:/Program Files/Native Instruments/ Guitar Rig 4/Documentation. The other is Cakewalk's own Amp Sim plug-in. Because SONAR X1 Studio has only the Cakewalk sim, for the benefit of both Studio and Producer owners, we'll build an effects chain around the Cakewalk Amp Sim. This is a no-frills plug-in, with only amp and cabinet sounds, along with tremolo. However, we can use SONAR's additional effects to create an effects chain where the whole is *much* greater than the sum of the parts.

The Importance of Effects Chain Gain-Staging

As guitar players, we tend to favor distortion. However, digital distortion is different from analog distortion and has an unpleasant quality. We want the amp sim's intentional distortion, but unless we're careful, it's possible to generate unintentional distortion within an effects chain. Proper gain-staging avoids this.

Before examining an FX chain for distortion, check your audio interface to make sure you're not overloading it with your guitar signal. Often a clipping indicator will alert you to distortion.

Aside from the Amp Sim, most plug-in effects we'll be using have output meters and output level controls. You don't want output meters to go into the red, as that creates internal distortion.

As to setting levels within the Amp Sim itself, in these chains it's invariably followed by a post-amp equalizer. So, monitor the Equalizer output level while adjusting the Amp Sim output; turn up the Amp Sim output until the Equalizer shows the desired output level. With these chains you can often set a fairly high Amp Sim output level because the subsequent EQ is generally cutting, not boosting, so it's attenuating the signal.

Cakewalk Amp Sim Controls

Before constructing our chain, let's look at the Cakewalk Amp Sim controls (see Figure 10.1).

There are eight basic amp models and a "direct box" (no amp) model. Each amp also has a bright switch. The four cabinets are 1×12, 2×12, 4×10, and 4×12. These have an Open Back option (don't expect too much from this, but there are ways to tame it somewhat) and an Off-Axis setting for the single virtual mic. Off-axis gives a duller, more resonant sound, whereas on-axis is more "in your face."

A Drive control sets the distortion amount, and there are also basic Bass, Mid, and Treble EQ sliders. The Tremolo includes Rate, Depth, and Bias.

Figure 10.1
The Cakewalk Amp Sim isn't very pretty and doesn't look very sophisticated—but as you'll discover, you can do a lot with it.

Create a Crunch Effects Chain

For a refresher on effects chains basics, see Chapter 8. Now, I'll give you some real-world examples of creating chains using FX Chains 2.0, starting with a Crunch guitar amp channel effects chain.

Drag the following effects from the browser into an FX Bin:

▷ Sonitus:fx Equalizer   ▷ Sonitus:fx Equalizer

▷ Cakewalk FX2 Amp Sim   ▷ Sonitus:fx Modulator

Once effects are in the FX Bin, if needed you can reorder them via drag-and-drop into the recommended order in Figure 10.2.

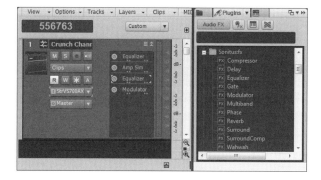

Figure 10.2

The browser is open to the right to show the available audio FX. Several processors have been dragged into the guitar track's FX Bin.

Now let's edit the processors to create our sound. For starters, adjust the settings to match those in the screenshots. The first equalizer tailors the sound going into the Amp Sim (see Figure 10.3).

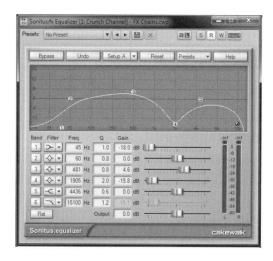

Figure 10.3

The first EQ conditions the pre-sim signal.

Rolling off the low and high end concentrates on distorting the midrange to give a "crunchy," midrange-y sound. The dip at 2 kHz promotes a smoother sound; these frequencies are above the guitar's note range, so preventing the amp sim from distorting these frequencies can reduce unneeded harmonics. (Note: The Amp Sim settings are the same as shown in Figure 10.1.)

The post–Amp Sim equalizer (see Figure 10.4) has a notch to reduce some high-frequency "fizz" and a low-pass filter to create a warmer timbre. Of course, this response doesn't look very flat, but the response of instrument amp speakers and cabinets is typically far from flat anyway.

Finally, there's modulation. This would usually add chorus, flanging, or some other thickening effect. It follows the amp because the effect is more dramatic that way; if it precedes the amp, the amp's distortion tends to mask the effect.

However, this particular effect takes advantage of the two delay lines to create a bigger stereo image and add some simulated "room reflections" to provide a feel of ambience (see Figure 10.5).

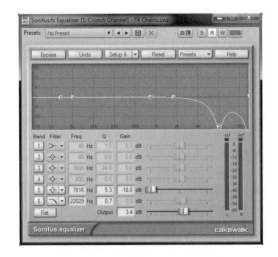

Figure 10.4

Post-sim EQ can make a huge improvement to the sound.

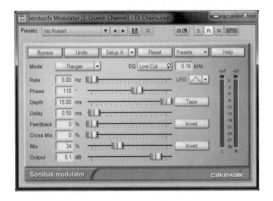

Figure 10.5

Modulation is good for more than just adding chorusing, because it can also create an acoustic space.

When all the effects are in place and edited, it's time to convert them into an effects chain—and take advantage of the FX Chain 2.0's ability to add knobs and buttons that control particular parameters, as well as customize the FX chain's skin. But first, save the chain.

1. Right-click in the FX Bin and select Convert Bin to FX Chain.

2. Right-click on the FX chain and choose Save FX Chain Preset. Name it and click on Save; this renames the chain and then saves it to the C:\Cakewalk Content\SONAR X1 Producer\FX Chain Presets folder.

Add FX Chain Controls

Double-click on the chain in the FX Bin, and the basic FX Chain 2.0 interface will open (see Figure 10.6)

Figure 10.6

The basic FX Chain 2.0 shows the effects used in the chain, as well as the input and output faders and meters.

Now you can bring particular controls from the chain's processors to the FX Chain 2.0 interface. For example, in the first Sonitus EQ, being able to edit the gain for Band 4 varies the guitar's presence. So, let's bring that out to a knob.

1. Right-click on a blank space within the FX Chain 2.0 interface and select Add Knob from the context menu.

2. The Control Properties dialog box will appear. Select the destination. (In this case, choose the first equalizer and the Sonitus:fx Equalizer:1 Gain 4 parameter; see Figure 10.7).

Figure 10.7

You can assign a knob to most effect parameters.

3. The Name field shows the name of the parameter you selected; change this by dragging over the Name field and typing in a new one. For example, because this changes the presence, call it Presence.

4. The Position field places the knob in one of six positions in a row, with 1 to the left and 6 to the right. Because this knob is in the first effect, we'll put it first.

5. The Type field determines whether the control is Unipolar (goes from full off to full on) or Bipolar (center is zero, and the value goes positive when turned clockwise and negative when turned counter-clockwise). In this case, either one would work, but Bipolar makes sense because the center position gives a flat response for that band.

6. Similarly, add a knob in the second position for the second EQ to control the Band 2 gain. This provides a bass cut that sounds more like an open-back amp, or bass boost for more oomph. We'll call this Bass.

7. Now add some controls from the Modulator. The Mix control acts like a mono/stereo control, so add a knob in position 6 and assign it to Sonitus:fx Modulator:1 Mix. Name it Width.

8. The Modulator's Mix Invert button can change the sound by throwing the processed signal out of phase. Because FX Chains 2.0 can also add buttons, right-click in the FX chain and select Add Button.

9. The buttons go above the knobs. Because we want to associate this with the Width control, assign the button to position 6, and for the destination, choose Sonitus:fx Modulator1: Invert Mix. Let's name this button Phase Flip. The FX chain now looks like Figure 10.8.

Figure 10.8

Our FX chain now has four effects and four ways to control them: three knobs and a button.

Add Another Effect

Suppose you'd like to add a Compressor at the beginning. No problem—just drag it before the first equalizer in the row of effects at the bottom (see Figure 10.9). You could also drag it between effects.

Figure 10.9
You can add an effect to the FX chain by dragging it in from the browser.

Now suppose you want to make the Compressor's Input Gain control accessible to control Sustain, but you also want it in Position 1—which is already occupied by the Presence control. Simply assign it to Position 1, and it will "bump" whatever control is in that position to the first open position (in this case, 3). In fact, you can edit any knob or button parameter by right-clicking on the control and entering new data in the Control Properties dialog box.

Personalize the Look

Finally, you can customize the user interface for your own look. Right-click on the FX chain and select Customize UI. You can edit the background image, preset name background, fader cap, buttons, knobs, and text colors. Several options are available in the folder C:\Cakewalk Content\Sonar X1 Producer\FX Chain Graphics, but if you're handy with a paint program, you can create your own .PNG files. See Figure 10.10 for the end result of moving some knobs around and using a background of a glowing tube to give that guitar-amp vibe.

Figure 10.10
The Crunch 2.0 FX chain has been customized for a cool look, not just a cool sound.

Create a Clean Channel

Now that you know how to create a version 2.0 FX chain, try your hand at creating a clean channel with a bright, animated sound that works well for rhythm guitar.

This channel needs only two effects:

▷ Sonitus:fx Equalizer

▷ Sonitus:fx Modulator

The Equalizer has a major high-frequency boost to create a bright, glassy sound (see Figure 10.11).

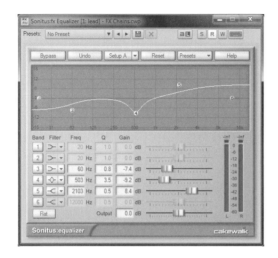

Figure 10.11
This setting produces a bright sound.

This channel was developed for humbucker pickups; single-coil pickups tend to be a bit brighter, so if you're using them, you might want to reduce the brightness a bit. The midrange cut around 500 Hz thins the sound somewhat, which emphasizes the brightness. Similarly, the low-frequency shelf reduces the very lowest frequencies.

The Modulator settings in Figure 10.12 are from the default Ensemble mode. After all, if something sounds right, there's no reason to change it!

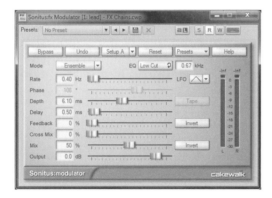

Figure 10.12
These are the default Ensemble settings.

More Effects Chains!

The next chapter, on track templates, explains how to build a four-channel amp track template. Here are some ideas on effects to use in additional chains.

Overdrive Effects Chain

This chain is designed to give both rhythm and lead sounds; a good effects order is:

1. Cakewalk Compressor/Gate
2. Sonitus:fx Equalizer
3. Cakewalk Amp Sim
4. Sonitus:fx Equalizer
5. Sonitus:fx Reverb

Use an EQ similar to the Crunch chain, but bypass Band 1 for more lows. For the Compressor, use a low threshold and a high ratio. Try Fuzz 2 for the Amp Sim; it's kind of buzzy, but you can tame this with the post-sim EQ by adding a broad notch at 2 kHz and a sharper notch at 7.8 kHz to reduce high-frequency artifacts. Set the top band to a low-pass filter to remove the very highest frequencies, which will warm up the sound. Adding a little reverb spices up the chain with some room ambience.

Lead Effects Channel

Now let's go for some lead sounds. The order of effects this time is:

1. Cakewalk Compressor/Gate
2. Sonitus:fx Equalizer
3. Cakewalk Amp Sim
4. Sonitus:fx Equalizer
5. Cakewalk Tempo Delay

Use a high Compressor/Gate input gain setting, because this hits the compressor harder. For the pre-sim EQs, try the same settings as the Overdrive chain, and for the post-sim EQ, use similar settings to the Crunch chain.

For the sim itself, start with the Crunch settings, but set the Drive, Treble, and Presence controls higher. Also, uncheck the Bright option and choose the 4×10 cabinet instead of the 4×12, as this gives a tighter sound. Finally, adding some delay at the end can give a bit of a spacey ambience.

11

Creating Virtual Amps and Pedalboards with Track Templates

I N THE PREVIOUS CHAPTER, WE COVERED EFFECTS CHAINS and how to put together the equivalent of a virtual amp channel (and the same principle applies to creating virtual multi-effects). Now let's take that one step further and use the effects chains we created to make a four-channel amp we can save as a track template.

Before making your amp, note that you can also use a track template to make a "virtual pedalboard" that groups your choice of stompboxes together in a useful configuration. You can then save this and recall it later as a turnkey, ready-to-go track (including the cute little track icon, of course!). Note that this goes beyond creating effects chains, as track templates can also save busses and bus settings—so you can have pretty sophisticated setups ready to go, complete with series and parallel chains. In fact, we'll take advantage of bussing as we put together our four-channel amp with clean, crunch, overdrive, and lead channels, using effects that are included in both the Producer and Studio versions of SONAR X1. What's more, you can use all of these channels at once if you want.

Amp Architecture

You'll fabricate this amp by creating a track with four send busses—one for each "channel." You can then enable or disable an amp "channel" by enabling or disabling its associated send. Each bus has an effects chain loaded and terminates in the Master bus so you can adjust the output level of each channel independently.

Constructing the Amp

Now let's go through constructing the amp, step by step.

1. In Track view, insert an audio track and call it "4-Channel Amp."

2. Right-click within the track and choose Insert Send > Insert Send Assistant.

3. Create the Clean channel first (see Figure 11.1). Specify New Bus, choose Stereo, assign the Bus Output to Master, name the bus "Clean," leave Choose Effect as is, and then check Pre Fader and Match Track's Pan and Gain (assuming the audio track's Gain is 0.0 and Pan is at 0%). Click on OK.

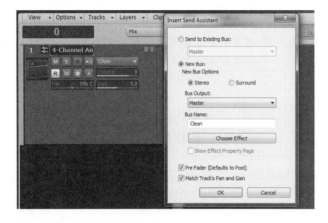

Figure 11.1

The Amp Send Assistant simplifies the process of creating each amp channel.

4. In the Clean bus FX Bin, insert the effects chain Clean that we created in the previous chapter.

5. Right-click within the track and again choose Insert Send > Insert Send Assistant.

6. Create the Crunch channel by entering the same parameters into the Send Assistant that you entered for the Clean channel, other than the bus name. When the bus appears, insert the Crunch effects chain.

7. Right-click within the track and again choose Insert Send > Insert Send Assistant.

8. Create the Overdrive channel by entering the same parameters into the Send Assistant that you entered for the Clean channel, other than the bus name. When the bus appears, insert the Overdrive effects chain.

9. Right-click within the track and again choose Insert Send > Insert Send Assistant.

10. Create the Lead channel by entering the same parameters into the Send Assistant that you entered for the Clean channel, other than the bus name. When the bus appears, insert the Lead effects chain.

11. You should now have a setup that looks something like Figure 11.2.

12. Turn off all the send "power" buttons in the 4-Channel Amp audio track, enable its Input Echo, and turn the main channel Volume fader all the way down. (Remember, all the sends are pre-fader, so you'll hear them regardless of the track's main fader setting.)

13. To turn a channel on or off, enable or disable its send, respectively.

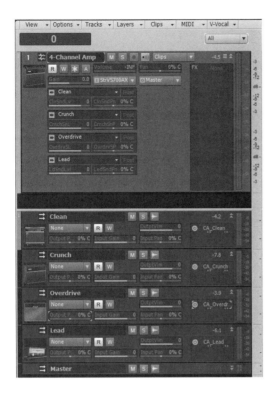

Figure 11.2
The audio track has four sends that go to four busses, each of which has an FX chain inserted.

Saving and Loading the Track Template

When all your effects are set up as desired, save the virtual amp as a track template. In Track view, right-click in a blank space (for example, between the track widgets and the FX Bin; in Console view, right-click to the left of the channel fader) and then select Save as Track Template. Navigate to Audio Track Templates, then to the Guitar folder, and then save the template as 4-Channel Amp.

Now you can call up the track template by right-clicking in an empty space in Track or Console view, choosing Insert from Track Template, and navigating to the track template you saved (see Figure 11.3)

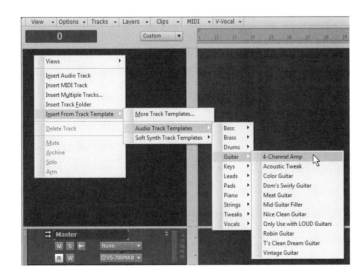

Figure 11.3
You can recall the track template into any project at any time.

However, note that there's a complication: Currently, if the track template includes a bus, and an effects chain is inserted into the bus, SONAR X1 will not recall the effects themselves—only the effects chain name. So, you'll need to use this information to reload the effects chain into the bus. This is not an issue if a track includes an effects chain in its FX Bin.

Additional Track Template Techniques

Here are some additional tricks you can do with this track template.

▷ The Send level control for each send in the 4-Channel Amp track now acts like a distortion drive control. For example, pull down the Overdrive to −15 or so, and the sound is well-suited to rhythm guitar parts; turn it up all the way, and you'll get a more sustaining lead sound.

▷ Try turning on more than one channel and panning them oppositely.

▷ If you want to add in some completely unprocessed guitar sound, turn up the 4-Channel Amp track fader.

▷ If the busses take up too much space for your liking, you can select Narrow Strip in Console view or even hide channels that you're not using.

Re-Amping with SONAR

WOULDN'T IT BE GREAT IF YOU COULD CHOOSE a guitar's amp tone while mixing down instead of being locked into the tone you used while recording? Thanks to plug-in technology and fast computers, you can.

For years, engineers and guitarists have used a technique called *re-amping.* With this, a guitarist splits the guitar signal in two: One feed goes directly to a guitar amp, and the other goes straight into the recorder via a direct box. As the guitarist plays, the amp signal is recorded—but so is the straight signal, on a separate track.

During mixdown, if the amp track sounds fine, that's great. But if not, the engineer can mute the amp track, feed the straight track's output into a different amp, and then record the output of the other amp. Or, another option is to keep the original amp track but add a new amp track to provide a stereo image or layered sound.

SONAR allows a twist on the traditional re-amping concept by doing it all virtually. The key to what makes virtual re-amping possible is that SONAR always records whatever is plugged into the audio interface input, *not the audio that's processed through any plug-ins.* (Of course, you can always bounce the track and incorporate the plug-in, but we're talking about recording in this situation.) So, any processing that occurs depends entirely on the plug-in(s) you've selected; you can process the guitar in any way you'd like during the mixdown process, including changing virtual amps, patching in high-quality reverb, or whatever.

In Chapter 17, "Control Surfaces and the Roland VS-20 Interface for Guitarists," we'll discuss re-amping with the Roland VS-20 interface in detail. This implementation is VS-20 specific, as it takes advantage of the onboard hardware effects to provide processing and minimize any latency that would otherwise occur when re-amping with software plug-ins. If you're using SONAR with a traditional interface and doing re-amping with plug-ins, the situation is somewhat different.

When recording through plug-ins, you need to be able to hear the processed sound. This requires enabling the Input Echo switch (see Figure 12.1) so you can send the guitar into the computer's signal path and monitor through the complete path, including any plug-ins. Make sure that any direct-monitoring option for your interface is disabled so you don't hear the dry guitar sound.

Figure 12.1

Enabling Input Echo lets you monitor the guitar sound as it's being processed by plug-ins.

Because the signal is now going through the computer and any plug-ins, there is a delay (latency) due to all the computations that are being done in real time. (See Chapter 2 for more information about latency.) With older computers, or if you're really picky, the delay might be unacceptably distracting. So if you find that playing through plug-ins has too much delay, yet you want to be able to hear yourself playing through an amp sound if for no other reason than to have the right feel when recording, then you'll need to go old school if you have an audio interface with more than one set of inputs and outputs.

Split your guitar signal and feed one audio interface input with the dry signal. Send the other split to an amp so you can play through the amp in real time, or into a multi-effects processor that adds the desired processing. (Of course, you can do this with the VS-20 as well.) It's also a good idea to send the processor or miked amp output to a second audio interface input and record this, just in case it turns out to be the sound you wanted after all. Or, even if you get the sound you want during mixdown with plug-ins, you might want to layer the original amp sound with it as well.

But here's one final thought: Just because you *can* re-amp doesn't necessarily mean that you should rely on this as your standard operating procedure. Sometimes committing to and recording a particular sound derived from an amp or multi-effects will shape the direction of a track; changing it might detract from any magic. I've run into this several times when using the VS-20—after recording the processed sound, that becomes the guitar sound for the track, and I don't look back. This can really help maintain the flow of recording and avoid interrupting the creative process.

How to Improve Amp Sim Tone

AMP SIMS ARE CONTROVERSIAL, AS SOME GUITARISTS say the experience of playing through a sim is not the same as playing through a physical amp. But it can't be: An amp goes through a big speaker and cabinet and moves lots of air, while an amp sim plays back through speaker monitors or headphones. If you feed a sim into a power amp and cabinet, it starts to get that "feel."

But few would dispute that amp sim tone has improved dramatically since amp sims were first introduced and that a track recorded with a miked guitar amp doesn't sound all that different (if there's any audible difference at all) compared to one recorded through an amp sim.

However, just as you wouldn't just pick a mic at random and point it in the general direction of an amp, amp sims require some setup and optimization as well. There are many ways to improve the sound of amp sims, so let's get started.

Raise the Sample Rate

Physical amps don't have a lot of energy above 5 kHz because of the physics of cabinets and speakers, but amp sims don't have physical limitations. So even if the sim is designed to reduce highs, sometimes there will still be high-frequency artifacts.

One way to obtain a more pleasing distorted amp sim sound is to run any projects using amp sims at an 88.2-kHz or 96-kHz sample rate. This is not about a "golden ears" thing regarding frequency response; it's just that sometimes, higher sample rates seem to handle the harmonics generated by high-gain amp sim settings more elegantly. It's easy to check this out for yourself—run Guitar Rig 4 LE in stand-alone mode using a high-gain amp at 44.1 kHz, then do the same thing at 96 kHz and draw your own conclusions.

However, because it's not always practical to run projects at elevated sample rates, you can also improve amp sim tone by enabling any internal oversampling options. In Guitar Rig 4 LE, there's a HI (as in High Quality) switch at the upper right. Enabling this doubles the CPU consumption but improves tone (see Figure 13.1).

Figure 13.1

Guitar Rig 4 LE's HI switch helps improve tone.

Other amp sims include similar features. For example, IK Multimedia's AmpliTube 3 has a Preferences menu where you can specify oversampling for several different components, as well as different resolutions. If that's too much to deal with, there's a toolbar that simply chooses between Hi, Mid, and Eco resolution, which chooses various combinations of preferences automatically. Peavey's ReValver has the option to choose real-time, 32-bit processing, or for mixdown, 64-bit processing with four times oversampling. Also, Waves GTR includes an HD button that works similarly to Guitar Rig's HI switch (see Figure 13.2).

Figure 13.2

AmpliTube's hi-res options are outlined with rectangles, Peavey's is circled, and GTR's HD button is outlined with a triangle.

Avoid Unintended Distortion

One reason guitarists can get bad amp sim tone is from not realizing there's the potential for two types of distortion within modules such as amp and cabinet emulators: the good amp distortion we know and love, and the nasty digital distortion that results from not setting levels correctly inside the sim.

With analog technology, if you overload an amp input, you just get more distortion. Because you're hearing that sweet analog distortion, it sounds fine—just more distorted. But if you overload a digital amp's input, remember that digital technology has a fixed, and unforgiving, amount of headroom. If you don't exceed that headroom, the amp sim will sound as the designers intended. But if your signal crosses that threshold, the result is ugly, non-harmonic distortion.

To avoid digital distortion, optimize levels as you work your way from input to output; it's crucial to do so in the following order.

First, make sure the guitar isn't overloading your audio interface, which will probably have a small mixer application with metering. Set the audio interface preamp gain so the guitar never goes into the red, no matter how hard you hit the strings. Be conservative, as changing pickups or altering your picking style might change levels.

Second, your sim will likely have an input meter and level control; adjust this so that the signal never hits the red (see Figure 13.3).

Figure 13.3
Make sure that Guitar Rig 4 LE's input levels never trigger the red LEDs toward the right of the input level meter—if needed, pull down the level slider located inside the meter.

Some sims other than Guitar Rig (such as Peavey's ReValver) include an input "learn" function. Click on Learn and then play your guitar with maximum force. Learn analyzes your signal and then automatically sets levels so that the peaks of your playing don't exceed the available input headroom.

Third, you need to trim within the amp itself. Like their real-world equivalents, amp sims can be high-gain devices—high enough to overload their headroom internally. This is where many guitarists take the wrong turn toward bad sound by turning up the master volume too high. The cabinets in Guitar Rig 4 LE include a volume control with the Learn function (see Figure 13.4).

Figure 13.4
The Learn function, included in both individual amps and for the overall output, optimizes gain within Guitar Rig.

The final stage where level matters is the output. Guitar Rig has a special Preset Volume output module, which also has a Learn function. This matches levels among patches but also prevents distortion.

It's crucial that you adjust the amp Learn first, and only after that's set, adjust the Preset Volume Learn.

Trim Post–Amp Sim High and Low Frequencies

Another tweak is removing unneeded high frequencies. With the ProChannel, enable the LPF option (see Figure 13.5) and choose the 48-dB/octave response. Lower the frequency control until you get a warmer sound, without buzziness—this will likely be around 8 to 12 kHz.

Figure 13.5

The ProChannel allows for steep high-frequency cutoffs—up to 48 dB/octave.

With the Studio Edition, use the Sonitus:fx Equalizer to trim highs. Choose the Lowpass filter option, experiment with lowering the frequency until any high-frequency buzziness goes away, and then adjust the Q control to alter the cut's sharpness. Although the rolloff isn't as sharp as with the ProChannel, you can "stack" two or more bands to create a sharper response (see Figure 13.6).

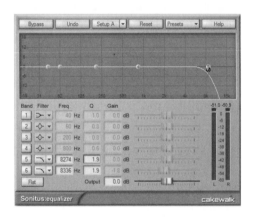

Figure 13.6

Bands 5 and 6 are edited for identical settings to create a steeper high-frequency cutoff.

Similarly, it's sometimes a good idea to trim the very lowest bass frequencies. Physical cabinets—particularly open-back cabinets—have a limited low-frequency response; besides, recording engineers often roll off the low frequencies a bit to give a "tighter" sound. The ProChannel has a dedicated Highpass filter that works similarly to the Lowpass filter, and with the Sonitus:fx Equalizer, you can choose a Highpass response from the Filter drop-down menu. Because a guitar's lowest string is just below 100 Hz, set the frequency for a sharp low-frequency rolloff around 70 Hz or so to minimize any "mud" or possible subsonics.

Trim Pre–Amp Sim High and Low Frequencies

Sometimes it helps to put an EQ before the amp sim, particularly if you have a guitar with really bright pickups. Most guitarists know that turning down the tone control prior to feeding distortion can give a smoother sound; we're dealing with the same principle here. If you send lots of highs into distortion, then you're adding distortion to those highs and generating even higher harmonics. This can result in a harsh sound.

I've also found that many sims seem to like having a bit of a notch around 2 kHz preceding the sim. Why? I don't know! Just give it a try—create a notch (not too broad, not too narrow) and sweep it between 1 and 4kHz while playing full chords. If you find a frequency where the tone sounds better, leave the EQ in place and note the setting for future use.

Remove "Fizzy" Frequencies

Most amp sims I've used exhibit, to one degree or another, what I call "the annoying frequency." This adds a sort of "fizzy," whistling sound that I find objectionable. It may be the result of pickup characteristics, musical style, playing technique, and so on adding up in the wrong way and therefore emphasizing a resonance; or it may be something else, such as a sound that was part of the amp being modeled, and therefore was faithfully reproduced. It also seems like an unpredictable problem—one amp might have this fizz only when using a particular virtual mic or cabinet, but the same mic or cabinet on a different amp might sound fine. In any event, it detracts from the amp sound's potential richness.

Normally, if you experience this sound, you'd probably just say, "I don't like that," and try a different cabinet, amp, or mic (or change the amp settings). But, you don't have to if you know the secret of fizz removal. All you need is a stage or two of parametric EQ from the ProChannel (Producer Edition) or Sonitus:fx Equalizer (Studio Edition), a good set of ears, and a little patience. These need to go after the amp sim, so with the Studio Edition, simply insert the EQ in the FX Bin after the amp sim. With the Producer Edition, you need to make sure the ProChannel is in the Post FX Bin position (see Figure 13.7).

Figure 13.7
Toward the left, you'll see the collapsed version of the ProChannel in the Inspector, with Post selected. Toward the right, the same channel is shown in the Console view, again with Post selected.

Now let's find any annoying frequencies and remove them.

1. Turn down your monitors, because there may be some really loud levels as you search for the annoying frequency (or frequencies).

2. Enable a parametric equalizer stage. Set a sharp Q (resonance) and boost the gain to at least 12 dB.

3. Sweep the parametric frequency as you play. There will likely be a frequency where the sound gets loud and unpleasant—more so than any other frequencies. This will typically be between 2 and 10 kHz.

4. Now use the parametric gain control to cut gain, thus reducing the annoying frequency.

You may find it easier, especially after you have some experience with this technique, to start off with a notch response. (Again, use a fairly high Q and at least –12 dB of gain.) As you adjust the frequency control, at some point the sound will become warmer; lowering or raising the frequency will no longer notch out the annoying frequency, and you'll lose the warmth.

Sometimes finding and removing a second (or even a third) "fizz frequency" can improve the sound even more. This is a somewhat more advanced technique and requires both practice and sharp notches; but when done right, the difference is beneficial and definitely not subtle. Generally, the more notches you need to use, the narrower they need to be.

To refine this technique, experiment with the notch bandwidth. You want the narrowest notch possible that nonetheless gets rid of the whistle; otherwise, you'll diminish the highs—although that may be what you want. As usual, experiment!

Tweak the GR4 LE Jump Amp

Let's apply this technique to Guitar Rig 4 LE.

1. Insert Guitar Rig 4 LE into a channel's FX Bin.

2. Under the Components tab, select and "unfold" Amplifier.

3. Drag the Jump amp into GR4 LE's "rack."

4. Move the mic slider fully to the B position, as this produces a more obvious fizzy frequency than the A position.

5. Create the first notch. Enable LMF and set Q to around 6.7 and Level to –12 or so.

6. Sweep the associated Freq control slowly. You'll probably hear the tone get a little less harsh around 2.6 kHz.

7. Now let's set another notch. Enable HMF and set Q to 7.0 and gain to +12 dB. Sweep the Freq control, and you'll likely hear a whistling sound around 4.0 to 4.5 kHz. Zero in on the frequency; you may find it helpful to hold down the Shift key so you can fine-tune the frequency. Once you find the frequency, turn Level all the way down.

8. Bypass the equalizer and strum all six open strings forcefully. Now enable the equalizer; the tone should be sweeter and less harsh.

9. Next, we'll shave off the very high frequencies. Enable the LFP filter, choose a slope of 48 dB, and then set the Freq control to around 10 to 12 kHz.

10. Our last EQ tweak is to trim the low frequencies. Enable the HPF filter and set slope to 48 dB and Freq to about 70 Hz.

11. Let's also make a few final tweaks at the Jump amp itself. Move the A-B slider to taste (I like it about halfway) and add some Air to give ambience.

12. Now when you enable/disable the EQ, you should hear a distinct difference, with the EQ'd sound being a bit richer and warmer (see Figure 13.8).

Figure 13.8
Here's what the ProChannel EQ looks like after notching out some frequencies in GR4 LE's Jump amp to "warm up" the sound.

When you're finished with the high-/low-frequency trims, midrange notches, and choosing either a higher sampling rate or using an amp sim's oversampling options, your sim sound should be smoother, creamier, and more pleasing.

The Care and Feeding of Plug-Ins

Y ES, THIS IS A SOMEWHAT MORE ADVANCED TOPIC—but as music software becomes more complex, it becomes necessary to tune your software as well as your instrument. Plug-ins are a huge part of today's computer-based recording, and they're particularly important for guitar players; how you work with, manage, and select them can have a major impact on workflow. Let's investigate how to make using and managing plug-ins as simple and effective as possible.

Simplify Organization with a Common VST Plug-Ins Folder

When VST plug-ins first appeared in programs by Steinberg, they were installed in a folder at C:\Program Files\Steinberg\Vstplugins. When installing a non-Steinberg program, some would install their plug-ins into this existing folder, while others would create their own Vstplugins folder.

Like all programs that can host VST plug-ins, SONAR needs to know where to look for plug-ins, using the path specified in Preferences. So, it simplifies matters if you create one Vstplugins folder, put all your VST plug-ins there, and then point all your programs that host VSTs to this folder. (Note that if you're using a 64-bit operating system, you'll need separate folders for 64-bit and 32-bit plug-ins, as SONAR can work with both.) Here's the procedure.

1. Create the folder or folders. My 64-bit one is at C:\Program Files\Vstplugins, and for 32-bit plug-ins, C:\Program Files (x86)\Vstplugins.

2. Use your computer's search function to find all Vstplugins folders.

3. Copy all the plug-ins from all these folders into your main folder.

4. In SONAR, choose Edit > Preferences > File section > VST Settings. To add your new folder(s), click on Add, navigate to the folder, click on it, and then select OK. Do the same for the second folder, if needed. Now SONAR will look for VST plug-ins within that specified folder or folders (see Figure 14.1).

5. Remove any Vstplugins folders that no longer need to be scanned by highlighting the folder and then clicking on Remove.

Figure 14.1
Specify where SONAR will look for plug-ins under Preferences, where you can also specify scan behavior on startup.

Once you've verified that all the plug-ins load correctly, you can delete the old folders that contained the plug-ins you moved. Of course, you'll need to change the file path to the new folder(s) in any other programs you have that host VST plug-ins.

With multiple programs installed, you may have some surprises. Some plug-ins are "keyed" to specific programs and won't work in SONAR, while plug-ins from other programs (for example, most plug-ins from Acoustica's Mixcraft) will work just fine when SONAR knows where to find them.

You can also specify additional folders for SONAR to scan for plug-ins, but usually it's easiest just to throw everything in one place (or two places with 64-bit systems).

Plug-In Scanning during Startup

To make sure SONAR sees newly installed plug-ins, while you're in the VST Settings section of Preferences, check Scan for VST Plug-Ins on Startup. SONAR will scan only those plug-ins that have been added since you last opened SONAR.

I recommend against checking Re-Scan Existing Plug-ins, as you'll have to wait for SONAR to scan all your plug-ins on startup—which can be time consuming.

However, if you have a fairly stable setup and don't add a lot of plug-ins, you can save a few seconds each time you open SONAR X1 by unchecking Scan for VST Plug-Ins on Startup. When you do add a plug-in, run the VST scan manually by clicking on the Scan VST Folders button.

Handling Problematic Plug-Ins

Although plug-ins are supposed to conform to an established specification, not all plug-ins follow that spec to the letter (especially free ones). As a result, some plug-ins may work in some programs but not in others. Problems can manifest themselves in a few different ways.

Loading a Plug-In Crashes SONAR

This happens when you load a project: SONAR gets to a certain point in the loading process and then freezes or crashes. Fortunately, it's easy to track down which plug-in is causing the problem.

1. Before opening the project file, hold down the Shift key.

2. Choose File > Open and open the project while still holding the Shift key.

3. A window will open each time SONAR is instructed to load a plug-in, and you'll be asked whether you want to load that plug-in. If you click Yes and SONAR crashes, there's your answer.

Rescanning Failed Plug-Ins

If SONAR won't recognize a plug-in, there could be an incompatibility, but it also might be that some kind of glitch happened when SONAR was scanning the plug-ins. Before you give up on a plug-in, check Re-Scan Existing Plug-Ins (again in the VST Settings part of the Preferences window). The next time you boot SONAR, it will try again to recognize the plug-in.

If that doesn't work, create a separate VSTplugins folder for these "problem children" and include it as a VSTplugins path for programs that are compatible with the plug-in(s).

Plug-Ins Don't Work at 88.2-/96-kHz Sample Rates

Although SONAR's plug-ins work at 88.2- and 96-kHz sample rates, some third-party plug-ins may not. If you plan to record at these higher sample rates, create a project and load plug-ins, one at a time, while passing audio through them. Keep track of which ones pass and which ones fail. If desired, you can exclude the ones that don't work in SONAR (as described later, in the "Managing Effects and Plug-Ins with the Plug-In Manager" section).

Dealing with Missing Plug-Ins

When opening a project, SONAR will inform you if it can't find a plug-in that's used in the project. SONAR is outstanding in how it handles this situation; it installs a placeholder that maintains the plug-in settings so that if you do restore the plug-in and open the file, it will carry on as if nothing happened.

The Errant Folder Problem

Moving the plug-in to a different folder can cause the plug-in to be missing in action. Check the VSTplugins folder SONAR points to and make sure the plug-in is located there. If not, reinstall it into that folder (or if you know where the plug-in lives, move a copy into the folder). If you don't know where a plug-in is located, the Plug-In Manager can help—check out the section about it at the end of this chapter.

Installing Non-Default SONAR Plug-Ins

If a plug-in is missing that you've used in previous versions of SONAR, the plug-in may not have been installed when you installed SONAR itself. This is because SONAR includes most older plug-ins for compatibility but may not install them if newer, improved versions exist. To install all plug-ins included with SONAR:

1. Start installing SONAR from the distribution DVD-ROM.
2. When you reach the Select Components screen, click on the Options box in the Plug-Ins category.
3. Check any older plug-ins you want to install.
4. Click on OK and then complete the installation process.

Registering DirectX Plug-Ins

This section is *really* esoteric, so feel free to skip it—you'll probably never encounter this problem. But if you *do* run into it, you'll be very glad this section exists, because you'll have a hard time finding this information elsewhere.

If a DirectX plug-in doesn't load, it may not be properly registered with Windows (host software knows where to find DirectX effects via the registry, rather than dealing with a file path). This is extremely unlikely to happen with SONAR plug-ins, as Cakewalk has their act together about making sure they're registered. But, this can happen with plug-ins from other manufacturers or ones you download from the Internet. Here's how to register a DirectX plug-in.

1. You will need to have administrator privileges on your computer. If you're the only user, you're probably an administrator.
2. Locate the DirectX plug-in's DLL you need to register and write down or copy the file path. You'll find Cakewalk's DirectX plug-ins at C:\Program Files\Cakewalk\Shared Plugins. If you don't know where to find the plug-in, see the "Managing Effects and Plug-Ins with the Plug-In Manager" section toward the end of this chapter.
3. Click the Start button and then type CMD in the Search field—but *don't* press Enter yet.
4. Above the Search field, under Programs, right-click on CMD and choose Run as Administrator.
5. If you're asked whether you want to allow the program to make changes to the computer, click on Yes.
6. A command-line interface box will appear. Yes, it's scary and vaguely prehistoric, but don't worry.
7. After the prompt, type **regsvr32 "file path"**. (You must use quotes, such as **regsvr32 "C:\Program Files\Cakewalk\Shared Plugins\Aliasfactor.dll"**.)
8. After typing this, press Enter. You should see a message that says the registration succeeded (see Figure 14.2). You might want to reboot the computer to make sure that the registration "sticks."

You may want to *unregister* a DirectX plug-in if you don't use it anymore or if it's corrupted. Follow the same steps as earlier, but type **regsvr /u "file path"**. In stubborn cases, you may need to unregister a plug-in before you can register it.

An alternative way to unregister registered plug-ins automatically is to use the Plug-In Manager. Choose Utilities > Cakewalk Plug-In Manager. Choose the DirectX Audio Effects category, click on a plug-in, and then click on Exclude. If the plug-in isn't found, SONAR will ask whether you want to permanently unregister the plug-in (see Figure 14.3). This removes the plug-in's registry keys.

Figure 14.2
Make sure you type the file path exactly as specified.

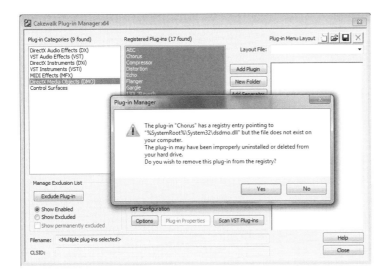

Figure 14.3
This message shows up if you try to exclude a DirectX plug-in and SONAR can't find it on your machine.

Managing Effects and Plug-Ins with the Plug-In Manager

Effects and signal processing are important to guitar players, so it's helpful to have plug-ins arranged in a way that makes it simple to call up the effect you want, when you want it.

That's exactly what the Plug-In Manager is all about. As your collection of plug-ins grows, you may want to sort them according to particular functions or by manufacturer, create a folder of "favorite" plug-ins, or exclude plug-ins that aren't designed to work with SONAR (such as some that accomplish specific functions in other programs, like video filtering that has nothing to do with audio).

Consider Figure 14.4, which shows the audio FX that SONAR X1 found when it was first installed. Clearly, some of these have nothing to do with audio processing. It doesn't hurt anything if they show up, but you can prevent SONAR X1 from listing them, thus making for a neater listing.

To start managing your effects, open the Plug-In Manager. You can do this in two ways: Choose Utilities > Cakewalk Plug-In Manager or right-click on an FX Bin, choose either Audio FX or Soft Synths, depending on which layout you want to edit, and then select Plug-In Layouts > Manage Layout. You'll see a window with three main columns (see Figure 14.5).

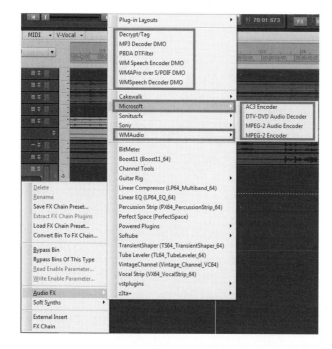

Figure 14.4
These outlined plug-ins are part of Windows and have nothing to do with SONAR. We can tidy up the display by excluding them with the Plug-In Manager.

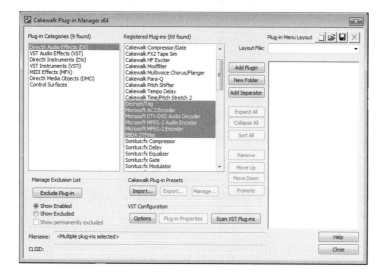

Figure 14.5
Cakewalk's Plug-In Manager lets you rearrange, rename, and exclude plug-ins. The highlighted plug-ins are about to be excluded.

The leftmost window shows various plug-in categories. Clicking on one of these shows plug-ins registered under that category, in the middle window. These will generally be relevant to SONAR except for the DirectX Media Objects category, which may include video-oriented or proprietary plug-ins that SONAR can't use.

Most of what you do to manage plug-ins will occur in the rightmost window, where you can build up a custom menu layout for plug-ins. (Conveniently, SONAR X1 already comes with one layout that lists only the plug-ins included with your version of SONAR X1.) We'll describe how to create layouts shortly, but first, let's exclude plug-ins that aren't relevant to SONAR so they don't clutter up our layout.

Excluding Plug-Ins

Although you can add and remove plug-ins from the layout in the right-hand column to create custom menus you call up when inserting effects in the FX Bin, excluding a plug-in is different from removing a plug-in from a layout—it's removed from the list of source effects that you use to create layouts. This prevents them from showing up in the plug-in menu that gets called up when you right-click on the FX Bin.

In Figure 14.5, DirectX Audio Effects is selected as the plug-in category, so that's what you see in the middle column. The Cakewalk ones are clearly labeled, as are the Sonitus ones, but you can see unrelated plug-ins from other companies.

To exclude a plug-in, click on it in the Registered Plug-Ins window (the middle one) and then click on Exclude Plug-In. You can Shift-click to select contiguous plug-ins or Ctrl-click to select noncontiguous plug-ins. Note that this affects SONAR only; any programs that showed the plug-in before will continue to show it. If you excluded a plug-in accidentally, click on the Show Excluded button, and you'll see a list of all excluded plug-ins. You can then highlight the plug-in and click on Enable Plug-In to make it visible again.

Creating Effects Layouts

You build the custom layout in the right column. For example, suppose you want to organize some plug-ins by manufacturer and some by function. You create folders by clicking on the New Folder button and then add plug-ins to the folder by clicking on the desired plug-in in the middle column, clicking on the folder, then clicking Add Plugin (see Figure 14.6).

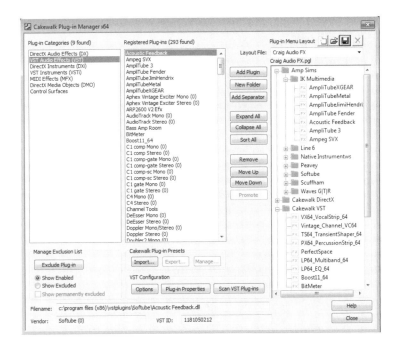

Figure 14.6

The custom menu on the right is in the process of being built and puts a folder of Amp Sims toward the top. Note how you can have folders within folders.

Don't worry about over-editing; you can always return to the FX Bin, choose Audio FX or Soft Synths, and then select Plug-In Layouts but instead of choosing Manage Layout choose Default—All Plug-Ins. As expected, removing a plug-in doesn't actually delete it, but only makes sure its name isn't displayed.

Within the layout, you can select/remove individual effects, multiple effects (Shift-click to select contiguous effects or Ctrl-click to select noncontiguous ones), or entire folders. To remove, simply highlight what you want removed and then click on Remove or press Delete. Be careful, though; you can't undo, so if you make a mistake, hopefully you saved the layout previously, or you'll have to add the effect back in manually.

The whole drag-and-drop aspect is very flexible. You can drag folders into any desired location, drag folders within folders or out of folders, and basically arrange everything as desired. What's more, you can add the same plug-in to multiple folders. For example, you could create a folder called Favorites and add all the plug-ins you use the most—even if they're also represented in other folders.

There are other helpful editing options: Expand All to open up all the folders, Collapse All to do the opposite, Move Up and Move Down if you want to move a highlighted plug-in up or down in the hierarchy (although I find using drag and drop easier), as well as create new folders, add separators, and sort alphanumerically within all folders.

When you've organized the plug-ins as desired, you can save the layout—or even save multiple layouts and choose the one you want (see Figure 14.7).

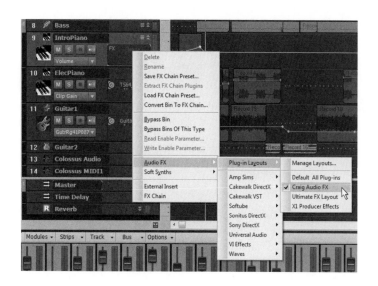

Figure 14.7

When choosing audio FX, there are four possible plug-in layouts. Craig Audio Effects includes all effects, sorted the way I want. Ultimate FX Layout is a "greatest hits" collection. X1 Producer Effects ships with SONAR, and Default All Plug-Ins is all plug-ins.

Renaming Plug-Ins

The Plug-In Manager lets you rename plug-ins in two ways—friendly names and display names. This can be very helpful if you like to, for example, organize plug-ins by function. If four different manufacturers call something "Compressor," you can rename these to be more descriptive—perhaps by preceding it with the manufacturer's name or indicating functionality (for example, Guitar Sustainer, Vintage Compressor Emulation, Multiband Compressor, and so on). Note that this affects only how the plug-in is seen in SONAR; it will have its standard name in all other applications.

Changing the friendly name edits the registered plug-ins in the middle column. To rename the friendly name, double-click on the name in the middle column, enter the new name, and then click on OK.

The display name appears in the rightmost column and, most importantly, is the name that's displayed in the FX Bin when you choose an effect. To rename, double-click on the name in the right column, enter the desired name in the Display Name field, and then click on OK. (You can also right-click on the name and choose Rename from the context menu, or click on the name, pause, click again, and once the name is highlighted, type in a new one.)

Note that if you double-click on a name in the right-hand column, a dialog box will appear that shows not only the editable Display Name field, but also its unique CLSID (whatever that means!) identifier, actual file name with path, category, friendly name, and for DirectX effects, the option to choose a default preset (see Figure 14.8).

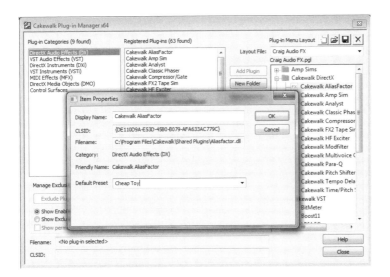

Figure 14.8

The Plug-In Properties box allows you to edit the Display Name and default preset for DirectX effects, but it also shows a variety of useful information about the plug-in.

How to Find Plug-Ins That Won't Load

In addition to renaming, the Plug-In Manager's Properties window also makes it easy to find where plug-ins are located. Double-click on the plug-in in the Registered Plug-Ins column and then look in the Filename field to display the plug-in's path.

MIDI-Controlled Audio FX Plug-Ins

Not too many audio processors include MIDI control. However, this is becoming more common, and SONAR itself has a MIDI-controlled audio effect: the z3ta+_fx, which is the effects section of the z3ta+ synthesizer.

Normally, you'd use its effects section to process audio, as you would any other audio effect. When used this way, you can provide MIDI control over parameters, but it takes some work—you need to assign a parameter to automation, then enable Show Assignable Controls in the Console, then assign one of those controls to a Remote Control, which you specify via MIDI. (See Chapter 16, "Mixing and Effects Automation.") It may be easier to simply consider the z3ta+_fx as a MIDI-controlled effect, not unlike a synthesizer.

Furthermore, some audio effects plug-ins respond to MIDI in other ways, such as a plug-in that reacts to pitch and therefore responds to MIDI notes. Installing this kind of plug-in as a standard audio plug-in doesn't expose the MIDI inputs.

But there's a workaround: Tell SONAR it's a virtual instrument.

1. Choose Utilities > Cakewalk Plug-In Manager.

2. Under Plug-In Categories, select VST Audio Effects.

3. Click on the plug-in in the Registered Plug-Ins column.

4. Under VST Configuration, click on Plug-In Properties.

5. In the Properties window, check Configure as Synth (see Figure 14.9).

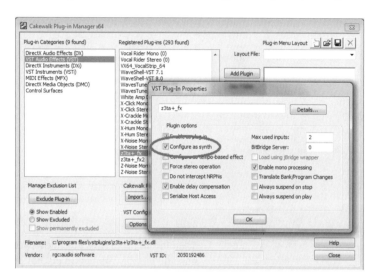

Figure 14.9
If a VST audio plug-in responds to MIDI, tell SONAR it's really a virtual instrument.

6. Click on OK.

7. The list of plug-ins will refresh, and you'll now find the plug-in under the VST Instruments plug-in category.

However, as the effect is still intended to work as an audio processor, don't use the Insert > Soft Synth method to add it to a track. Instead, right-click in the FX Bin and select the processor from the Soft Synths choices. You can then create a MIDI track, set the MIDI track input to listen to your MIDI controller, and select the signal processor as the track's MIDI output. Now your MIDI controller can control parameters in the z3ta+_fx processors.

A similar trick works for effects that respond to tempo. If the effect doesn't respond to tempo of its own accord, do the same steps as above, but in Step 5, check Configure as Tempo-Based Effect.

The Preset Librarian

The Plug-In Manager also includes a Preset Librarian. This is of limited use, as it works only with presets for Cakewalk and Sonitus DirectX effects—not plug-ins from other companies or VST plug-ins. However, it does allow you to exchange presets with other users or bring custom sets of presets with you when you work in other SONAR-based studios.

To use this:

1. Under Plug-In Categories, click on DirectX Audio Effects.

2. Under Registered Plug-Ins, click on the plug-in for which you want to import or export presets.

3. Below the Registered Plug-Ins pane, you'll see a Cakewalk Plug-In Presets section. This indicates whether any presets were found and has buttons for the Import, Export, or Manage presets.

4. To import, click on the Import button and navigate to where your Cakewalk Plug-In Preset files (.spp filename extension) are located. Click on the file and then on Open.

5. To export, click on the Export button, navigate to where you want to save the preset, name the file, and then click on Save.

6. To rename or delete presets, click on the Manage button, make your changes, and then click on Close (see Figure 14.10).

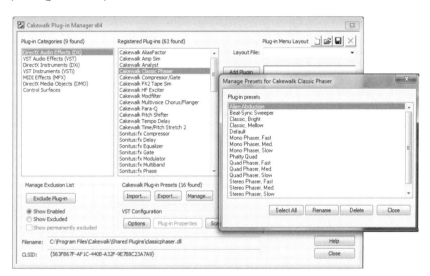

Figure 14.10
If DirectX effects have presets, you can manage them by exporting, importing, renaming, and deleting them.

Plug-In Manager Strategies

I always liked the idea of the Plug-In Manager for creating custom plug-in layouts, but with hundreds of plug-ins, I never could get a grip on the best way to organize them. However, I found there's an easy way to put together a custom layout.

1. With the Plug-In Manager open, select a new Plug-In Menu Layout.

2. Select DirectX Audio Effects under Plug-In Categories.

3. Select all registered plug-ins in the middle column. (Click on the top plug-in and Shift-click on the bottom one.)

4. Click on Add Plugin. This populates the right column with all DirectX plug-ins.

5. Select VST Audio Effects under Plug-In Categories.

6. Select all registered plug-ins in the middle column. (Click on the top plug-in and Shift-click on the bottom one.)

7. Click on Add Plugin. This will populate the right column with all VST plug-ins.

8. Now create folders—for example, by manufacturer—and start dragging the plug-ins into folders as appropriate.

9. Save the layout and then continue refining it.

10. As soon as you install a new plug-in, add it immediately to the appropriate folder so you don't lose track of it.

Part III

Recording Techniques

Perfect Takes with Composite Recording

*C*OMPOSITE RECORDING **IS THE PROCESS OF RECORDING** multiple takes—usually in quick succession—and then editing the best sections together into a single, cohesive part. This is extremely useful because you can record an unbroken series of lead or rhythm parts and really get into a "groove," rather than having to continually stop and start. For example, if one take has a great beginning and another has a great ending, you can combine the two into a single, composite take. Let's discuss the available tools for composite recording, but first, it's time for a quick detour into the artistic ramifications of composite recording.

Just Because We Can, Should We?

Of course, there are no rules in recording, and the following is a personal opinion. Still, I hope you find these thoughts helpful as you work with composite tracks.

Composite recording used to be done with fairly large chunks of music, like piecing together different verses and phrases. But nowadays, I've seen engineers slave over piecing together vocals and leads on an almost note-by-note basis. In particular, vocalists sometimes come into a session, sing a dozen takes or so, and then let the engineers apply pitch correction and composite editing to create the "perfect" vocal.

There's only one problem: Musical parts aren't necessarily meant to be perfect at the expense of expressiveness. A good vocal or lead part has expression that evolves over a period of time, with high points and low points—not just in terms of dynamics, but in terms of emotional impact.

We have technology that's very powerful, but it's important to use that power to serve the listener more than the musician. A good producer recognizes a great take and knows when to leave well enough alone. You can't *create* a great take; you *record* a great take.

Any editing is at its best when it gives something already great the extra 10 percent needed to make it transcendent, not when it tries to salvage a vocal from a series of haphazard takes.

Okay, rant over.

The Composite Recording Process

What makes composite recording possible is *loop recording*, which allows you to record take after take without having to stop.

With loop recording, you define the region you want to loop (that is, repeat over and over, with the loop jumping back to the loop beginning after reaching its end) using the right and left loop locator points. The easiest way to do this is to drag across the timeline to define the region you want to loop and then click on the Set Loop Points to Selection button or press Shift+L (see Figure 15.1). This also turns on looping automatically (the button directly above the Set Loop Points to Selection button).

Figure 15.1
In this example, the first eight measures of a drum intro are being looped so that an intro lead guitar part can be overdubbed.

It's generally a good idea to leave a measure or two before the part begins, and maybe a measure or two afterward, so you have a bit of a chance to regroup after doing each take.

Next, decide whether you want each take to go in its own track or be layered with other takes in a single track. You set this by choosing Edit > Preferences > Project > Record (this is available in both the Basic and Advanced Preferences) and then selecting the desired option under Loop Recording. (The Recording Mode setting doesn't matter.) Although it may seem that storing takes in separate tracks would be ideal because that makes it easy to differentiate among tracks, SONAR allows "opening up" an individual track to display each take as a separate layer. This is very convenient for editing, so I'd advise selecting Store Takes in a Single Track (see Figure 15.2). Click on Apply and then Close.

Record-enable the track and then click on the Transport's Record button. Recording will begin, and each pass will create a new layer within the track. However, you won't actually see the layers while recording; it appears that you're recording into the track, and new takes wipe out previous takes, but that's not the case. (Incidentally, if you have an older or slower computer, or you are starting to "red-line" your CPU, you can turn off waveform drawing by choosing Edit > Preferences > Customization > Display and unchecking Display Waveform Preview While Recording. This takes a bit of a load off the CPU.)

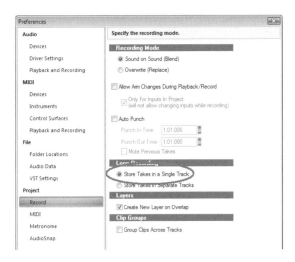

Figure 15.2

Storing takes in a single track is usually the most convenient way to work with composite recording in SONAR.

I suggest doing no more than a half dozen takes at a time, for three reasons:

▷ You don't want to have to wade through too many takes when you're trying to locate and isolate the best sections.

▷ If you can't get a good performance in six or seven takes, then you may need to practice the part more or rethink it.

▷ You'll want to hear what you've done before committing to too many tracks. Otherwise, you'll just be wasting your time if you do 20 takes, and they turn out to be going in the wrong direction.

After you stop recording, turn on track layers (see Figure 15.3). There are three ways to do this:

▷ Click on the Show Layers button in the track header.

▷ Choose Show Layers from the Layers tab at the top of the Track view.

▷ Right-click anywhere within a clip in the track and check or uncheck Show Layers.

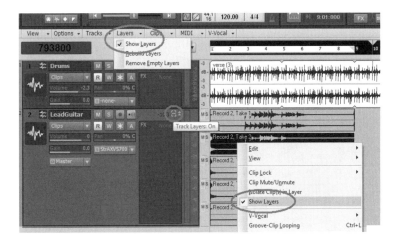

Figure 15.3

This montage of screenshots shows the three ways to display layers.

Note that if you turn off layers, any selected layer will be the one that displays as the foreground layer. If no layer is selected, than the last recorded layer will show.

Editing Time

Now it's time to take advantage of SONAR's Mute tool. Generally, I expand the track height to make it easy to see the waveforms of the various loop-recorded takes.

To select the Mute tool, right-click on the rightmost tool button in the Tools section of the Control Bar and select Mute (see Figure 15.4). You can also press F10 to toggle between the Mute and Erase tools.

Figure 15.4
Choose the Mute tool from the toolbar or press F10.

The Mute tool changes its function depending on its position in relation to the clip's height.

  ▷ Dragging over the clip's lower half mutes the clip audio where you dragged (and conforms to any snap setting). Sections muted with the Mute tool are outlined with dashes, and waveforms have "hollow" insides.

  ▷ Dragging over the upper half unmutes any audio that was previously muted.

There are also options to mute and solo entire clips.

  ▷ Click in the layer's clip with the Mute tool to mute an entire clip if unmuted and to unmute if the entire clip is muted. Note that any mute selections persist when you mute or unmute the entire clip.

  ▷ Clicking the M button to the left of a layer mutes that layer.

  ▷ Clicking the S button to the left of a layer solos that layer. If the layer has Mute selected, Solo takes precedence, but when you un-solo, the track reverts to being muted.

Now it's time to compare sections of each take to decide which you like best. Reset the loop points around the area being evaluated—a verse, a phrase, and so on. There are several possible workflows for figuring out which sections to mute, but I usually solo an individual clip, listen, and then mute all sections that I don't like. This gets repeated for all the tracks until I have a collection of "good" sections. Then it's time to compare the different "candidate" sections, choose the winners, and mute the rest (see Figure 15.5).

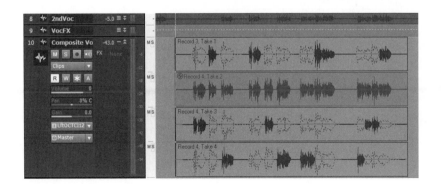

Figure 15.5
Muted audio is outlined with dashes, while unmuted audio is a solid waveform. As you can see from the international "no" symbol, Take 2 is muted in its entirety—it had nothing worth using.

Cleanup Time

Next, let's tidy things up. Select the Smart tool, and now you can trim the unused parts of clips, as well as add fades if needed. Sometimes you'll get the best transition if you enable Auto Crossfade and crossfade two clips. The important point is that you can edit the clips in layers the same way as clips in individual tracks (see Figure 15.6).

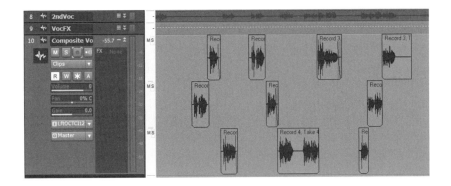

Figure 15.6
The previous example has now been trimmed and edited. Take 2 was deleted and its layer removed; some clips have had fades added.

Note that there are several options to manage layers. Right-click on the splitter bar between the track and the clips pane, and you'll see options to Show Layers, Rebuild Layers, Remove Empty Layers, Insert Layer, Delete Layer, and Select Layer (see Figure 15.7). These are all fairly obvious except for Rebuild Layers; this puts non-overlapping clips in a single layer, with overlapping clips placed in a separate layer (or layers, if necessary).

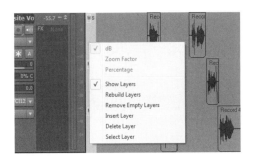

Figure 15.7
A context menu provides for a variety of layer-oriented operations.

The Track view Layers tab also offers the most commonly used layer options—Show, Rebuild, and Remove Empty Layers.

At this stage in the editing process, if you uncheck Show Layers, the remaining regions will collapse into a single track; overlapping clips will crossfade if you've selected an Automatic Crossfade option. Although collapsing to a single track is useful, you're still seeing individual clips. Therefore, if you want to manipulate the clips (process them, move them, and so on), you have to make sure that you select them all prior to doing any editing. I find it more convenient to bounce all the pieces into a single clip, which is easier to manipulate.

So, select all clips by drawing a marquee around them with the Smart tool and then select Apply Trimming from the Track view Clips tab. This deletes all unused audio. Then (also from the Track view Clips tab), choose Bounce to Clip(s). This consolidates all clips into a single layer. To remove the other layers, with the track selected from which you want to remove the layers, use the right-click context menu described earlier or choose Remove Empty Layers from the Track view Layers tab.

Additional Tips

At this point, you have a track that (hopefully) represents the pinnacle of musical expressiveness—or at least something worth hearing! But you may want to take the process just a bit further.

Quite a few musicians double their parts (in other words, play the same part twice) to create a thicker, more animated sound. Although this can be done electronically, "real" playing sounds better to my ears.

One of the advantages of composite recording is that you can easily find not only the best version of a take, but also whether any of the other takes work well with the chosen take. If so, you can simply drag the take out to another track and assemble a second track with the doubled take.

However, because you don't hear previous takes as you play new ones, it's not a given that the phrasing will be exactly the same. It's also possible that the reason you chose a particular take as optimum is because it stood out from the others for one reason or another, making it less likely that there will be any other matches in the collection of takes.

One technique to try is that after you put together the composite part, listen to it and play along until you've learned the new, improved part. At that point, play the part again to create the doubled track.

In any event, always remember to choose individual phrases based on musical continuity, not just musical perfection. The technology should be there to serve you—not the other way around.

Mixing and Effects Automation

THE MIXING PROCESS USED TO INVOLVE TURNING KNOBS, sliding faders, and pushing switches on a physical mixing console (or what the British call a *mixing desk*). We can still work that way, thanks to control surfaces, but we can also edit virtual knobs, faders, and switches onscreen.

During the mixing process, lots of "moves" are necessary—bringing instruments in and out, bypassing effects, altering pan position in the stereo field, and, of course, changing levels. Automation is what allows SONAR to "remember" your various moves. For example, if a track's level (or bus level) needs to vary throughout a piece, you can concentrate on getting those changes perfect while the automation records your moves. On playback, the level will vary exactly as you specified. (The virtual onscreen fader or other control will even move to reflect the changes.) You can then work with other tracks, or if your moves weren't perfect, you can edit the automation or redo portions of it.

But what's equally important for guitar players is that automation extends beyond mixing to changing processor settings. For example, you might prefer to have your distortion overdrive build up over a few measures leading up to a solo than to just have it switch in all of a sudden, or you might want to drop the midrange on your rhythm guitar a little bit when the vocal comes in to create more "space" for the voice. However, some aspects of effects automation work somewhat differently compared to automating mixer parameters; see Chapter 18, "ACT: The Key to Hands-On Control," on SONAR's ACT protocol for more information.

MIDI tracks implement automation too, but they have a somewhat different repertoire of parameters they can control, compared to audio tracks. Volume, pan, mute, reverb, and chorus are the "stock" automatable parameters, but you can automate parameters such as virtual instrument settings via MIDI controllers and create automation envelopes for these controllers.

Automation is one of the keys to a pro-sounding mix. If on playback you decide that a track should have been softer or louder, no problem: Just redo the automation.

Eventually, you'll get all the levels exactly the way you want.

There are five ways to automate parameters in SONAR. The method you choose will depend on the circumstances, what you're trying to accomplish, and personal preference.

Method One:
Record Onscreen Control Moves in Real Time

This is the easiest option for many people, and it's very intuitive. It's also the primary way of doing automation with the Mixer, as well as effects and virtual instruments.

Enabling Mixer Control Automation

To find out whether you can automate a mixer parameter (in Track view or Console view) by moving its associated control, right-click on the control. If you can select Automation Write Enable, then the parameter can be automated (Figure 16.1)

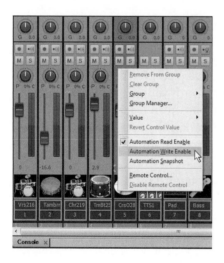

Figure 16.1

Right-clicking on the pan control (hidden by the context menu) allows you to select Automation Write Enable from the context menu. Therefore, the control is automatable.

After the control is selected, small red brackets will appear at its corner. You can select multiple parameters for automation. To select *all* automatable track parameters (Level, Pan, Mute, Send Level, and Send Pan), click a track's W button (as in Write) in Track or Console view—see Figure 16.2.

Figure 16.2

Look closely at the Volume, Pan, Send Level, and Send Pan controls, as well as the Mute button; the small brackets in each parameter's corners indicate that these are enabled for automation, and the W button is lit.

There are some fine points involved with enabling mixer automation:

▷ In Console view, you must have Wide strips selected to see the Automation Write and Read Enable buttons. In the Console Edit View menu, choose Strips > Widen All Strips.

▷ If all track parameters are automation-enabled, the W button is red. If some, but not all, parameters are automation-enabled, half of the W button is red.

▷ The Mute button can be automated or operated manually. Right-click on the Mute button and select Switch to Manual Mute or Switch to Automated Mute, as appropriate.

Enabling Plug-In Control Automation

With plug-ins—either effects or instruments—if the W button appears toward the upper right of the instrument's window and is enabled, then any onscreen controls that respond to automation will have their moves recorded when you move them. If no W button is present, no automatable parameters will be available (see Figure 16.3).

Figure 16.3
Guitar Rig 4 LE has a W (automation write) button, which means you can simply move the onscreen controls, and if they're automatable, your moves will be remembered as automation data. However, the TTS-1 in the background does not have a W button, so its parameters can't be automated by moving controls.

Here are some details regarding effects and virtual instrument automation.

▷ Automating some signal processor and soft synth parameters may produce clicks or other glitches as they're changed. This is a technical limitation of the plug-in design, so there's not much SONAR can do about it.

▷ Clicking in a plug-in's W button enables *all* automatable parameters. However, you may want to enable only certain parameters. To restrict the number of automatable parameters, right-click on the plug-in in the FX Bin and choose Write Enable Parameter from the context menu. A dialog box will appear that lists all automatable parameters; uncheck a parameter to disable, and check to enable it (see Figure 16.4)

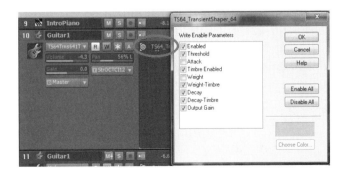

Figure 16.4
It's possible to restrict the plug-in parameters that are enabled for automation.

Recording Onscreen Control Moves

Recording automation moves couldn't be simpler. Click Play and then, to start recording automation data, click on a control and move it. Any moves will be remembered as automation data. To stop recording automation data, release the mouse button or stop moving the control. To resume writing automation moves, click on the control again and move it. Remember, Record mode does not need to be active to record automation. As long as the W button is red (or half-red), automation will be recorded.

As you record automation, a dark-reddish overlay will appear on the track when you start writing automation moves, and it will disappear when you stop recording automation. You'll also see a curve being drawn in real time that corresponds to the control movements; this curve is called an *automation envelope*.

SONAR handles automation overdubs intelligently. If playback occurs over an area that has automation data and the mouse button isn't pressed, then the existing automation data will remain unchanged. As soon as you push down on the mouse button, any moves will overwrite existing automation data. However, note that if you're overwriting existing automation data, you'll see the new data being drawn, but the previous data will remain visible until you stop recording automation and also stop the Transport.

When you've finished recording automation, remember to turn off the Write Enable button so you don't accidentally overwrite any automation you've recorded.

Method Two: Draw Envelopes or Modify Existing Ones

As described in the previous section, moving an onscreen control while recording automation will create a corresponding automation envelope that appears in the track. You can edit an existing envelope or draw a new one from scratch, as well as show, hide, copy, and paste envelopes.

Because moving onscreen controls creates envelopes, and drawing or editing envelopes moves the onscreen controls they affect, these methods are somewhat interchangeable. The method to use depends on the application. To add an expressive wah-wah effect, I'd go for recording control motion; but if I wanted to have a fade-in that lasted exactly one measure (or if I wanted to edit an existing envelope), the envelope-drawing approach would likely be easier and more precise.

The Edit Filter

Before going any further, we need to cover the Edit Filter, as it's the key to seeing and modifying particular envelopes. The Edit Filter chooses what you'll be editing in Track view and lets you create envelopes. It's especially handy if you have "envelope clutter" in a track, because you can isolate specific envelopes to view and edit without having to be concerned about editing the wrong envelope by mistake.

There are four Edit Filter options:

▷ **Clips.** Choose this to move, trim, and otherwise manipulate clips.

▷ **Audio Transients.** This essentially turns on AudioSnap for the track and shows the transients within a clip. This doesn't relate to automation; AudioSnap relates to quantizing audio and is an advanced technique. If you want to learn about AudioSnap, refer to SONAR's Help menus.

▷ **Automation.** This selects any one of all available track automation envelopes. If an automation envelope exists in the track, either because you drew it or moved controls, then when you navigate to the menu listing all available automatable parameters, a small colored square will appear next to the envelope name. The envelope in the track will be the same color as the square. If you want to create an envelope, use the Edit Filter Automation option to select a particular parameter (see Figure 16.5); a default envelope (in other words, a straight line) will appear in the track after you've selected the parameter.

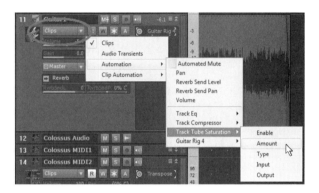

Figure 16.5

The Edit Filter currently shows Clips but is about to change to Automation. Automated Mute has a square to its left that shows the envelope color, meaning that automation envelope already exists. Meanwhile, an automation envelope for the track's ProChannel Tube Saturation Amount is about to be created.

▷ **Clip Automation.** This is automation that exists within individual clips rather than the track. We'll cover this type of automation later in this chapter.

Editing Envelopes

After creating the envelope, you can modify it in multiple ways. The Smart tool can do the needed editing.

▷ Double-click anywhere on the envelope with the Smart tool to add a breakpoint (node).

▷ Click on the node and drag to move it.

▷ Right-click on the envelope between two nodes and specify a particular shape (see Figure 16.6).

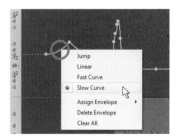

Figure 16.6

Right-click on a segment between nodes to specify the shape of the curve. Jump means that the envelope will continue at the same level as the first node on the envelope line and then when it reaches the second node it will jump immediately to that value.

▷ Click on the envelope line or curve segment between two nodes and drag up or down to move the segment up or down.

▷ Nodes can move freely, but if Snap is turned on, they can snap to the grid when they get close to a grid point.

▷ To select multiple nodes, either use the Smart tool to draw a marquee around the nodes or Ctrl-click or Shift-click to select noncontiguous nodes. Click on any selected node and drag to move all selected nodes simultaneously.

▷ Nodes can move horizontally until they encounter the vertical axis of an adjacent node.

▷ To delete a single node, either click on it to select it and then hit your keyboard's Del key or right-click on the node and select Delete Node from the context menu.

▷ To delete multiple nodes, Shift-click or Ctrl-click on the nodes to be deleted or select them by drawing a marquee around them. Then, hit the Del key.

Copy and Paste Envelopes

There are many situations where it's convenient to be able to copy and paste envelopes; here are some possible applications.

▷ You might want two parameters to change in tandem, such as echo feedback and echo mix, so that as the effect becomes more intense, there's more feedback.

▷ Suppose you've recorded a rhythm guitar part and used an envelope to reduce the level somewhat when the singer starts singing. Then you decide to record another rhythm guitar to double your first part. You don't have to spend time re-creating the envelope; just copy it from the original track to the new track.

▷ After recording a lead vocal and using envelopes to get rid of noise between phrases and such, I often double the vocal by singing it again. After singing the part, I can copy the level envelope to the new vocal. Usually, only a few small tweaks are necessary.

▷ In one song, I recorded two rhythm guitar parts playing power chords in opposite channels. I wanted to add some rhythmic "chopping" effects, so I did that for four measures on one of the tracks and then copied the envelope to other parts in the track where it would sound good. Next, I copied the same pattern, but offset by an eighth note, into the other channel so there was a panning/chopping effect.

To copy a track or bus envelope, select the range of nodes to be copied (or select the entire track by clicking on the track number in the track header). Do not select nodes by drawing a marquee around them, as you need to select a region containing these nodes. There are two ways to do this:

▷ Position the cursor in the clip's lower half and then drag right or left to select an entire region containing nodes.

▷ Click on the envelope segment that defines one end of the region and then Shift-click on the segment that defines the region's other end.

You'll know a region has been selected because not just the nodes will be selected, but the entire region within that track will be shaded.

Next, right-click within the track and choose Edit > Copy (or press Ctrl+C). In the dialog box that appears, uncheck all boxes except Track/Bus Automation and then click on OK (see Figure 16.7). The envelope data will be copied to the clipboard.

Figure 16.7

Select an envelope range to copy, choose Edit > Copy, and then check the Track/Bus Automation box to copy the selected envelope range while leaving all other boxes unchecked.

To paste the envelope region at the beginning of a track, select the track. To paste it somewhere other than the track beginning, place the now time where you want the envelope region to be pasted (see Figure 16.8). Choose Edit > Paste, either from the Edit menu or from the context menu obtained by right-clicking in the track. (Alternatively, you can press Ctrl+V.)

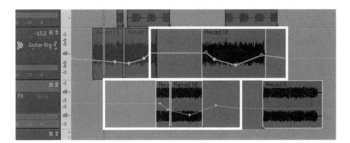

Figure 16.8

It's a little difficult to see the region shading against the background, so in the upper track, the selected region with automation has a rectangular outline. This automation has been pasted in the track below, with the region (also outlined) starting at the now time. The now time is shown with a thicker vertical line so it's more easily visible.

There's also a Paste Special option (see Figure 16.9) that lets you specify a particular starting time (in Measures:Beats:Ticks; default is the now time), enter a number of repetitions, place the data in a different track or bus, and so on. Most of the time you probably won't need this, but it's there if you need to do more than just paste the envelope.

Figure 16.9

Paste Special provides sophisticated ways to paste envelopes.

Moving Envelopes with Clips

When you move a clip, you can choose to have the envelope sitting on top of the clip move with it, or you can choose to have it remain fixed, regardless of how you move the clip. In the Track view Edit menu, go to Options and either check or uncheck Select Track Envelopes with Clips (see Figure 16.10)

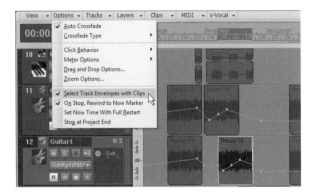

Figure 16.10

The outlined clip in the lower track is the same as the clip directly above it, but moved to be offset somewhat later. Note how it has the same envelope as the non-offset clip, because Select Track Envelopes with Clips is checked.

Reassign an Envelope

You can reassign an envelope to a different parameter. Right-click on the envelope or envelope node, select Assign Envelope, and then choose the appropriate destination.

Delete an Envelope

Right-click on an envelope or envelope node and select Delete Envelope. Poof! Gone!

Clear All Nodes

Right-click on an envelope or envelope note and select Clear All. This will remove all nodes, returning the envelope to a straight line.

Method Three: Clip Automation

The standard envelopes we've discussed so far extend for a track's entire duration. However, SONAR also offers gain and pan envelopes that affect only individual clips and are independent of whatever is happening with the track envelopes. For example, you might want to add a radical stuttering effect to a clip through clip automation but have it fade out over a time specified by a track envelope.

Audio clips have automatable pan and gain (see Figure 16.11), while MIDI clips have only automatable velocity.

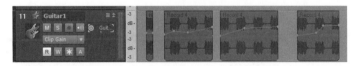

Figure 16.11

Each clip has Clip Gain automation applied. Note that the Edit Filter is set to Clip Gain.

In most other respects, they are like track or bus envelopes in that you can add nodes, delete nodes, move nodes, and so. However, there are two main differences.

▷ Clip envelopes always move with the clip.

▷ If you select a region to copy, you will always copy the selected part of the clip and any automation data. You cannot copy a clip envelope independently of the clip.

Method Four: Recording Track Automation Data from an External MIDI Controller

Any SONAR track parameters that can be write-enabled for automation (in other words, the ones that have brackets around them when write-enabled) are eligible for control from an external MIDI-based remote control box. Although this section covers recording automation data from an external remote control device, a parameter does not have to be write-enabled to be remote-controlled.

Using an external MIDI controller for automation follows the same basic procedure as recording a control's onscreen motion, because the onscreen control mirrors the external controller. After setting up a parameter to respond to an external control signal and enabling write automation, the data generated by your controller will appear as an automation envelope—just as if you'd moved an onscreen fader.

To control a parameter via a MIDI controller (usually a MIDI continuous controller, such as a fader or knob):

1. Go to Preferences > MIDI > Devices and make sure your MIDI controller is enabled as a MIDI Input device.

2. Right-click on the parameter you want to control and select Remote Control. The Remote Control window will appear (see Figure 16.12).

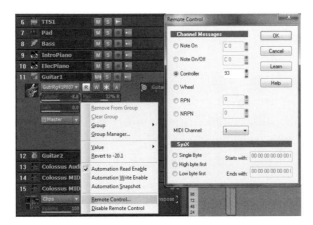

Figure 16.12

The guitar track's volume control is being enabled for Remote Control, and through the miracle of cut-and-paste paint programs, you can see the Remote Control window as well. Controller 93, which was determined by turning a control and then clicking on Learn, will control the volume.

3. Click the radio button for the MIDI message you want to use (typically a controller, although you might want to use a MIDI note for a switched function such as Mute). You can enter the controller number in the associated field, but if you don't know what the number is, just move your hardware controller first and then click on the Learn button. For example, if you want to control a parameter with a synth's data slider, but you're not sure what controller number it generates, move the slider and then click on Learn.

4. Arm the onscreen control for automation by right-clicking on it and selecting Automation Write Enable.

5. Click Play on the Transport and move your hardware controller as desired.

6. Click on Stop when you've finished your automation moves, and turn off Write Enable so you don't record additional automation moves accidentally.

Method Five: Snapshot Automation

Snapshot automation isn't a dynamic process, but instead it captures the automation setting for a particular setting at a particular now time. This automation value remains at a constant value until the next snapshot; in other words, the automation value is a straight line until it jumps instantly to the next value. Of course, you can always click on the segment between the two automation values and specify a linear, fast, or slow curve.

A typical application would be if you want the levels on multiple tracks to change at the same time when a song goes into, say, the chorus. Set up all the parameters exactly how you want them at the beginning of the chorus and then take an automation snapshot of each parameter.

Here's how to take an automation snapshot.

1. Place the now time where you want to enter the automation event for a parameter.

2. Adjust the parameter (for example, fader, pan, or whatever) to the desired value.

3. Right-click on the parameter and select Automation Snapshot (see Figure 16.13). Note that you don't need to write-enable the track or bus.

Figure 16.13

The top guitar track's Volume slider has been set to a position that will become an automation snapshot.

4. If an automation envelope for the parameter already exists, a node will be added at the value you specified. If no envelope exists, one will be created with a node at the specified value.

5. When you play back your project, whenever the now time goes past a snapshot, the parameter automated by the snapshot will jump to the snapshot value.

Incidentally, if two or more controls are grouped, taking a snapshot of one does not take a snapshot of the other. Each snapshot has to be taken independently.

Control Surfaces and the Roland VS-20 Interface for Guitarists

W ITH COMPUTER-BASED RECORDING, you have to decide which interface is best for you. There are many choices, but very few are designed specifically for guitar players. Of these, the Roland VS-20 is one logical choice for SONAR users, as it was developed in conjunction with Cakewalk and is a turnkey hardware/ software package for Windows. (What's more, many of its functions also work with the Mac.) More importantly, it has several features that are ideal for guitarists.

Although this chapter focuses on using the VS-20 with SONAR, because it includes a control surface we can take advantage of this to explain how to hook up a control surface to SONAR—the same principles apply to any SONAR-compatible control surface.

Although marketed as an intermediate-level package and optimized for use with the bundled Guitar Tracks software, the VS-20 also works well with SONAR X1. Initially, the hardware looks like a standard audio interface: It connects to your computer via USB and offers both mic and guitar inputs (as well as two built-in mics for "instant stereo recording"). But the eight front-panel faders and Transport buttons hint at more—a control surface that ties in with Cakewalk software to write automation to a track and do transport control. Furthermore, the VS-20 is compatible with the Mackie Control protocol, which means it can control non-Cakewalk programs, such as Propellerhead Reason, Sony ACID, and many more.

The faders control level for four banks of eight tracks (32 tracks total), accessed with four Track Group buttons; there are also input selectors, track select buttons to arm for recording, and various level controls (see Figure 17.1).

Figure 17.1
The VS-20 is an interface that incorporates a control surface for doing hands-on mixing and automation.

But it's what you don't see that provides something extra compared to other interfaces: built-in hardware BOSS multi-effects. This means the VS-20 isn't dependent on amp and effects plug-ins, so if you're really picky about latency, the hardware effects get around this. As in standard recording, you can process your sound with effects and then record the processed sound—while monitoring (with zero latency) what you're playing.

However, one advantage of computer-based recording is the ability to record your guitar dry and then add amp and effect sounds when mixing. The VS-20 covers that, too; you can play (and monitor) with a processed sound but record it dry and then route the dry signal through the effects later if you want to try different effects.

Incidentally, the VS-20 also does double-duty for live performance: You can open the VS-20 editor by itself, call up presets with the footswitch, and run an effects system with just a netbook or modest laptop and the VS-20 interface.

However, note that the VS-20 doesn't support sample rates above 44.1 kHz, which may be an issue for some people. A more minor issue is that the output jacks are RCA phono types, not 1/4-inch phone jacks, so you may need adapters or adapter cables.

Digging deeper, built-in vocal processing uses the available guitar effects (except for the amp sims), but also provides parallel harmonies and pitch correction, from the subtle to the "hard" pitch correction that's a hip-hop staple. Having vocal processing in the same package as guitar effects hardware is convenient and increases cost-effectiveness. What's more, the XLR mic input can provide phantom power, so it's compatible with condenser mics—a common choice for miking acoustic guitars—as well as dynamic mics.

Control Surface Basics

One of the problems with software-based, virtual recording is that it lacks the hands-on, real-time control of traditional recording or live performance setups. However, there are many SONAR-compatible control surfaces, including the one in the VS-20 interface, Roland's top-of-the-line V-Studio 700, various synthesizers that include faders and/or knobs, and Mackie's line of control surfaces. Not only can they help you create a more "hands on" mix, they can even speed up your workflow and allow for more efficient operation. Thanks to automation—SONAR's ability to remember and edit your mixing moves—if you make a mistake in just a couple of places, you can go back and make any necessary fixes. You do this by punching in new automation mixing moves or by redrawing the graphic envelopes that SONAR creates from your mixing moves.

In practice, if you use a control surface, it's likely that you'll record the automation for your real-time moves and then use graphic editing to fix small details.

How to Add a Control Surface

Control surfaces interact with SONAR via MIDI. In other words, the control surface generates MIDI data, which SONAR interprets and applies to a project. SONAR accommodates different control surfaces by loading an associated control surface plug-in (not to be confused with audio effect or virtual instrument plug-ins). After specifying the control surface as a MIDI device, the plug-in handles all communications with SONAR from that point on.

SONAR X1 currently has plug-ins for the TASCAM US-428, Joystick Panner (for surround), Red Rover, CM Labs MotorMix, Roland VS-20/VS-100/VS-700, Edirol PCR-M30 and PCDR-300, Roland A Pro series keyboards, Peavey StudioMix, Radikal Technologies SAC-2K, Mackie Control, Mackie Control XT, and Mackie Control C4. If your control surface isn't supported, no worries; there's also a Generic Surface plug-in you can adapt to whatever you're using. What's more, many control surfaces are compatible with the Mackie Control protocol.

To add the VS-20 (or any other compatible device) as a control surface, do the following (see Figure 17.2).

1. Choose Edit > Preferences.

2. Under MIDI, click on Control Surfaces.

3. Click on the star icon in the upper-right corner to add a new control surface.

4. In the dialog box that appears, choose VS-20 as the Controller/Surface. If VS-20 does not appear on the list, you can download the plug-in from the Cakewalk website. Install the plug-in in accordance with the instructions that come with the download, and VS-20 will appear on this list the next time you open SONAR.

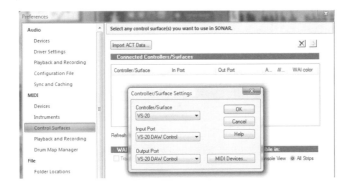

Figure 17.2
Start the control surface installation process with the Preferences menu.

5. In both the Input and Output Port fields, select VS-20 DAW control. This tells MIDI to listen to the VS-20.

6. Click on OK, and the VS-20 will be listed as a Controller/Surface.

7. Click on Apply and then Close.

Control Surface Functions

Once the VS-20 is functional as a control surface, you can do the following:

▷ Use the Transport controls to play, stop, rewind, fast forward, return to the beginning, and start recording.

▷ Select groups of eight tracks for fader control (A = Tracks 1–8, B = Tracks 9–16, C = Tracks 17–24, D = Tracks 25–32).

▷ Select a track with the Track Select 1–8 buttons.

▷ Use the Mic 1, Mic 2, Guitar/Bass, or Line switch to select which input SONAR will receive when you choose Stereo VS-20 In as a track input.

▷ Monitor the signal appearing at the selected VS-20 input with the Direct Monitor control.

▷ Monitor the signal coming out of SONAR with the DAW output control.

▷ Adjust the level of the incoming signal with the Sens control. (The Peak LED lights if the incoming level is too high.)

About the VS-20 Effects

The hardware guitar effects offer four effects slots. The included editing software (see Figure 17.3) lets you choose one effect per slot, each with appropriate controls.

Figure 17.3
The VS-20 effects editor looks almost exactly like the BOSS ME-70 multi-effects and works almost identically—except you control it all in software. In this screenshot, a new patch has just been selected.

The first slot offers 10 dynamics/wah/EQ effects, the second 10 distortion effects, the third 7 modulation effects and EQ, and the fourth 6 types of delay. There's also a reverb and noise gate, and the amp sim modules have Gain, Bass, Treble, Middle, Presence, and Level controls. As to the sound, if you've heard BOSS effects, you know what the VS-20 sounds like.

To use this with SONAR X1, choose Edit > Preferences > Audio > Devices and then enable VS-20 In as the input driver and VS-20 Out as the output driver. The VS-20 has a single stereo output that sends a signal to SONAR; what you assign to that output (guitar/bass, mic 1, mic 2, or line in) is done at the VS-20 by enabling the associated front panel switch. So when you want to record a signal from the VS-20, choose the input from the VS-20 front panel and then set an X1 audio track input field to VS-20 (1 in, 1 out) and select Stereo VS-20 IN (see Figure 17.4).

Figure 17.4
How to select the VS-20 output from within SONAR.

To process the guitar signal going into SONAR:

1. Open the VS-20 Editor program by pressing the big COSM button on the VS-20. (Remember, the VS-20 must be hooked up as a control surface for its buttons to do anything useful in conjunction with SONAR.)

2. Look for Setup in the menu bar and choose Set Up MIDI Devices.

3. For Input and Output, choose VS-20 Effect Control.

4. Now you can use the front panel Patch Select buttons (or the Editor's Patch Select buttons) to choose different patches.

When you record using the VS-20, you'll be recording the processed sound, whether for guitar or vocals. You can monitor this processed signal with no latency by using the Direct Monitor level control.

Re-Amping with the VS-20

While recording the processed signal has the advantage of being able to be monitored with no latency, the disadvantage is that you can't change the sound after the fact. Or can you? Through the process of re-amping, you can monitor the guitar sound with processing but record your guitar track without processing. On playback, you can then re-amp the dry track with the VS-20 patch of your choice—not necessarily the one you used for monitoring—and record the track with the new patch. Here's how. (We'll assume that SONAR X1 is open, you've inserted an audio track, and that its input is set to Stereo VS-20 In.)

1. Check that your instrument is plugged into the VS-20 Guitar/Bass input and that the VS-20 Guitar/Bass Input button is enabled.

2. Click on the VS-20 COSM button to open the onscreen VS-20 Editor.

3. Click on the VS-20 Setting button toward the right side, under the Patch Select button area. Then, in the System Setting window, click on Dry Rec (see Figure 17.5).

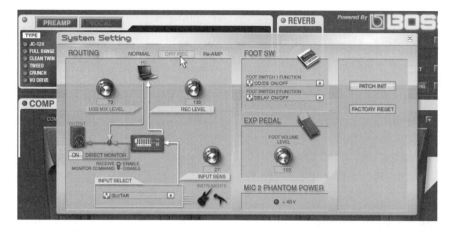

Figure 17.5
With Dry Rec selected, you can monitor the guitar through effects but record the dry guitar sound.
You can then play back this dry sound through the BOSS effects and choose which effect to use
for your final recorded sound.

4. To set levels properly, strum your guitar as hard as you expect to play and adjust the Input Sens
control in the System Setting window (or on the VS-20 itself) so that the VS-20's Peak LED lights
only briefly (if at all) and only on the loudest peaks.

5. Enable a track (for example, Track 1) for recording with its Track Select button. While observing the
track's meter and strumming your guitar hard, adjust the System Setting window's Rec Level control
for proper recording levels on the selected SONAR audio track's meter.

6. Click on the Record button (on the VS-20 Transport or in the SONAR Transport) and start playing.

7. When you're finished recording and the Transport is stopped, go to the VS-20 Editor's System Setting
screen and then click on Re-Amp (see Figure 17.6). Close the System Setting screen.

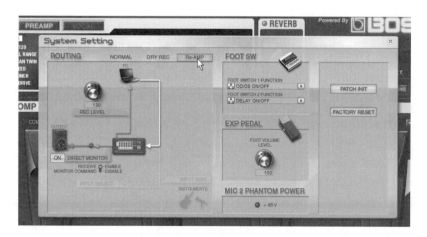

Figure 17.6
With Re-Amp selected, the dry signal comes out of your computer, goes into the VS-20
for processing, and then gets recorded back into a SONAR track with the processed sound.

8. To hear the guitar track you recorded, click on the Play button (on the VS-20 Transport or SONAR's Transport) or press the spacebar.

9. To change the re-amped guitar sound, choose a new patch using the < and > buttons. Alternatively, click on the Preset or User button, click on List, and then click on a patch name and click OK to select it.

10. Once you've chosen your new patch, click on a different track's Track Select button (for example, Track 2). The re-amped sound will be recorded into this track.

11. Click on the Record button (on the VS-20 Transport or in SONAR's Transport). The dry guitar track will be recorded into the new track through the processor you selected in Step 9.

12. When you're finished recording and the Transport is stopped, choose which track you want to hear. To hear only the re-amped track, mute the track containing the dry sound (in this example, Track 1). If you're satisfied with the re-amped track's sound, you can delete the dry track or leave it as is (but muted) in case you change your mind later and want to re-amp it through a different processor.

Using a Footpedal and/or Footswitch with the VS-20 and SONAR X1

You can use an optional expression pedal, such as the BOSS EV-5 or FV-500H, to control volume and wah with the VS-20. (Other expression pedals may work, but proper operation is not guaranteed.) You'll also need an optional stereo (three-conductor) cable. Make sure the plugs have three sections (tip, ring, and sleeve), not just two. Patch the stereo cable from the pedal's Expression jack to the VS-20's Exp Pedal jack, and make sure the VS-20 Editor is open.

The Expression pedal defaults to controlling level. To set the maximum level (in other words, when the pedal is pressed all the way down), click on the VS-20 Editor's Setting button and then in the System Setting window, adjust the Foot Volume Level control for the maximum desired volume (see Figure 17.7).

Figure 17.7
Use this setting to determine the maximum volume when the pedal is pushed all the way down.

To use the pedal for wah instead of volume, click on the VS-20 Editor's Detail button to show the various available effects for each effects block and then select the Pedal Wah effect in the Comp/FX block (see Figure 17.8).

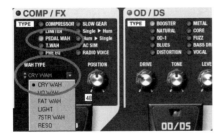

Figure 17.8
The pedal can control wah instead of volume.

Several different wah types are available. Note that the Position knob corresponds to the pedal angle and can serve as a manual wah control if you don't have a pedal.

You can also control VS-20 functions with a footswitch (bypassing effects, stepping through patches, and so on) or two SONAR Transport functions (play/stop and go into record mode).

For the optional footswitch, Cakewalk recommends the BOSS FS-6 Dual Footswitch, as it provides the most flexible control options. As with the pedal, other footswitches may work, but proper operation is not guaranteed. You also need another stereo (three-conductor) cable. Patch the stereo cable from the FS-6's middle jack (A & B) to the VS-20's Foot Sw jack and make sure the VS-20 Editor is open.

Click on the VS-20 Editor's Setting button and then, as shown in Figure 17.9, choose the desired function for each footswitch from the drop-down menus under Foot Sw.

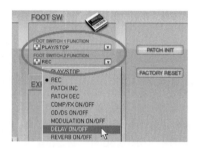

Figure 17.9
You can choose two different functions for footswitch control.

Incidentally, note that each FS-6 footswitch has a switch for momentary or latched operation. With momentary, the switch is closed as long as you hold it down. With latched, stepping on it once closes it, and stepping on it again opens it. The polarity switches reverse the open and closed states.

ACT: The Key to Hands-On Control

O NE OF THE ADVANTAGES OF PHYSICAL HARDWARE as opposed to virtual, plug-in devices is the ability to grab controls and tweak them in real time—no mouse required. It's fast, it's intuitive, and it's the way guitar players are used to "editing" effects.

If you thought using a computer meant you had to give up that kind of convenience, fortunately that's not the case. You can use a control surface not just to change mixer and track parameters, as described in Chapter 17, but to provide hands-on control for effects (and virtual instruments), thanks to SONAR's ACT (*Active Controller Technology*) protocol. As a bonus, ACT provides an alternative way to do hands-on mixing.

How ACT Works: Under the Hood

You don't have to understand the following to use ACT, but if you have an inner geek, you might find this interesting.

A plug-in will show up under ACT if the plug-in has automatable parameters and ACT can access the automation. So far, ACT works with every automatable VST plug-in I've used; DirectX plug-ins may or may not be accessible via ACT, but most are.

SONAR contains a database of ACT data. When you give focus to a plug-in, SONAR looks at the ACT data to see whether there's a specific mapping of your control surface to that particular plug-in. If there is no learned mapping, SONAR looks at a second set of data for "generic" control. More importantly, you can also set up your own mappings using ACT's Learn function, as described later in this chapter, and modify the database to include your own custom mappings.

ACT Setup

ACT is a very deep protocol that can offer a huge amount of control over all aspects of SONAR. However, let's keep it simple and concentrate mostly on the task at hand—providing hands-on control over effects. If you encounter any problems, check the "Troubleshooting" section at the end of this chapter.

SONAR offers are several ACT templates for different control surfaces from a variety of manufacturers. There are some definite advantages to using Roland's A-Pro series, because they're designed to integrate with SONAR, but it's not necessary to use a supported control surface. In fact, the simplified approach to ACT described in this chapter works with pretty much any control surface that generates MIDI.

To make this section as "generic" as possible, I decided to use a non-supported control surface—in this case, Arturia's Analog Laboratory controller, which had just been introduced when I was writing this chapter. Other controllers work similarly, so here's how to do quick tweaks of your processors using ACT.

Getting SONAR to Recognize Your Controller

1. Open SONAR.

2. Your controller communicates with SONAR via MIDI, so go Edit > Preferences and under MIDI > Devices Inputs, enable your controller's MIDI in (see Figure 18.1). If there are multiple MIDI inputs, you can check all of them if you're not sure which one to use. For example, the Roland A-300PRO keyboard has two MIDI ports and defaults to sending slider and rotary-knob data over Port 2. If you didn't realize this, then you could simply select both Port 1 and Port 2 to make sure ACT receives the incoming data, regardless of which port carries it. Technically speaking, you don't need to enable MIDI out to use ACT, but it's probably a good idea to enable it anyway, in case you need to use the controller's MIDI out for some other, non-ACT purpose.

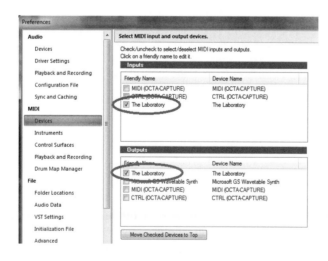

Figure 18.1

To use a controller for ACT, you need to enable at least its MIDI input in SONAR's Preferences menu.

3. After making your assignments, click on OK.

4. You now need to designate your controller as an ACT controller surface. Choose Edit > Preferences > MIDI > Control Surfaces and then click on the Add New Controller/Surface button. (It looks like a little gold star.)

5. A dialog box will appear that lets you choose the desired controller/surface; select ACT MIDI Controller—*not* the name of your particular hardware controller. Also, choose the device's MIDI input and output (what you enabled previously as MIDI devices—see Figure 18.2).

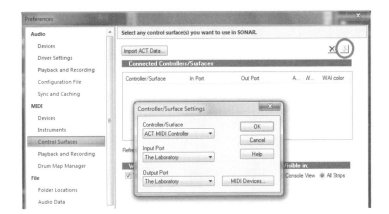

Figure 18.2

The Add New Controller Surface button is circled. After adding a new control surface, a dialog box will appear (the foreground window) where you can specify that your controller/surface should serve as an ACT MIDI controller, as well as specify the input and output MIDI ports.

6. Click on OK in the Controller/Surface Settings box, and you'll see the ACT MIDI controller listed under Connected Controllers/Surfaces.

Linking Your Controller to ACT

If you're using a supported control and have selected its corresponding preset, click on the Options tab and look at the Comments field. Often, there will be instructions about loading a particular preset on your controller or other aspects of using that controller with ACT. You may even have the option to send a MIDI Initialization Message to the controller to set it up for ACT.

If you're using the Default template and an unsupported controller (and sometimes even if your controller is supported), you'll need to make sure the hardware controls are "linked" properly to ACT. Choose Utilities > ACT MIDI Controller, and you'll see something like the following: a group of "cells" for each parameter that can be controlled (see Figure 18.3).

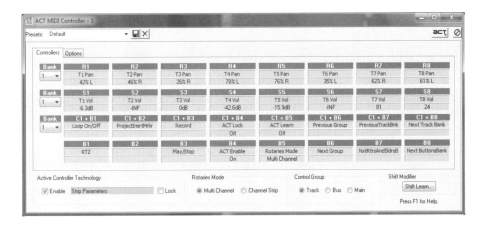

Figure 18.3

Each cell represents a parameter that can be controlled by ACT.

In this example, the dialog box is showing track parameters and their current values. If an effect had the focus, it would be showing effect parameters and their values. It doesn't matter what's being shown for now.

As this is the default preset, ACT is guessing that you're using a relatively common controller configuration—eight rotary knobs (hence the designations R1–R8) and eight sliders (the S1–S8 row). The bottom two rows relate to buttons, which is a different aspect of ACT that we'll skip over—if you want to get deeper into ACT, there's always the online help.

If we had a Peavey PC 1600 controller with 16 sliders, there's a dedicated template for that, so the labels would read S1–S8 along the top and S9–S16 along the bottom to represent the 16 sliders. If your controller uses something other than eight rotary knobs and eight sliders, you can change the cell label by clicking on the label (not within the cell itself) and typing in a new name.

Now let's see whether the controller is linked. Turn a knob and see whether any of the cell values change. If not, let's start linking.

1. Click within the cell. The other cells will go blank, and the cell you clicked on will say MIDI Learn. Move the hardware control you want to assign to that cell, and the cell parameter value should change. (If not, there's a problem with the MIDI communication between your controller and SONAR.) For example, if you clicked on R1, you'll probably want to rotate the leftmost rotary knob.

2. Repeat this process for the remaining 16 cells.

3. Verify that each control affects the desired cell.

4. Now you've linked your controller and ACT. Save this preset by typing in a new name in the Presets field and then clicking on the Save (floppy disk) button.

Controlling an Effect with ACT

There's a "standard" way to use ACT, and we'll describe that toward the end of this chapter; however, I prefer a more custom approach. I don't think the main reason ACT exists is to assign every single parameter to a control, even though it can. My favorite use of ACT is as a temporary way to tweak an effect or virtual instrument, or to provide hands-on control while recording. For example, suppose I want to adjust delay processor parameters. I'll temporarily set up my control surface to control those parameters, do my tweaking, and then move on to the next processor. For this type of control, I feel using the Learn function for individual parameters is the easiest, quickest way to do ACT mappings.

This approach is particularly useful because with default ACT mappings, the parameters aren't always mapped to controls the way you'd like. For example, suppose you have a controller with eight rotary knobs and eight sliders, which is what the generic ACT template accommodates. If you have ACT enabled, call up an effect, and move eight rotary controls sequentially on your controller, going from left to right on the controls won't necessarily go through the parameters from left to right on the effect (which is likely what you want). So, here's how to create a custom mapping.

Custom ACT Assignments

1. With the effect open that you want to control, click on the effect's ACT Learn button. (There's also an ACT Learn button in the Control Bar's ACT module and an ACT button in the ACT MIDI Controller dialog box. These are identical from a functional standpoint.) We'll use the Compressor/Gate as an example and assume you have a controller with at least eight rotary knobs.

2. Move the compressor's onscreen knobs (or switches) you want to control, *in the order you want to assign them to hardware controllers.* For example, with the Compressor/Gate, I moved Attack, Release, the three Compressor controls, Gate Mode, Threshold Gate, and Level. You can't just click on these for ACT to recognize them; you actually have to change their existing values. I didn't select Manual Trigger because it's not something I really need on a controller, and also, by choosing what I did, all the compressor controls fit within eight knobs. As ACT's default template also allows for eight sliders, I could of course have assigned Manual Trigger to a slider if available.

3. Move the hardware controllers you want to assign to these parameters, again *in order.* For example, to control the first eight parameters going from left to right with the rotary knobs, you'd move rotary knobs 1–8, in that order.

4. After you've chosen your parameters to assign and your controllers, disable ACT Learn by clicking on the ACT Learn button again.

5. A dialog box will appear that says "[X] parameters and [X] controls were touched. Do you want to keep these assignments?" (see Figure 18.4). If X represents the number of parameters and controls you moved, click on Yes. Otherwise, click on No and start over.

Figure 18.4

The Compressor/Gate parameters have been remapped from the default settings to something that seemed more logical to me, and SONAR is asking whether I want to keep those assignments. Note that the ACT Learn button, which was disabled prior to this dialog box appearing, is circled.

Incidentally, you can assign a parameter to more than one hardware controller. For example, if you wanted to be able to control the compressor with either eight rotary controls or eight sliders, use ACT Learn to assign the rotary knobs, turn off ACT Learn, turn it on again, and then assign the eight sliders and turn off ACT Learn.

This approach is great for a sort of "ACT on demand." If I'm tweaking a particular group of controls, I'll assign them to the physical controls, do my tweaks, and move on. With a few exceptions, I don't worry too much about consistency from plug-in to plug-in, and I regard most ACT mappings as temporary, to be used as needed.

However, note that SONAR does remember the mappings you've created with the ACT Learn option until you change them, even if you choose the Clear MIDI Learn button described in the next section. So if, for example, you created a custom mapping for the Compressor/Gate and another for the Classic Phaser, when you move back and forth between them, the custom mappings you made will be retained.

ACT Options

There are several useful ACT options. To access these, choose Utilities > ACT MIDI Controller.

Controllers Tab

▷ **Lock.** This is toward the lower left. Enable Lock while an effect is selected, and your hardware will control only that instance of only that effect. Disabling Lock returns full control.

▷ **Bank.** There are four banks for each row of controls (for example, a row of knobs and a row of sliders, two rows of sliders, two rows of knobs, or however your controller is configured), so you can assign up to 64 different effects parameters total. For example, suppose an effect has 16 parameters that you want to assign to rotary controls, but your controller has only eight knobs. Use MIDI Learn to assign the eight controls to eight effect parameters. Then, from the Bank drop-down menu, select another bank (for example, Bank 2) and do eight more assignments. Now your eight knobs will control either the first set of eight parameters or the second set, depending on which bank you've chosen in the ACT MIDI Controller dialog box.

Options Tab

▷ **Capture mode.** There are two choices, Jump or Match. With Jump, if you move a hardware control, the parameter value jumps immediately to the physical control setting. With Match, the physical hardware control position has to match the parameter value before you can adjust the parameter value. For example, suppose a hardware knob is all the way up to its maximum value. Now you switch to a different effect, and that control is mapped to a parameter that's currently at its minimum value. With Jump, as soon as you move the hardware control, the parameter will jump to whatever parameter value the knob's position represents. With Match, you'd have to move the knob to its minimum position to match the existing parameter value, at which point the knob would take over control of the parameter value.

You can choose a different capture mode for each bank of controls. Match is particularly appropriate for rotary controllers that are "endless encoders"—if these are set to Match, and you want to do something such as tweak the distortion drive, you'll get a smooth transition and will not experience any jumps from the existing value to the new value. However, it can sometimes be disconcerting to move a control and have nothing happen until you reach the matching value, so each option has advantages and disadvantages.

▷ **Clear MIDI Learn.** Click this to clear all existing mappings from your hardware controller to ACT's cells.

▷ **Defaults.** Click this to restore ACT to its basic, default settings.

▷ **ACT Follows Context.** It's bonus time—if this is checked, then even if a plug-in has the focus, clicking on a track will allow ACT to control track parameters. The default mapping is eight pan and eight level parameters, but you can change this. For more information, see the upcoming section, "Mixing with ACT."

▷ **Exclude this Bank from ACT.** Checking a bank's Exclude box means that a particular bank will not follow the focus. For example, if you want to use the rotaries to control plug-in parameters but reserve the sliders exclusively for Console view mixing, you'd exclude the Sliders bank that controls Console view levels from ACT so it's always available.

Traditional ACT Control

With traditional ACT control, all parameters are already preassigned to particular cells and banks. To see which hardware controllers are mapped to which parameters, open the effect's user interface and click on it to give it the focus. Then choose Utilities > ACT MIDI Controller (if the window isn't already open) and click on the Controllers tab (see Figure 18.5).

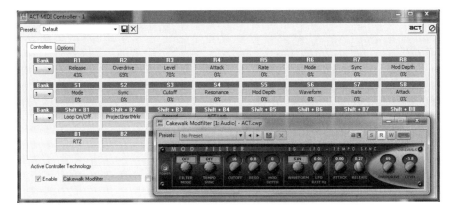

Figure 18.5
When you put the focus on an effect, the ACT MIDI Controller dialog box correlates any
rotary controls and/or sliders to the effect parameters.

The advantage of using traditional ACT control is that you don't have to spend time making custom mappings
or dealing with MIDI Learn. The disadvantage is that the mapping may not be intuitive, so you'll need to
open the ACT MIDI Controller dialog box to see the relationship between particular controls and parameters.

If you're just tweaking a parameter here and there, then the traditional mapping might save you some time. If
you find these mappings non-intuitive, or you do a lot of tweaking, it's probably worth the effort to set up your
own custom mappings.

In any event, SONAR will remember the custom mappings you make, and once they're made the ACT MIDI
Controller dialog box will show your assignments rather than the defaults. Therefore, if you create enough
custom mappings, over time the "standard" mappings will simply reflect your custom mappings anyway.

Mixing with ACT

We've covered ACT in terms of controlling effects, but ACT also works for controlling track parameters, such
as levels and pan for mixing. If ACT Follows Context is checked on the Options page, you really don't have to
do anything—if you click on a track or mixer channel, your ACT controller will then control mixing and will
continue to do so until you return focus to an effect.

There's some intelligence built into the way SONAR handles ACT, although it can be a little confusing at first
because sometimes ACT makes decisions for you. For example, the first time I fired up the ACT MIDI
Controller page and checked out the Controllers tab, the pan and volume parameters were available for only
four tracks, even though there were eight slots in the ACT MIDI Controller window. Eventually, it dawned on
me that this was because the project had only four tracks! As soon as I inserted more tracks, additional pan
and volume assignments showed up until all eight slots were filled.

If your project has more tracks than the number of controls in your controller, SONAR's WAI (*Where Am I?*)
feature comes into play. This places a colored band next to the tracks being controlled; in the Preferences
menu, under Control Surfaces, you can choose whether the WAI display shows up in the Track view or the
Console view, neither, or both by checking the appropriate boxes. In Track view, the WAI strip appears to the
left of the tracks; it appears below channels in Console view—see Figure 18.6.

Figure 18.6
The WAI strip, shown here in Console view below mixer Channels 3–10, indicates which tracks are being mapped to your controller for mixing.

If you want to control a different group of tracks, just drag the WAI strip so it's under the desired tracks. Assuming an eight-channel controller, you could drag the WAI strip so that the controller affects Tracks 7–14, 9–16, or any other contiguous combination of eight tracks. However, you're not limited to eight tracks: If you hook up two eight-channel controllers, one could control Channels 1–8, and the second could control 9–16.

Another useful feature is that on the ACT MIDI Controller page, you can shift the controller among different control groups. This option is located toward the bottom right of both the Controllers and Options pages; your choices are Track (which we've already looked at), Bus (where the faders and pans affect busses), and Main (your controller affects the main outs).

Furthermore, although for track parameters the upper row of cells defaults to controlling pan and the lower row defaults to controlling level, you can change this through the drop-down menu located under the Parameter field (accessed via the ACT MIDI Controller dialog box's Options tab; see Figure 18.7).

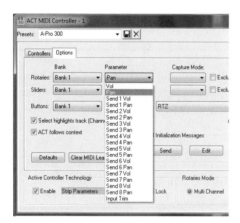

Figure 18.7
You can change the default track parameters controlled by ACT.

The Differences between Mixing Methods

When you add a new control surface in Preferences, you may have noticed you can choose ACT MIDI Controller or a specific hands-on control device, such as the Mackie Control or VS-700. Both let you do mixing, so what's the difference?

Part of it is the physical configuration. A control surface such as the VS-700 or Mackie control has the "look and feel" of a mixer. An ACT control surface may be the knobs and sliders on your keyboard controller rather than a device that's supposed to feel like using a traditional mixer.

But there's one other important point. ACT is not intended for bidirectional communication—your ACT controller sends MIDI data to SONAR, and SONAR acts on it. That's fine for tweaking parameters, but many mixing-oriented control surfaces include motorized faders that track the motions of your automation moves. These are very convenient for mixing, as punching in a new mixing move simply involves punching in and grabbing the fader—you don't have to concern yourself with matching levels before punching in, because the motorized fader will, by definition, be at the existing automation value when you punch in. Motorized faders require bidirectional communications, because SONAR has to tell the control surface where the fader should be based on automation data within SONAR, and the control surface has to tell SONAR the current physical fader position if you want to edit the automation data.

As a result, it makes sense to have one controller for ACT and another for doing mixing with motorized faders. The one exception to this is Roland's VS-700 controller, which was designed specifically to complement SONAR and incorporates both types of functionality in a single control surface. Once enabled as a control surface, pressing the VS-700's ACT button allows the channel strip controls to serve as ACT controls; you assign them to parameters in the same basic way as you would with any other controller.

Troubleshooting

If you move controls and the ACT parameters don't change, here are some possible reasons why:

▷ The Capture Mode option under the Options tab is in Match mode, and the controls haven't matched their associated values yet.

▷ The hardware controls aren't linked properly to ACT; refer to the section "Linking Your Controller to ACT."

▷ If you clicked on the Clear MIDI Learn button on the Options page or chose a different controller preset, you'll likely need to relink your controller to ACT.

▷ Under Connected Controller/Surfaces, make sure the ACT MIDI Controller has the correct input port assignment.

▷ The Lock option was invoked, so only one instance of one possible ACT destination will respond to controller changes.

Part IV

SONAR's Bundled Effects

SONAR's Bundled Plug-Ins: Common Elements

THE NEXT FIVE CHAPTERS COVER MOST OF THE PLUG-INS bundled with SONAR, with an emphasis on those of interest to guitarists.

SONAR's plug-ins cover a wide variety of signal-processing needs. Of course, one advantage of the plug-in concept is that you're not limited to what comes with the program—SONAR can run literally thousands of plug-ins from hundreds of manufacturers. But given that third-party plug-ins can be expensive (although many free and shareware ones exist as well), it's convenient to have a wide variety of options bundled with the program.

Regarding the chapters on individual effects, there's no real point in simply repeating what's in the help menus and documentation. So, each effect description includes information on where to find help on the effect. (It's not in the same place for all effects.) Where appropriate, we'll concentrate on additional tips and applications that let you get the most out of these effects.

Although the documentation and tips can help point you in the right direction, in many respects the best way to learn what these plug-ins do is to experiment. Edit the controls, try different effects on different instruments (even ones that don't seem logical, such as a guitar amp simulator on drums), and if you come up with a preset you like, save it.

Some of SONAR's older effects have help files written in Microsoft's .hlp format, which is not supported in Windows versions newer than XP. To read these files, go to www.microsoft.com/download and search the Microsoft Download Center for winhlp32.exe. Download the appropriate version for your operating system (make sure you download the 32-bit version or 64-bit version, as appropriate) and then double-click on the downloaded winhlp32.exe file to install it. You will now be able to read .hlp files. Note that you will need to complete the Windows Validation process to download the file.

We'll start off describing elements that are common to all effects and then proceed to the chapters dedicated to particular effects categories.

The Common Plug-In Header

Most plug-ins included with SONAR have a common header with plug-in-oriented functions. Note that the following applies to 32-bit SONAR running 32-bit plug-ins and 64-bit SONAR running 64-bit plug-ins; the situation is somewhat different for 64-bit SONAR running 32-bit plug-ins, as described later.

Going from left to right across the header, you'll first see a Presets selector (see Figure 19.1).

Figure 19.1

Many plug-ins include presets for common applications.

Select Presets

If a plug-in has presets available, you can choose one from the Presets drop-down menu.

Click on the down arrow in the Presets field, and you'll see a drop-down menu listing the presets, if any are available. There can be up to three sections of presets, each separated by a line:

   ▷ Up to eight recently used presets

   ▷ Factory presets

   ▷ User presets

Click on the preset you want, and its settings will load into the effect.

The left/right arrows to the right of the Presets field select the previous and next preset in the list, respectively. This is handy for when you want to try out presets in rapid-fire succession.

Save Presets

You can also create your own presets; saving them adds them to the list. Having a library of custom presets can save time when mixing, as you'll often find that certain instruments tend to get along well with particular effects settings, even in different songs. When you find an effects setting that works well, save it, because you may need it again. You can also save presets that are "points of departure"—for example, EQ curves that have a somewhat generic purpose (brighter, more bass, and so on), which you then tweak for a specific application.

Note that there are differences between how saving works with VST and with DirectX effects. (You can tell an effect is VST because it has a VST drop-down menu in the middle of the header; DirectX effects don't.)

The basic save procedure for either type of effect is:

1. Double-click in the Presets Name field.

2. Type in the desired preset name (or don't, if you just want to overwrite the existing preset).

3. Click on the Save (floppy disk) button to the right of the right arrow button.

However, there is an exception with VST effects. If there are no user presets, you call up a factory preset, and you follow the save procedure above, you will end up renaming a factory preset rather than creating a new user preset. So, if you open the Presets drop-down menu and don't see any user presets, call up any factory preset but don't type a new name, and save it. This will create a user preset, thus creating a section of user presets. From here on, when you save one of your presets, it will go in the list of user presets. After you have at least one user preset in the list, you can delete the factory preset that you saved into the user preset list.

With DirectX effects, as soon as you save a preset, it goes into the list of presets and is sorted alphanumerically within the list.

Preset Dirty Flags

I don't know why Cakewalk chose this name, but it is a really cool feature. If an asterisk appears next to a preset name, it means the preset was saved and referenced by a different project, but that the current settings differ from the saved version referenced by the other project. If you want to make sure you don't change the settings, which might alter the sound in the other project, then change the name before saving. If you do save, the asterisk will disappear, but when you open the other project and call up the plug-in, its name will have an asterisk, as its settings will be different from what you just saved.

Delete Presets

To delete a preset, select it in the Presets Name field. Then, click on the X (Delete) button. If the X button is grayed out, then you have selected a factory preset, which cannot be deleted.

The VST Drop-Down Menu

The VST drop-down menu provides an alternative way to save presets with VST plug-ins. One of the advantages of saving using this method is that you create a discrete file that can be shared easily with other SONAR users and backed up easily. You can save and load presets from this menu, and for effects (or VST instruments) that contain banks of presets, you can save and load these as well.

Randomize

This little-known feature of the VST drop-down menu randomizes parameter values every time you invoke it. The odds of getting something great are remote, but sometimes a little extra editing can produce something truly novel. Remember that randomization affects everything, so if parameters seem grayed out, it may be because the power switch became randomized to off.

Plug-In Properties

This duplicates the Plug-In Properties section of the Cakewalk Plug-In Manager, which is described in Chapter 14.

Other Header Buttons

Let's check out the five buttons toward the right of the preset header.

▷ **ACT.** Click on this to learn ACT settings for an external controller. For details on using ACT, refer to Chapter 18.

▷ **S.** This is equivalent to a track's Solo button—in other words, you'll hear only the track containing the effect if you click on the effect's Solo button. This is for convenience, so you don't have to go find the track containing the effect and solo that.

▷ **R.** This lets the plug-in respond to (read) any automation data recorded in the track.

▷ **W.** Click to enable automation writing. As you move plug-in controls, they will write automation control signals to the track. On playback, the controls you moved will play back the automation. For more information on automation, see Chapter 16. Note that this button isn't available with all plug-ins.

▷ **Give All Keystrokes to Plug-In.** This is the button that looks like a QWERTY keyboard. A plug-in may have keyboard shortcuts that conflict with the keyboard shortcuts dedicated to SONAR. Enabling this button directs the QWERTY keyboard exclusively to the plug-in, not to SONAR.

Header Appearance with 64-Bit SONAR

An application included in SONAR called BitBridge enables 64-bit SONAR to run 32-bit plug-ins. However, a limitation is that 32-bit plug-ins can't dock, and the header is minimal (see Figure 19.2).

Figure 19.2
The header appearance changes when running 32-bit plug-ins with a 64-bit version of SONAR.

There's an on/off button, a preset selector, and a File button for saving and loading VST presets and banks.

Fortunately, this isn't as much of a limitation as it might seem. You can use a track's Read and Write Automation buttons for effects and virtual instruments. (Also with virtual instruments, you can use the Synth Rack Read/Write Automation buttons.) Furthermore, you can right-click on an effect in the FX Bin and choose which parameters to enable for read and write.

Although there's no Solo button, you can just use the track Solo button instead. And for ACT, you can click any ACT button (for example, in the Control Bar), as they all operate in parallel. So the only functionalities that aren't available are the ability to delete presets from the list of presets and the option to give all keystrokes to the effect.

Sonitus Effects Preset Management

The Sonitus effects supplement the standard methods of preset management with an additional, quite sophisticated preset management system.

With a Sonitus effect, click on the Presets button toward the right. From the drop-down menu that appears, you can create a preset based on the current settings (Add Preset), call up one of the existing presets as shown in Figure 19.3, or use the Preset Manager to delete, update with current settings, rename, import, or export presets.

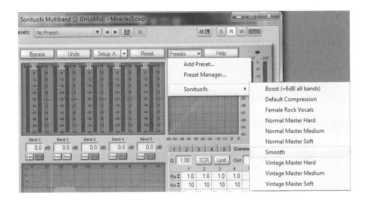

Figure 19.3

Sonitus effects have a tool that, among other functions, provides for preset management.

These effects also have a useful compare mode, accessed via the effect's toolbar. There are two independent parameter setups for each effect (three if you also count Bypass)—Setup A and Setup B. You can toggle between them by clicking on the Setup A/B button; the drop-down menu to the right of this button provides the option to copy one setup to another.

As to how you'd use this, suppose you're comparing two EQ settings, you have B selected, and you decide you like B better than A—but you think you can still do better. From the drop-down menu, select Copy to A, and the curve in B will be duplicated in Setup A. Now you can keep tweaking B, knowing that the original is safely stored in Setup B if you want to revert to it. Note that you can also copy from the other setup into the current setup (for example, copy Setup A's curve into Setup B). If you change your mind, Undo will work with this function, but Undo affects only the last operation.

Finally, the Reset function restores all effects parameters to their defaults.

SONAR's Equalizers

W HEN MIXING, EQUALIZATION IS ONE OF THE MOST IMPORTANT processors you'll use. This is because the frequency spectrum that we hear (from about 20 Hz to 20 kHz, depending on a variety of factors, such as age and how many loud concerts you've attended) has only so much bandwidth for particular sounds. For example, the bass and kick both occupy the low frequencies; vocals, rhythm guitar, piano, and many other instruments occupy the midrange; drums cover the range from very low (kick drum) to very high (cymbals), and so on.

Equalization can help differentiate among these different instruments. For example, a common technique with a singer/songwriter is to reduce the guitar's response a bit where it overlaps with the voice, thus creating more sonic space to emphasize the voice. To differentiate between kick and bass, some engineers will emphasize the bass's highs to bring out pick and string noise, while others will boost highs on the kick to bring out the "thwack" of the beater.

I'll start off by describing the Sonitus:fx Equalizer, as its functions are representative of equalization in general. I'll cover these functions in depth, so that when describing other equalizers in this chapter or the equalizers included in channel strips (as covered in Chapter 23, "SONAR's Channel Strips"), you'll already be aware of how equalization works, and I won't need to repeat the same material.

Sonitus:fx Equalizer

The Sonitus:fx Equalizer has a comprehensive help menu you can access simply by clicking on the Help button. It's a very capable equalizer (see Figure 20.1) that offers six stages of EQ, each of which can have one of five possible responses (Peak/Dip or parametric response, Shelving Low, Shelving High, Lowpass, and Highpass).

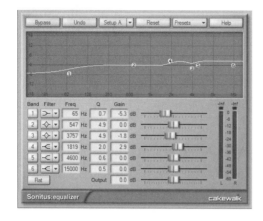

Figure 20.1

The Sonitus:fx Equalizer offers a very
useful complement of controls.

A parametric response is a versatile way to adjust frequency response, as it can boost (make more prominent) or cut (make less prominent) specific parts of the frequency spectrum. With six independent EQ stages, you can apply equalization to six different parts of the frequency spectrum for each audio track. You'll find three main parameters in each stage of parametric equalization.

▷ **Frequency.** This control determines where the boosting or cutting takes place. For example, if the high frequencies need boosting, you would dial in a high frequency. With the Sonitus:fx Equalizer, this is a field where you can type in the desired frequency in hertz. Or, on the graphic view of the frequency-response curve, you can simply drag the "button" associated with one of the six stages to the desired frequency (as described in more detail later).

▷ **Gain (also called Boost/Cut).** Use a stage's associated slider to adjust boost or cut. Boosting increases the level in the chosen frequency range, while cutting decreases the level; the Gain field to the left of the slider displays the amount of boost or cut, with negative values indicating a cut. You can also enter a value here.

Gain is specified in decibels (dB). A change of 6 dB doubles the level (–6 dB halves it), which is a considerable amount. Changes of no more than 1 or 2 dB are common when mixing and mastering. Even changes of less than 1 dB can make an audible difference.

▷ **Q (also called Resonance or Bandwidth).** This sets the range of frequencies affected by the boost or cut, from broad (smaller numbers) to narrow (higher numbers). Broader settings are gentler and are used for general tone shaping. Narrow settings generally help solve specific response problems. For example, suppose there is some 60-Hz hum on a recording. Setting a very narrow cut at 60 Hz will reduce the hum.

Figure 20.2 summarizes peak and dip response characteristics.

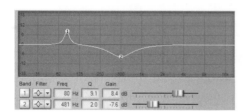

Figure 20.2

Band 1 is set for a narrow peak with a high Q,
while Band 2 is set for broad dip with a lower Q.

Choosing EQ Responses

You select the type of filter response by clicking on the drop-down menu for the Filter parameter and selecting the type (see Figure 20.3). As I've already covered the Peak/Dip response, let's look at the other ones.

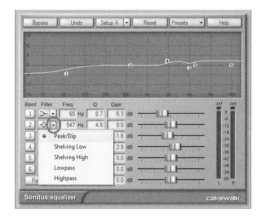

Figure 20.3

Each EQ stage offers five different ways to modify the frequency response.

A shelf response starts boosting or cutting at the selected frequency, but this boost or cut extends outward toward the extremes of the audio spectrum. Past a certain point, the response hits a "shelf" equal to the maximum amount of cut (see Figure 20.4).

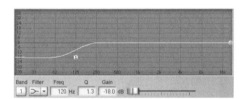

Figure 20.4

The low shelf in this screenshot is set to reduce low-frequency response.

Any Equalizer stage can be set for a low-shelf response; you set frequency as you would with a parametric stage, while Q determines the slope of the curve before it levels off into the shelf.

The high-shelf response (see Figure 20.5) is similar to the low shelf and offers the same parameters but affects the high frequencies.

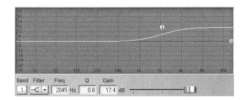

Figure 20.5

The high-shelf response can boost or cut high frequencies.

A high-pass response (see Figure 20.6) progressively reduces response below a certain frequency (called the *cutoff frequency*)—the lower the frequency, the greater the reduction. (This is unlike a shelf, where past a certain point the amount of gain reduction stabilizes to a constant amount.) A high-pass filter is sometimes used to remove subsonic (very low-frequency) energy.

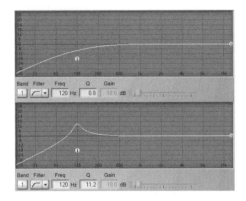

Figure 20.6

The upper graph shows a high-pass response with a low Q value, which gently rolls off low-frequency response. In the lower graph, increasing the Q creates a peak at the cutoff frequency.

The gain (boost/cut) control is not applicable because the high-pass filter can only attenuate below a certain frequency. However, as with the low shelf, the Q parameter determines the slope of the response reduction. High Q values add a resonant peak at the selected filtering frequency.

The low-pass response is the mirror image of the high-pass response, as it progressively reduces response above a certain frequency (see Figure 20.7). The reduction in response is greater toward the spectrum's higher frequencies. A typical application is removing hiss or excessive brightness.

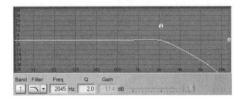

Figure 20.7

Low-pass response filter, set for a sharp high-frequency cut.

Other Sonitus:fx Equalizer Controls

Each stage has its own set of parameters. If a button under Band is yellow, the stage is on. To turn it off, click on the button, and it will turn gray. To conserve DSP power, turn off any unused stages.

The Flat button resets all gain controls to 0 and disables any high- or low-pass filters but leaves the frequency and bandwidth settings intact.

You can edit most parameters directly on the EQ graph. To select a band for editing, click on its small button, which turns black. Change Frequency by dragging left or right, Gain by dragging up or down, and Q with either a mouse wheel or by holding down Shift while dragging left or right. Note that these buttons don't have to be arranged sequentially—for example, the Band 2 button can be to the right or left of the Band 3 button.

To copy one band's setting to another band (or all bands), right-click on the associated band's square button under Band (not the button in the EQ graph) and choose the desired copy function. You can also reset an individual band from the same pop-up menu (see Figure 20.8).

You can change the resolution of the EQ's graph. It defaults to an amplitude axis range of ±20 dB, but it's possible to right-click anywhere in the graph and choose ±40, ±10, or ±5 dB as the range. The finer resolutions are extremely helpful with subtle settings; I usually use ±5 dB, with occasional forays into ±10 dB.

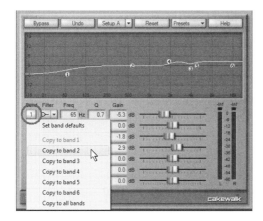

Figure 20.8

A pop-up menu lets you copy settings from one band to another or reset a band to its default (flat) setting.

Using the Sonitus:fx Equalizer with SONAR X1 Studio Edition

There are some special considerations when using the Sonitus:fx Equalizer with X1 Studio Edition or pre-X1 versions where the Sonitus EQ was hard-wired into the console channels.

Even though you see only four stages of track EQ in the Inspector or Console view, you can actually use all six stages of the Sonitus EQ by opening up the per-track EQ to its full interface view. Furthermore, this gives you all the other advantages of the full interface: You can call up presets, use undo, have separate settings for Setup A and Setup B, and so on.

It's possible to open up the full EQ view only if the EQ is enabled. To enable, either right-click on the plot and select Enable EQ or click on the EQ module's power button toward the bottom of the EQ module.

There are two ways to open the view. In the Inspector or Console view, double-click on the EQ plot, and you'll see the full equalizer. The other option is to right-click on the plot and select Show EQ Properties.

Para-Q

This effect is like a subset of the Sonitus:fx Equalizer; it includes two parametric EQ stages that are used for tone shaping. If clicking on the GUI and hitting F1 doesn't open the help, you can find the paraq.chm help file at C:\Program Files\Cakewalk\Shared Plugins. Double-click on the help file to open it.

This particular effect is very light on CPU power, so you can use lots of them in a project without hassling your computer. The Para-Q has the same basic parametric EQ controls per stage as the Sonitus Equalizer: Frequency, Gain (also called Cut/Boost), and BW (for Bandwidth, also called Resonance or Q). Figure 20.9 shows the two sets of these controls, as well as an overall Level control.

Figure 20.9

The Para-Q includes two parametric EQ stages.

HF Exciter

This effect adds brightness (HF stands for High Frequency), but not in the same way as EQ; instead, it adds a gentle amount of high-frequency distortion that adds sparkle to a track. If not overused, it can restore some of the brightness associated with acoustic instruments that sometimes seems to get lost during the recording process.

The controls are pretty intuitive, but if you need help, click on the GUI and press F1. If for some reason that doesn't open the file, you can find the hfexciter.chm help file at C:\Program Files\Cakewalk\Shared Plugins. Double-click on the help file to open it.

The control complement is very basic (see Figure 20.10).

Figure 20.10
The HF (High Frequency) Exciter is the audio equivalent of those "washday whiteners and brighteners" for laundry you see advertised on TV.

▷ **Frequency.** This determines the range of frequencies that will be "excited." Usually you'll want this set fairly high unless the track you're processing is really muffled. In general, a lower Frequency setting means you might want to pull back on the Drive control a bit to avoid an overly crispy sound.

▷ **Drive.** Use this to alter the character of the high-frequency emphasis.

▷ **Spread.** This increases the apparent stereo width. Because high frequencies are more directional than low frequencies, increasing the amount of Spread can give a wider high-frequency stereo image.

▷ **Mix.** Lower Mix control settings blend in less of the excited sound and more of the original (unprocessed) signal.

LP-64 Equalizer

SONAR is inching ever closer to being a mastering program (for some people, it's probably already there) and part of what makes that possible are the LP-64 EQ and LP-64 Multiband (compressor). Let's look at the EQ part of the pair (see Figure 20.11). You can open the very complete help menu by clicking on the GUI to give it focus and then hitting F1.

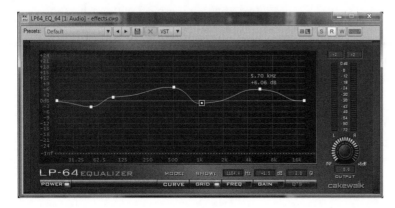

Figure 20.11
The LP-64 is a highly advanced equalizer that lets you create any number of bands.

The LP-64 is quite different from the Sonitus:fx Equalizer, starting with CPU consumption—it requires much more power. It also has a "look-ahead buffer" to anticipate processing that needs to be done, so if you alter a parameter using the graphical interface, the output will mute while the parameter is moving. This makes the LP-64 unsuitable for automation, so you'll likely not use it as a track EQ, unless it's to make a permanent change to a track—the LP effects in general are designed to be mastering and bus effects.

Comparing the LP-64 and Sonitus EQ, I'd say their "personalities" are audibly different; the Sonitus has a certain quality in the upper midrange that adds a bit of an edge, whereas the LP-64 is more neutral in how it affects the sound. However, for almost all applications, the ProChannel (or the Sonitus:fx Equalizer) will do the job; as this is a more advanced EQ, if you really want to dig deep into it I suggest studying the help file—it would take a lot of pages to get into the details.

SONAR's Dynamics Processors

O NE OF THE FIRST USES OF DYNAMIC RANGE COMPRESSION, the most common form of dynamics processing, was to shoehorn the dynamics of live music (which can exceed 100 dB) into the restricted dynamic range of radio and TV broadcasts, vinyl, and tape. Compression lowers the peaks of signals while leaving lower levels relatively unchanged and then boosts the overall level to bring the signal peaks back up to maximum. (Bringing up the level brings up any noise as well, but you can't have everything.)

As guitars can be percussive in nature, compression is used often to tame peaks and bring up the average level. It also increases sustain; most "sustainer" pedals for guitar are really just compressors set for a lot of compression. However, compression isn't the only kind of dynamics control; there's also expansion, multiband compression, limiting, loudness maximization, and gating.

I'll begin by describing the Sonitus:fx Compressor, as it's a typical compressor in terms of functionality (although it does have some interesting additional features). By covering this compressor in depth, I won't need to repeat basic concepts when I describe other compressors in this chapter or the dynamics processors included in channel strips (Chapter 23, "SONAR's Channel Strips").

Sonitus:fx Compressor

The Sonitus:fx Compressor has sophisticated metering, a choice of vintage or normal response, and other useful features (see Figure 21.1). To check out the help menu, click on the question mark in the upper-right corner; the documentation explains the various module parameters from a technical standpoint and provides useful background information. We'll concentrate on the musical implications of these parameters.

Figure 21.1

The Sonitus:fx Compressor can smooth out
a guitar's dynamics, as well as increase sustain.

Note that compression is not always a transparent process. Over-compressing can give a pinched, unpleasant sound that exhibits "pumping" and "breathing." In fact, one of the more difficult decisions for beginning engineers is how much to compress, which is made even more difficult because the ear is not that sensitive to level changes. If you adjust the compressor so you hear it "working," it's probably over-compressing. My attitude is that you shouldn't really know a signal is compressed until you bypass it, at which point you should note a reduction in punch and overall level. (If not, then you're probably under-compressing.) Until you've trained your ears to recognize subtle amounts of compression, keep an eye on the gain reduction meters (described later) to avoid over-compressing.

Compression works mainly by lowering a signal's peaks. For example, suppose some peaks reach 0, and compression manages to reduce those by –5 dB, so the loudest peaks hit at –5 dB. You can now turn up the signal's overall level by +5 dB, at which point the peaks once again hit 0. In other words, you've been able to add +5 dB of gain to the overall signal level simply by reducing the peaks.

Compressor Controls

Let's look at what the various controls do.

▷ **Threshold.** This sets the level at which compression begins. Above this level, the output increases at a lesser rate than a corresponding input change. With lower thresholds, more of the signal gets compressed, and the peaks become lower.

▷ **Ratio.** This parameter defines how much the output signal changes for a given input signal change. For example, with 2:1 compression, a 2-dB increase at the input yields a 1-dB increase at the output. With 4:1 compression, a 16-dB increase at the input gives a 4-dB increase at the output. Higher ratios increase the effect of the compression and tend to sound less natural.

Some compressors allow an infinite compression ratio, where the output will refuse to go past a certain point, no matter how much you pump up the input. This is the same function as a *limiter*. The Sonitus:fx Compressor has a Limiter switch that clamps signals to 0 dB (signals that exceed 0 dB with the limiter disabled are clipped, which creates distortion); note that this adds a little bit of processing delay.

▷ **Graph display.** The graph shows the threshold (where the curve has a "knee," and bends). Signals below the threshold aren't affected by the compressor. The slope to the right of the knee shows the ratio of output level to input level. This slope shows an 7:1 ratio of input level to output level—in other words, increasing the input by, for example, 7 dB causes only a 1-dB increase at the output. This is what compression is all about: The output level increases at a slower rate for higher input levels.

▷ **Attack.** This control determines how long it takes for the compression to start affecting the signal once it senses an input-level change. Longer attack times let more of a signal's natural dynamics through, but remember, those signals are not being compressed. This is where the Limiter switch can really come in handy, by trapping excessive transients even if you have a slow attack time.

▷ **Release.** This parameter adjusts the time required for the compressor to stop affecting the signal once the input passes below the threshold. Longer settings work well with program material and guitar chords, as the level changes are more gradual and produce a less noticeable effect.

▷ **TCR.** The Transient Controlled Release switch automatically optimizes the release time based on the levels of the incoming program material.

▷ **Output Gain and Gain Reduction meter.** After using Threshold and Ratio to squash the peaks, it's necessary to turn the signal's overall level back up again—which is the output Gain control's function. To help in proper level setting, observe the Gain Reduction meter. This works oppositely from most meters; the highest setting is 0, and as more reduction is applied, the meter moves downward from 0. You generally want to set the Output control to a little less than the amount of reduction. (For example, if the gain reduction meter shows about 5 dB of reduction, a good output Gain setting is around 4 dB.)

▷ **Knee.** This softens the compression curve so that the compression ratio increases over time around the threshold, rather than switching instantly from no compression ratio to full compression ratio at the threshold point. Any changes to the knee are reflected in the graph.

▷ **Type.** Choices are Normal and Vintage. Vintage gradually reduces the compression ratio a certain amount above the threshold, allowing it to eventually return to a 1:1 ratio for the highest peaks. This lets loud peaks pass through with much less compression, thus mimicking the compression action of old-school compressors that used electro-optical compression elements, and can give a bit more punch.

Compression Parameter-Setting Tips

Compression can be difficult to set up correctly, so here are some tips.

▷ Unless you're looking for a compressed sound, you usually don't want more than 6 dB of gain reduction. To reduce the amount of gain reduction, either raise the threshold or reduce the compression ratio.

▷ For a more natural sound, use lower compression ratios (1.5:1 to 3:1). Bass typically uses a ratio of around 3:1, voice 2:1 to 4:1—but these are approximations, not rules. To increase guitar sustain, try a ratio in the 4:1 to 8:1 range.

▷ With minimum attack time, peaks are clamped almost instantly, producing the most drastic compression action. If it's crucial that the signal never hit 0, yet you want really high average levels, you're probably better off using the Boost 11 Limiter described later in this chapter. For most sounds, you'll have a more natural effect with an attack time of 3 to 10ms to let through some peaks, even if it means a somewhat lower average signal level. The Sonitus:fx Compressor's Limiter switch can help preserve the punch from the peaks, yet minimize the chance of distortion.

▷ Decay is not as critical as attack. Start in the 100 to 250ms range. Shorter times sound livelier, while longer times sound smoother. But too short a time can give a choppy effect, while too long a release time homogenizes the sound.

▷ Use the Sonitus:fx Compressor's TCR switch rather than setting a Release time if you're new to compression.

▷ The Bypass switch is your friend—check it frequently to compare the compressed and non-compressed sounds. You may find that just a little bit of compression gives the desired effect.

▷ When using compression as a track effect, place it early in the chain so it doesn't bring up the noise from any effects that precede it.

▷ When increasing guitar sustain, remember that compressor/limiters are not miracle workers. They can't make your guitar's strings vibrate any longer; they can only increase the apparent sustain. No compressor can compensate for dead strings or guitars with poor sustain characteristics.

▷ Add compression before distortion for a smoother sound with more sustain.

▷ If it seems as if there's been a sudden increase in compression, but you didn't increase the compression amount, then the input signal going to the compressor may have increased.

Sonitus:fx Multiband

Multiband compression is a very powerful form of compression, as it splits the signal into individual frequency bands and then applies individual dynamics control to each band. Thus, unlike a standard compressor, you can have a huge amount of compression happening in the bass range without having this affect, say, the treble. The drawback is that five times the parameters need to be set, so tweaking can take a while. This is where presets come in handy—both the ones that come with the plug-in and those you create. Although you likely won't be able to use these exactly as is in every situation, they will at least serve as a point of departure.

The Sonitus:fx Multiband (for more information, click on the Help button) is very much like five Sonitus:fx Compressor modules, tied together with a common interface. Although you can do graphic editing by dragging the threshold, frequency-band crossover point "dividers," and gain, I spend a lot of my tweak time on the Common page. Here you can adjust individual parameters by clicking on a value and dragging up or down to change it. But more importantly, if you click on the parameter abbreviation (for example, Ra for Range, Ty for Type, and so on) and drag up and down, related values for all bands will change linearly. If there's an offset between values, this offset will be maintained until a value hits the maximum or minimum possible level. If you continue to increase or decrease respectively, values that have not hit a limit will continue to increase or decrease, while the value that has hit a limit will stay on that value. See Figure 21.2, which indicates how you edit various parameters.

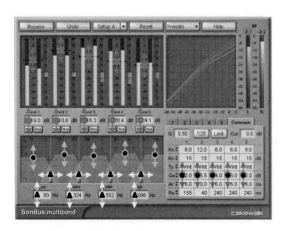

Figure 21.2
The arrows with internal dots indicate where you can adjust gain, both graphically (left) and on the common page (right). The arrows with internal triangles indicate graphic (upper) and numerical (lower) places to adjust the frequency crossover split between bands. The plain arrows show the graphic (upper) and numerical (lower) places to adjust the threshold. On individual pages (in other words, not the common page, but pages 1–5), the Ratio, Knee, Type, Gain, Attack, and Release parameters are available for editing.

You can adjust a band's threshold and keep the Common page on top by clicking and dragging on the threshold numerical for the band. Or, you can drag the band's graphic threshold adjustment, which instantly puts the page for the band being adjusted (1–5) on top instead of the Common page.

To adjust a band's frequency, click and drag on the frequency numerical below the frequency band graphic, or drag the graphic crossover frequency splitter. If you want fewer than five bands, drag the lower-frequency crossover splitters all the way to the left to reduce the number of bands. For example, if you drag band splitters 1, 2, and 3 all the way down to 20 Hz, the fourth splitter sets the dividing line between two bands. Just make sure that the values for bands 1, 2, and 3 are set so they have no effect on the sound (Threshold and Gain at 0, Ratio at 1:1).

The Limiter, Type, and TCR functions work as they do in the Compressor (including the slight delay with limiting enabled), except that they affect all bands simultaneously. The metering is a bit different, though; the yellow meter associated with each threshold slider shows the level in each band, while the blue meter that goes downward from the threshold shows the amount of gain reduction being applied.

The Solo and Bypass buttons for each band are crucial when doing multiband compression, as they let you monitor what's going on in individual bands. Using Solo also simplifies adjusting the frequency crossover points, as it's easier to hear the frequency range being affected.

Sonitus:fx Gate

The typical use for a gate is to reduce noise. It works by muting ("gating") the audio output when the input drops below the level set by a threshold control. If you set the threshold just above any background hiss, then the gate closes when only hiss is present but opens up when there's an input signal that's above the level of the hiss. However, gates can also produce special effects. If you have a signal with a long decay, setting the threshold fairly high can cut off the decay and create a more percussive sound.

The Sonitus:fx Gate (see Figure 21.3) is more sophisticated than the average gate; for more information, click on the Help button.

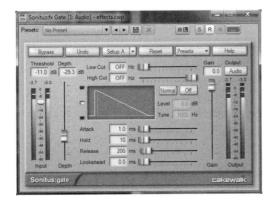

Figure 21.3
The Sonitus:fx Gate does all the basic gate functions and then some.

The Threshold parameter works as expected—it sets the level a signal must exceed to open the gate—while Depth determines how much the signal will be attenuated when the gate closes. At the maximum depth setting, –Inf, the signal path is essentially turned off with the gate closed.

Although you normally want a fast attack, setting a short Attack time (0.1 to 2ms) can eliminate clicks at the beginning of the audio when the gate cuts in. As this control is automatable, you can do tricks such as add dynamics to electronic drums by doing the equivalent of changing the "sample start point." When you want the drums to sit a bit more in the background, increase the attack time; to move them to the front, reduce the attack time. You can also use this to soften pick attacks.

Another cool attack technique is that adding an attack in the 100ms range or greater causes a signal to swell to its maximum level. For instance, if you pause briefly between notes when playing guitar or bass, when a new note exceeds the threshold, it will fade in over the specified amount of attack time. This can alter a guitar's attack characteristics, but there must be a space before every note that needs an attack, so the gate can reset itself. Also note that the Release and Hold parameters should be at minimum. Otherwise, the gate may remain open during the space between notes, which prevents triggering a new attack when a new note plays. However, too short a release time can result in a "chattering" effect. Use the shortest possible release time consistent with a smooth sound.

After a signal goes below the threshold, the Hold parameter determines how long the gate remains open before the release time kicks in. This is particularly helpful with signals that have long, slow decays (for example, long reverb tails) where the signal crosses over the threshold several times as it fades. This can produce a "chattering" type of effect if there's no hold option. Once the signal drops below the threshold for good, then after the hold time has elapsed, the Release phase begins.

To ensure the most accurate gating, the Sonitus:fx Gate has a "lookahead" function. This delays the audio going into the gate, but not the trigger signal, by up to 40ms. Thus, it's possible to open the gate just before any transients in the audio signal, as well as include a bit of an attack time, without cutting off the transient's beginning. If you find the resulting delay objectionable, you can slide the audio a bit to the left in the Clips pane so it plays earlier.

An outstanding feature is the ability to gate on the basis of frequency range as well as level. For example, suppose a bass amp sound leaks into a snare mic. If you restrict the gate's response to ignore the bass, then only the snare will trigger the gate, making it easier to reject the bass amp leakage. Note that this function does not affect the audio itself, only the control signal that triggers the audio.

Using this feature is simple:

1. Click on the Output button so it shows Sidech instead of Audio. This lets you monitor the trigger audio.

2. Adjust the low-cut and high-cut sliders to set the filter's low- and high-frequency limits, respectively.

3. Once you've isolated the sound you want to gate, click on Output again so it says Audio. You can now hear the noise gate output. Optimize the other parameters (Threshold, Attack, Decay, and so on) for the best results.

4. To disable the filter, slide Low Cut all the way to the left so its frequency says Off, and slide the High Cut filter all the way to the right so its frequency also says Off.

Gate mode's Duck option (click on the button that says Normal to select this) reverses the gate action, so that stronger signals close the gate, which then returns to its open position according to the Hold and Release times.

Finally, there's a "punch" mode button to the right of the Normal/Duck button with three possible settings: Off, Wide, and Tuned. Punch adds a brief burst of gain (up to 20 dB, as set by the Level parameter) at the beginning of the gating envelope. Wide is a broadband gain boost, whereas Tuned narrows the range (via a band-pass filter) to the frequency specified by the Tune parameter. This function has nothing to do with traditional noise gating, but it's cool. For example, you can accent the slap in a slap bass part by gating the bass and adding some high-frequency punch to emphasize the percussive slap.

Compressor/Gate

This provides a function similar to the Sonitus:fx Compressor but incorporates a gate function not found in the Sonitus processor (see Figure 21.4). To access the documentation, click within the GUI and press F1. (The actual help file, compgate.chm, is located at C:\Program Files\Cakewalk\Shared Plugins folder. You can double- click on the help file to open it.)

Figure 21.4
In addition to doing compression, the gate can help remove noise caused by heavy compression as well as provide special effects.

The Threshold, Ratio, Attack, and Release controls work the same way as the equivalent controls in the Sonitus:fx Compressor; Level does the same as Sonitus's Gain parameter.

One control that's different is Input Gain. This increases the level going to the compressor, so increasing this control also increases the compression. It's useful if you really want to squash the sound.

The Gate Section

This is much simpler than the Sonitus:fx Gate. If you want to use the Gate by itself, you'll need to bypass the Compressor; however, the Bypass control affects both the Compressor and the Gate. To neutralize the Compressor, set the Threshold to 0.00, Ratio to 1:1, and Input Gain to 0.00. In this case, the Attack and Release controls don't matter, and there's no compression.

Threshold works as described for the Sonitus:fx Gate. Gate mode offers Normal and Manual options (as well as Off, for when you don't want any gating). With Normal, the Threshold control affects gating, as expected. With Manual, you can gate the signal manually by clicking on the Manual Trigger button. This is automatable if you want to create "stuttering" effects, although you could also automate the track mute to provide the same type of function.

Boost 11

Boost 11 controls dynamics by reducing only peak levels, which allows you to bring up the overall level. For example, if the peaks are brought down by 6 dB, then that opens up 6 dB of headroom. Thus, the entire file can be brought up by 6 dB, making it sound considerably louder. While similar to compression, the curve is optimized to provide extremely fast control over the transient peaks.

You can access the Boost11.chm documentation by clicking in the GUI and typing F1, as well as within the Boost11 folder, located within the VSTplugins folder.

The help file is good for understanding the principle of operation, but it's easy to go through the basic operation—see Figure 21.5.

Figure 21.5

If used properly, Boost 11 can increase a signal's apparent loudness without impacting dynamics too much.

Look at the Waveform In meter. Note that some peaks of the incoming signal exceed a horizontal line; this line represents the maximum available headroom as set by the Output control. (In Figure 21.5, the peaks are colored white instead of red so they're easier to see in the book.) Compare this to the Waveform Out meter, where the peaks are no longer present; Boost 11 has reduced the gain of only those peaks so they would not exceed the available headroom.

Adjusting Boost 11 is easy: Just turn up the Boost control for the desired amount of boost. Be careful, though, because a little bit goes a long way. If you turn this up too far, the sound will become distorted—you can increase levels only so much without having undesirable artifacts. Typically, a few dB will be all you need. If the Waveform In has a ton of red peaks, you've probably gone too far.

The Reduction meter shows how much the peaks are being reduced downward. When no peaks are present, the meter doesn't show anything. As more reduction is applied, the bar moves downward; a longer bar represents more reduction. The numeric readout under the bar indicates the maximum amount of reduction that's been applied. To reset this, double-click on the number.

The Output control adjusts the output headroom. For example, if you set the output to −0.5 dB, no output signal will exceed −0.5 dB.

LP-64 Multiband

This processor has the same relationship to the Sonitus:fx Multiband as the LP-64 Equalizer has to the Sonitus:fx Equalizer: The LP-64 requires more CPU power, is more refined in its functionality, maintains a linear phase from input to output, and is ideal for mastering and bus processing. It also incorporates a look-ahead function to prevent clipping, so it can apply compression in time to catch any transient peaks. As this contributes a delay of about 20ms, this is one reason why you'd want to use the LP-64 Multiband for tasks such as mastering rather than as a track effect.

The LP-64 Multiband has the same general controls as other multiband compressors (see Figure 21.6). There are five bands that split the signal, and each band has its own compression controls. For more information, click on the GUI and type F1.

Figure 21.6

The LP-64 Multiband has a similar complement of controls to the Sonitus:fx Multiband but offers more refined—and CPU-hungry—processing.

TS-64 Transient Shaper

The TS-64 Transient Shaper (see Figure 21.7) is virtually identical to the Transient Shaper section of the PX-64 percussion strip, which is described in Chapter 23. As with most other processors, you can click on the GUI and press F1 to see the documentation or locate it within the TransientShaper folder in the Vstplugins folder.

Figure 21.7

The TS-64 is essentially the same as the Transient Shaper included in the PX-64 channel strip.

The two main differences (aside from the user interface) are:

▷ A Threshold control sets a threshold above which transient shaping is applied. Anything below the threshold is unprocessed. The PX-64 does not have this control.

▷ The PX-64's Color controls are referred to in the TS-64 as Timbre controls, and there's a switch to activate the Timbre section.

TL-64 Tube Leveler

The TL-64 can add subtle (or grotesque, if that's what you like!) distortion effects that are useful for guitar, synth, and bass (see Figure 21.8). Again, check out the documentation by clicking within the GUI and pressing F1.

Figure 21.8
The TL-64 serves a function similar to the ProChannel Saturation module but offers more control.

In addition to giving crunchy sounds, with subtle settings the TL-64 can add a really nice bite to make any sound a little less sweet. While the TL-64 is fairly straightforward, there are a few features that are particularly useful.

The Dynamic Response section offers a low-cut filter; drag the little square for the desired response, as indicated in the fields at the bottom of the window. This is helpful if you want a thinner sound or to keep the bass out of the drive/distortion effect. However, if you don't want to distort the bass but you still want to keep the same amount of low end, enable the CMPS button. This compensates for cutting the bass response by adding undistorted bass back into the signal path.

It's also worth clicking on the Advanced button, as this brings up controls for Offset and Symmetry of the clipped waveform. Altering these can change the timbre in interesting ways, and they are good for making a "round" synth bass sound a little more jagged. You can even get very lo-fi, broken speaker-type sounds by turning the Offset control low and Symmetry high, or Symmetry low and Offset high.

SONAR's Time-Based and Modulation Effects

O F ALL OF THE EFFECTS BUNDLED WITH SONAR, these will likely be among the most familiar to guitar players—if you don't know what reverb, chorus, or delay are, then check out the help files. As a result, I won't spend too much time on these; instead, I'll showcase the most important or unconventional elements of the various effects.

Sonitus:fx Reverb, Perfect Space Reverb

There are two main types of reverb: algorithmic (also called *synthetic*) and convolution-based. Each uses different technologies, and both are represented within SONAR.

Algorithmic reverb—the technology used by the Sonitus:fx Reverb (see Figure 22.1)—synthesizes a room's characteristics through algorithms that emulate reflections, high-frequency damping, pre-delays, particular room sizes, and so on.

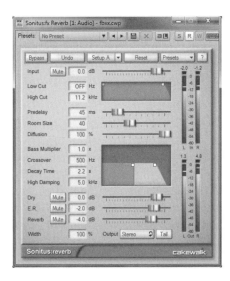

Figure 22.1

The Sonitus:fx Reverb, based on algorithmic reverb technology, can give rich reverb sounds while being light on CPU consumption.

Although this is an "imaginary" reverb, the algorithms are based on analysis of how acoustic spaces affect sound. For more information, click on the question mark in the upper-right corner (or press F1) to open the documentation.

A convolution-based reverb like the Perfect Space (see Figure 22.2) obtains its sound by loading an impulse, which is a sampled "snapshot" of a room's decay characteristics.

Figure 22.2

The Perfect Space convolution reverb gives realistic reverb sounds, but with fewer editing options than algorithmic types.

One way to create this sample is to record a starter-pistol shot and record its decay. Loading this impulse into a convolution reverb tells the reverb how to process an incoming signal so that it decays in the same way as the impulse. You can think of convolution reverb as similar to keyboard samplers, while algorithmic reverb is more like virtual analog synthesizers.

SONAR comes with a collection of impulses for the Perfect Space reverb that represent a variety of spaces, but one of the really cool features about convolution reverb is that you're not limited to loading only room impulses—you could load an impulse of an acoustic guitar's body, a piano chord, a drum pattern, or whatever. You can do some amazing sound-design work by choosing the "wrong" impulses for the Perfect Space reverb.

For more information about Perfect Space, click on the main screen's Info button; then when the Info page opens, click on the Help button.

As to which type of reverb to choose, convolution reverb is more "literal," while algorithmic reverb is more "impressionistic." Each type has its own sound quality, and neither one is wrong unless it doesn't sound right in the context of your music. Try both, and it should be obvious which works best with your recordings.

Inserting Reverb

Reverbs are often used as bus effects, so that signals from multiple tracks can feed into them, and create the illusion of existing in the acoustical space provided by the reverb. In this case, the reverb output includes no dry sound, as the reverb supplements the various dry sounds feeding the main output mixer. However, "special-purpose" reverbs, such as gated reverb for drums or a vintage spring reverb for guitar, may serve as insert effects on the appropriate tracks. The Sonitus:fx Reverb offers two folders of presets—one for aux bus applications and another for insert applications.

Sonitus:fx Delay

This delay has several features you won't find on the typical guitar delay stompbox (press F1 or click on the Help button for the documentation); see Figure 22.3.

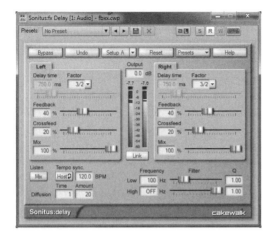

Figure 22.3

For more sophisticated delays than those obtainable with typical guitar effects, call up the Sonitus:fx Delay.

For use with SONAR, one of the most important features is tempo sync, so that delays can follow (or not follow) a rhythm; clicking on the Tempo Sync button cycles through three options.

▷ **Man.** This lets you set a tempo, independent of SONAR, that the delay can follow. After choosing the tempo, you set the delay with the Factor control. Factor represents the tempo as a rhythm—for example, a factor of 1/4 would be a quarter-note delay, while 1/8 would be an eighth-note delay. You probably won't use this much, as you'd more likely want the delay to follow SONAR's tempo. However, you can do some special effects, such as setting a tempo that's slightly faster than SONAR's host tempo so the echoes "push" the tempo a bit, or using a slightly slower tempo where the echoes "lag" the tempo somewhat.

▷ **Off.** With this setting, SONAR's tempo has no effect on delay. You set the delay time with the Delay Time slider (or by entering a value in the Delay Time field). The Factor control is still active, but it bases its timing on whatever tempo is shown next to the Tempo Sync box. Although this will be grayed out if Man is selected, it's still relevant.

▷ **Host.** The delay time follows SONAR's tempo, including any tempo changes, with the delay set by the Factor control.

Here's how to use some of the other controls.

▷ **Crossfeed** feeds back a percentage of one delay channel's signal into the other delay, creating interesting stereo echo feedback.

▷ **Link** ties the Delay Time, Feedback, Crossfeed, and Mix controls for the two channels so that adjusting a parameter in one channel causes the identical parameter in the other channel to assume the same value.

▷ **Listen** chooses between Mix, where you hear both the delayed and dry signals (their balance depends on the Mix control setting), and Delay, where you hear the delayed sound only.

▷ **Diffusion** builds a cluster of echoes around single echoes to more closely emulate the effect of echoes reflecting in a room. The Time parameter determines the time "spread" between echoes, while Amount acts like a feedback control that makes the sound more or less resonant.

▷ The **Filter** sliders set an upper and lower limit to the delayed signal's frequency response. This is useful if you want echoes that are brighter, duller, more bassy, and so on. Note that the filter does not insert in the feedback loop, but affects the delayed output only.

Stereo Delay (Tempo Delay)

This effect has an identity crisis: It's listed in the FX Bin as Tempo Delay, but its front panel says Stereo Delay. No matter—it's a useful stereo delay that can sync delay times to tempo (see Figure 22.4).

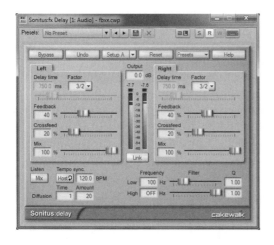

Figure 22.4
The Stereo Delay provides a simpler option for creating delay effects than the Sonitus:fx Delay.

This is another effect where the help menu (type F1) will tell you most of what you need to know, but here are a few hints on getting the most out of this effect.

▷ For dance music where you want to add some motion to the sound, try using the 1D Tempo Sync, in Stereo Delay mode, with a fair amount of Feedback.

▷ To take this one level further and add stereo effects, switch to 1/2D Tempo Sync and set the Delay Mode to Ping.

▷ The EQ section is very powerful. Check out the help menu for details on how to take advantage of it.

▷ For a sound that resembles old tape echo units for guitar, turn EQ mode to Wide, pull the Low and High EQ controls all the way down, turn Mid all the way up, and use a fair amount of feedback.

▷ With percussion, try EQ mode in the Wide position, with the High EQ control all the way up and the Low and Mid EQ controls all the way down. This adds a bright echo that sort of "floats" above the other sounds. In fact, if you apply this to a drum part with a fairly repetitive hi-hat part, it can almost sound like there's an additional shaker or perhaps maracas part.

▷ To add echo to a drum part but keep the kick solid, set EQ mode to STD, leave Mid and High up about halfway, and reduce the Low control.

Classic Phaser

And for those who love that classic '70s swooshing sound, meet the Classic Phaser (see Figure 22.5). Let's check out its main controls; for more info, press F1.

Figure 22.5
Phasing provides swooshing, "underwater"-type sounds.

> ▷ **Mode** progressively widens the stereo image as you switch from Mono to Stereo to Quadra.

> ▷ **Tempo Sync** is a crucial control, as it makes the Phaser's sweep relate to the song's tempo. You can choose common rhythmic values (such as having it sweep every quarter note) as well as dotted and triplet values. If set to Off, then the LFO Rate control sets the sweep period.

> ▷ **LFO Depth** determines the influence of any modulation, from subtle to a sweep that covers a wide range. This control is active regardless of whether you've chosen Tempo Sync or LFO Rate.

> ▷ **Waveform** provides one of three different "shapes" that determines how long the sweep stays at the top of the sweep, how long it stays at the bottom of the sweep, and how it transitions from top to bottom. This is one of those "try it and see what sounds best" controls.

> ▷ **Center** weights the phasing effect more toward the low (counterclockwise) or high (clockwise) frequencies.

> ▷ **Feedback** gives a sharper, more whistling tonal quality by increasing the phaser resonance as you turn the Feedback control clockwise.

Modfilter

If you're reading this book, I'd be willing to bet you know what a wah-wah pedal sounds like with guitar. For those who were born prior to 1965, fell asleep, and just woke just a few minutes ago, a wah-wah pedal imparts a sort of vocal quality to your playing.

This plug-in creates wah effects automatically in one of two ways: by sweeping a filter (similarly to how the Classic Phaser sweeps the signal phase) or by tying the filter frequency to the incoming signal level. In the latter case, louder signals kick the filter frequency higher, and the filter decays back to its initial frequency (as set by the Cutoff control) over a time specified by the Release control. See Figure 22.6, which shows a preset that creates an automatic wah effect similar to the '70s "Funk Machine" effect used by bassist Larry Graham and others.

Figure 22.6
This preset causes the Modfilter to respond to the incoming signal level, thus producing an automatic wah-wah effect.

The controls are fairly straightforward (press F1 to see the documentation), so let's talk about applications. When the Filter mode is set to LFO, the controls are similar to the Classic Phaser with respect to synching the LFO to tempo. One very cool application is to create a pulsing effect by synching to tempo and using a square wave as the LFO waveform. Use the Mod Depth to vary the depth of the pulsing, or better yet, enable automation Write and vary the depth to add variations. The Sample and Hold waveform can also be fun for creating random variations on each rhythmic interval (for example, every beat, every measure, and so on).

In EG Filter mode, the Attack and Release controls can have a major effect on the sound. If the settings are too fast, the envelope follower will try to follow every tiny little level change, which can produce a sort of warbling or choppy effect that's not particularly smooth. Increasing the attack time to 0.03 (30ms) will pretty much get rid of this, provided the release isn't too short. For percussive material, you'll want a relatively short release; for more complex sounds, you may need a longer release time to avoid an overly choppy sound.

Note that adding a little Overdrive can help thicken the overall filter sound. As for Resonance, be careful; too high a setting can produce massive peaks. If you want to use lots of resonance, you may need to follow the Modfilter with the Boost 11 to reduce the dynamic range.

When used subtly, the Modfilter can add "animation." For this application, set the filter Cutoff fairly high (around 4,000–5,000 Hz), with low Resonance and just a little bit of Mod Depth to make the filter wiggle a bit. Try this on vocals as a subliminal type of effect.

Sonitus:fx Wahwah

This provides effects similar to the Modfilter but with options to make the wah sound more customizable (see Figure 22.7). Also, instead of using an envelope follower to control the filter frequency, the Wahwah derives a pulse from the input signal and uses it to trigger an envelope with Attack and Release (decay) parameters. You can access the documentation by pressing F1 or by clicking on the ? button in the upper-right corner.

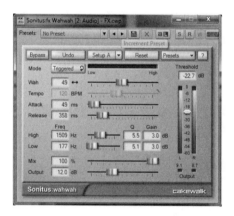

Figure 22.7
The Sonitus:fx Wahwah offers three different ways to modulate a wah effect, as well as ways to tailor the filter response.

Click on the Mode button to cycle through three ways to modulate the wah effect.

▷ **Manual.** Move the wah slider to change the wah frequency.

▷ **Auto.** This creates a periodic change, as determined by the Tempo slider. However, note that you can't sync the wah to the host tempo.

▷ **Triggered.** This controls the wah frequency with an Attack/Release envelope.

Adjusting the Envelope Parameters in Triggered Mode

Three parameters are exclusive to the Triggered mode.

▷ **Threshold.** The input has to exceed the threshold level to trigger the envelope. When set low, even soft signals will trigger the envelope; the envelope resets upon receiving the next trigger.

▷ **Attack.** This determines how long it takes for the wah filter to reach its high-frequency setting. A shorter attack time gives a more percussive effect, while a longer attack time causes the filter to take longer to reach its high frequency in response to an input signal.

▷ **Release.** After the attack time is complete, this sets how long it takes for the wah filter to return to the low wah setting in the absence of another trigger.

With really short Attack and Release settings, the effect may sound choppy. Lengthening the Attack and/or Release somewhat can solve this.

Adjusting the Filter Parameters

A wah's filter covers a range of frequencies, from low to high. In addition to sliders to control these frequencies, the high and low frequencies can have individual Q (resonance) and Gain settings.

The Mix control sets the balance between the dry and wah sounds. Fully dry is 0%, while 100% is fully wah. The output control can boost the level, which is often necessary because a wah "thins" the sound.

Multivoice Chorus/Flanger

The Chorus effect thickens sounds; think of a choir compared to a couple of people singing together, and you have the basic idea (see Figure 22.8). Flanging produces the "jet airplane" sound effect that was big during the '60s on albums by artists such as Jimi Hendrix, the Beatles, the Small Faces, and many others.

Figure 22.8
When you want to thicken a sound and make it swirl around the stereo field, the Chorus/Flanger is for you.

This plug-in benefits from an informative help file (press F1), so we don't need to get into details. In fact, this is another one of those effects where playing with the presets for a while is probably the best way to learn what it does. However, pay particular attention to the help file section on the EQ mode and EQ controls, as these can make a huge difference in the sound. As with the Modfilter, high Feedback settings can produce significant peaks (especially with the Flanger presets), so be careful of introducing distortion.

Sonitus:fx Modulator

This is a multi-effects—although it produces effects similar to the Multivoice Chorus/Flanger, it also does two different types of phasing and even tremolo, while offering more options and variable parameters (see Figure 22.9). The help file is quite complete, and you can access it by pressing F1 or clicking on the Help button in the upper right.

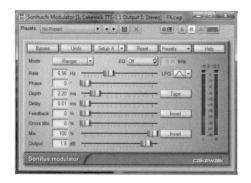

Figure 22.9
This shows the parameter settings for a vibrato effect.

In addition, there's an excellent selection of presets, so if you just want to "plug and play," you don't really need to spend too much time learning how the controls work. However, one effect that's not mentioned is vibrato, which the Sonitus fx: Modulator can also do.

Start with the Flanger algorithm. Set the Phase, Delay, Feedback, and Crossmix parameters to minimum, and Mix to maximum, so that you hear the processed sound only. EQ should be off. For LFO, choose the Sine waveform.

The crucial controls are Rate and Depth; you don't want to set Depth too high, or you'll get a "warped record" effect instead of vibrato. In addition to vibrato, you can also create a useful rotating speaker effect with the Modulator—see Figure 22.10.

Figure 22.10
This shows how to set the Modulator parameters to obtain a rotating speaker effect—with some added distortion, too.

This is also a variation on the Flanger algorithm but covers a more restricted range than flanging. The Depth and Delay controls are critical, so feel free to experiment for the most realistic rotating speaker effect. You'll also want to vary the rate to emulate the effect of the rotating speaker speeding up and slowing down.

One final comment about rotating speaker emulation: The classic models had a preamp that could be over-driven, and quite a few classic organ sounds involve using that feature to create distortion. To emulate this effect, insert the Cakewalk Amp Sim prior to the Sonitus:fx Modulator, set for a light amount of distortion, as shown in Figure 22.10.

SONAR's Channel Strips

SONAR INCLUDES SEVERAL CHANNEL STRIPS, which combine multiple effects within a single plug-in and are dedicated to a particular set of functions.

Even though the ProChannel is technically not a plug-in—it's "hardwired" into every SONAR track and bus and can't be inserted in the FX Bin—it's most definitely a channel strip and one of SONAR X1 Producer Edition's main features, so let's start there.

ProChannel

This channel strip offers seven bands of EQ, two types of compression (modeled on the UREI 1176 and SSL 4000G hardware processors), two types of saturation (modeled tube distortion), and the option to change the order of effects. You can find the documentation by choosing Help > What's New; under the Contents tab, you'll see a chapter for the ProChannel.

EQ Section

The EQ section (see Figure 23.1) has four main bands—LF, LMF, HMF, and HF, which stand for Low Frequency, Low Mid Frequency, High Mid Frequency, and High Frequency. However, these names are for reference only, as all bands can select any frequency from 20 Hz to 20 kHz. The LF band can switch to a low-shelf response, and the HF band to a high-shelf response.

Two more bands offer a high-pass filter (HPF) and low-pass filter (LPF). The frequency for these bands again extends from 20 Hz to 20 kHz, with adjustable slope from a gentle 6 dB to an ultra-steep 48 dB, in 6-dB increments. The final band, Gloss, is a fixed band with no adjustments other than on or off. It provides high-frequency "air" to add, well, "gloss" to a sound.

Figure 23.1
The equalizer section can create complex EQ curves. Note that the HPF is providing a sharp, low-frequency cutoff to minimize subsonics and room rumble.

A common high-pass filter technique is to set the frequency just below the lowest frequency contributed by a track's instrument; this tightens up the low end by minimizing hum, room rumble, subsonics, handling noise (with mics), and so on. The 48-dB/octave rolloff is much steeper than you'll find with most equalizers and is recommended for this kind of application. Adding a steep low cut to midrange instruments may not make too obvious a difference with individual tracks, but the effect is cumulative and opens up more "space" for bass, kick drum, and other low-frequency instruments.

The low-pass filter can sometimes reduce "brittleness" and create a warmer sound when used judiciously to cut a track's very highest frequencies.

Pure, Vintage, and Modern Response Options

The ProChannel EQ offers three different types of responses—Pure, Vintage, or Modern. Modern seems to be the most accurate response. Pure is the next closest but seems to give a slightly richer low end and smoother highs. It appears Cakewalk intended this option to be a more musical EQ than one for surgical precision.

Vintage seems to model control interaction, gives a fatter sound in the low end, and has a somewhat non-standard midrange response. According to Cakewalk, they weren't trying to model any specific piece of gear, but instead achieve a particular character they felt was desirable.

ProChannel EQ Module Options

ProChannel has a Display tab that lets you access Module options. Two of these are important for EQ.

Choosing Display > Module Options > ProChannel > Compact EQ Module shrinks the EQ size so that you see only enable buttons for the bands, along with the full high-pass, low-pass, and gloss options (see Figure 23.2).

You may need to use the Compact option if your monitor's vertical resolution is less than 1024 pixels (the minimum I've found that lets you see the full ProChannel) or if you're using a laptop and need more overall screen space.

However, note that this doesn't lock you out of making EQ adjustments, as you can make all needed adjustments on the plot itself—you won't see any numeric calibrations, but some would say this is a good thing because it forces you to use your ears!

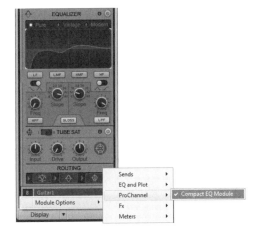

Figure 23.2

Choosing Compact EQ Module shrinks the amount of space required by the EQ, but you can still adjust all EQ parameters graphically by clicking and dragging in the EQ plot.

Note that the plot is divided into four rectangles, with each one representing one of the four EQ bands. Clicking within the band turns that band on or off. (This is the same as clicking on the label with the band name abbreviation—for example, LMF or HF.) Hovering the mouse within a band shows two ticks on the graph's top and bottom that indicate the band filter's frequency setting and a horizontal tick on the left that indicates the amount of boost or cut. Note that the frequency ticks can appear outside of the rectangle if the frequency is out of the range indicated by that rectangle.

If you click and drag within a rectangle, dragging horizontally adjusts the frequency, while dragging vertically determines the amount of boost or cut. If you hold down Alt while dragging vertically, you edit the Q instead. You don't have to lift your finger off the mouse button to switch between editing Q or boost/cut.

Display > Module Options > EQ and Plot offers a choice of EQ plot resolutions, which are global settings for all channels (see Figure 23.3).

Figure 23.3

The three mixer channels on the left have plot resolution set to 18 dB; you can clearly see the difference in amplitude among the three peaks (from left to right, +18, +12, and +6 dB). The three mixer channels to the right have plot resolution set to Auto, making it difficult to see the level differences among peaks at a glance.

I recommend *not* choosing Auto, because if a peak or notch exceeds 6 dB, then the plot will be rescaled to fit within the existing graph. As a result, if one channel is set for a peak of +18 dB and another for +6 dB, they will look as if they have the same amplitude, but the +18 peak—being scaled—will appear to have a higher Q. I prefer the 6-dB option because it gives the most detail to the graph, but more importantly, if you need drastic EQs that 6 dB won't show adequately, that's a hint that maybe there's a problem with your recording or mixing techniques. Unless you're doing something surgical, such as notching out hum, you shouldn't need radical amounts of EQ.

Dynamics Section

The ProChannel can switch between two compressors, which are intended for different applications (see Figure 23.4).

Figure 23.4

The 76 compressor (left) and 4K compressor (right) provide different compression effects. Both include a Dry/Wet control, which allows you to create the parallel compression effects described later.

The 76, which is the default compressor for individual tracks, has the potential for more drastic compression. When you want to set the compression so high it pops or gives a "pumping" drum sound, this is the one to use (although of course, you can also employ more subtle settings). It does not support sidechaining.

The 4K is often referred to as a *bus compressor*, which makes sense because it's less about dramatic compression effects and more about "gluing" complex program material together. As a result, this type of compressor is often strapped across the stereo bus to give program material more punch, or on individual tracks with complex material (for example, full mixed loops or even rhythm guitar). It's the default compressor when you select a bus in Sonar X1, and it supports sidechaining.

However, there's an important caution. If you intend to send a project to a mastering engineer, don't insert anything in the Master bus, particularly a compressor. This restricts dynamics in a way that's almost impossible to undo, whereas if you don't add compression, it can always be added during the mastering process (which it almost certainly will).

Parallel Compression

Parallel compression is a technique that splits a track to an effects bus that includes a compressor, which is mixed back in with the track's unprocessed sound. This is most often used with bass and drums so that the dry signal can provide dynamics and transients, while the compressed signal can bring up softer sounds and add more punch or sustain. However, it's also an excellent technique for rhythm guitar, as the compression evens out the dynamics, but the unprocessed path preserves the attack of the strums. Both ProChannel compressors provide parallel compression via a Dry/Wet control, as shown in Figure 23.4, that's continuously variable between 0% compressed sound and 100% compressed sound.

In between, with settings in the 30% to 50% range, you'll hear useful parallel compression effects. One side effect of using parallel compression is that the compressor settings can be more drastic than would be desirable if you were using the compressor by itself, because the dry signal will preserve the signal's dynamics.

Using the 76

The 76 doesn't have a traditional Threshold control; instead, an Input control increases the level going into the compressor. Turning this up "slams" the input more, thus increasing compression. (The Output control provides makeup gain to balance levels between the enabled and bypassed states.) Also, instead of having a continuously variable ratio control, you have a choice of 4:1, 8:1, 12:1, 20:1, and Infinity.

If you want a lower ratio—which I often use to give just a little lift to tracks—the 4K can give a 2:1 ratio. For an even lower ratio, you'll need to use the Sonitus compressor or the compressors in the VC64 vintage channel.

Using the 4K

Switching over to the 4K enters a different world, as you can tell by the change in color scheme and knob cosmetics. With the 76, the meter goes negative to indicate gain reduction; with the 4K, positive values indicate the amount of gain reduction. And while the 4K is billed as a bus compressor, it can give a sweet, gentle compression effect that leaves you wondering whether or not you really have the compression enabled—until you disable it, whereupon the 4K's sonic contribution becomes obvious. I like using the 4K with rhythm guitar and the 76 with lead guitar and bass.

The controls are the same as for standard compressors: Threshold, Attack, Release, Makeup Gain, and Ratio. However, Ratio options are limited to 2, 4, and 10, with 10 giving more of a peak limiter effect.

As to sidechaining, the 4K's detector input can appear as a destination for any track, bus, or send output, but the 4K won't respond to any signal being sent to it unless the 4K's S. Chain switch is enabled. Note that there's also a high-pass filter for the sidechain that's variable from 0 Hz to 2 kHz—ideal for keeping subsonics or kick drums from influencing the compression effect.

Another consideration with sidechaining is that it's helpful to "lock" the ProChannel view to the 4K being controlled. Otherwise, when you click on the channel sending the sidechain signal to adjust (for example) the output level, the ProChannel view will switch over to the newly selected channel and not show the one with the 4K you're controlling.

To lock the ProChannel view to a specific track, first select the track whose ProChannel you want to lock. With the ProCh tab showing in the Inspector, click on the track name at the bottom of the Inspector and choose Lock the Current Track or Bus from the pop-up menu (see Figure 23.5).

Figure 23.5
Normally, the Inspector shows the ProChannel for the currently selected track. However, you can lock the Inspector to the track of your choice by accessing the pop-up menu and selecting the track to which you want to lock the Inspector.

ProChannel Saturation

Saturation does not substitute for amp simulation or fuzz effects; SONAR includes Guitar Rig 4 LE for that. Saturation is more about vintage/tube warming and adding character to the sound. The most important aspect is choosing the right distortion type for the job—Type 1 for a more conventional distortion sound that distorts all frequencies and warms sounds that don't have a lot of highs, or Type II when you want the highs to remain more or less intact and tip saturation toward the lower frequencies.

Regarding Saturation controls (see Figure 23.6), Drive determines the degree of distortion, but this also interacts to some degree with the Input control, as more input signal subjects more of the signal to distortion. The Output control simply compensates for any gain differences created by saturation.

Figure 23.6
ProChannel's Saturation section is simple but effective. Note the "glowing tube" indicator toward the right; the brighter it glows, the greater the degree of saturation.

ProChannel Routing Section

In Track view, note the routing section toward the lower part of the ProChannel; you can rearrange the order of compression, saturation, and EQ by dragging their respective icons into the desired position. This can't be done in the Console view, but in the Console view you can decide whether the ProChannel should go before or after the FX Bin with the Pre (before FX Bin)/Post (after FX Bin) button just above the EQ plot.

Here are some tips on how different orders affect the sound.

EQ Before or After Compression

There is no universal answer for which of these should precede the other, because compression can serve different purposes. Consider this scenario regarding compression and EQ: You've recorded a resonant wah guitar part. On some notes, the level goes way too high when a note's frequency coincides with the filter frequency; otherwise, the signal is well behaved. But, you also want to boost the lower midrange a bit to give a beefier sound. In this case, try putting the compressor before the EQ to trap those filter resonances and then apply EQ to the more dynamically consistent sound.

Now suppose you don't have any problems with overly resonant filters, but you do need a massive lower-midrange boost. This much boost could greatly increase the amplitude at some frequencies, so putting compression after the EQ will help even these out a bit.

But there's a complication. Because significant boosts in a certain frequency range increase level in that range, the compressor will scale those levels back down a bit. So, this reduces the effect of what the EQ is trying to do—it tries to boost, but the compressor won't let it go beyond a certain point. However, signals below the threshold do remain boosted, and this just might give the sound you want.

Another reason to place EQ before compression is to make the compression more frequency-sensitive. Suppose you want to emphasize a guitar part's melody. By boosting EQ slightly for the range to be emphasized and then compressing, the boosted frequencies will go into compression sooner than the other frequency ranges.

EQ Before or After Saturation

Placing equalization before saturation can make the resulting distortion seem more "touch-sensitive" if you boost certain frequencies so they distort more readily than non-boosted ones. For example, you might boost a guitar around 900 Hz so that lead lines higher up on the neck saturate more readily than lower notes. With saturation before equalization, the equalization tailors the saturated sound's timbre.

Compressor Before or After Saturation

Placing the compressor before saturation gives a more consistent distortion timbre. Saturation before compressor provides a somewhat gentler sound than compressor before distortion.

ProChannel Studio Edition Compatibility

ProChannel is included only in Sonar X1 Producer Edition. Although Sonar X1 Studio can load projects created in the Producer version, any effects contributed by the ProChannel won't exist. However, this doesn't mean the settings are gone. If you save the Producer Edition project using Studio and then load it back into the Producer Edition, the ProChannel settings will appear, as they're saved regardless of which edition you use.

VX-64 Vocal Strip

Granted, this is the guitarist's guide to SONAR. But a lot of you probably sing too, so let's take a quick look at how to apply the VX-64. Using VX-64 is a highly convenient way to take care of most vocal processing needs with a single plug-in. To open the documentation, click on the VX-64 GUI (but not the header—you need to click within the interface) and then type F1. The documentation file VX-64_Vocal_Strip.chm is in the Vocal Strip folder in your Vstplugins folder.

The VX-64 vocal strip includes a DeEsser, Compander (Compressor/Expander), Tube Equalizer, Doubler, Delay, and Saturation (see Figure 23.7). I usually adjust dynamics first, then de-essing, EQ, and finally, anything else and then re-tweak if needed.

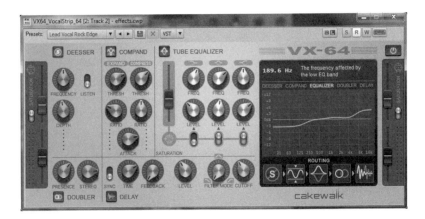

Figure 23.7

The graph toward the right provides details on whatever control you're editing; in this case, it's EQ.

Using the VX-64 Compander

Almost every vocal you hear has compression on it. My personal preference is a vocal that's compressed quite a bit, *but doesn't sound it.* Here's one way to approach adjusting compression.

1. Assuming your vocal is a nominal −3 dB below 0 (if you're slamming zero, you might reconsider—it's good practice to leave a little headroom), set the Threshold to around −15 dB. The top field of the big graph toward the right of the VX-64 shows precise parameter values.

2. Increase the Ratio from 1:1 upward until you find the "sweet spot" where the vocal sounds much more consistent but still natural and lacks any kind of pumping or artifacts (unless, of course, that's what you want). For natural-sounding vocals, the ratio is usually no more than 4:1; for rock/pop vocals, it can be as high as 10:1 and sometimes more.

3. The Attack control has a huge effect on vocals. With very short attacks (less than 0.5ms), the clamping on signal dynamics is instantaneous. Attacks of 1ms and above let through some of the dynamics, which gives the vocal more "life."

4. You may need to go back and re-tweak these controls, as they all interact.

The Compander also includes an Expander section. This is useful mostly for getting rid of mic preamp hiss, mic handling noise, and other low-level signals. To minimize this type of noise, try a Ratio of 1:10. Turn up the threshold from the lowest setting until there's no noise in the space between vocals. If you don't need expansion, disable the Expander section by setting the Threshold to −90 dB and the Ratio to 1:1.0.

De-Essing

The DeEsser, which is designed to reduce overly bright sibilants, does more than take care of only high sounds. On one song I was mixing, there was an overly loud "shh" sound that didn't reach particularly high frequencies. But the DeEsser (set to its lowest frequency) was able to reduce it.

The easiest way to optimize the DeEsser is to:

1. Turn on the Listen switch (up position), so you can hear what's being *removed* by the DeEsser.

2. Turn Depth up full, then sweep the Frequency until you hear the sound you want to minimize.

3. Turn off Listen. You may be surprised by how even a little bit of de-essing can sound like too much when the full vocal is happening, so pull back on the Depth control if needed.

Equalization

This is crucial for vocals, but the VX-64 includes a twist: You can saturate any of the three bands to add a sort of "exciter" effect.

Vocals often need a bit of upper-midrange boost, especially with dynamic mics. Set the middle band to between 2 and 4 kHz and start off with a couple dB of boost. Think of the high shelf as adding air, and use the low shelf to either cut bass if the vocals sound muffled or add bass if the vocals lack depth or warmth (or you want the stereotypical "FM radio DJ" sound).

Once the EQ is set, consider adding an extra 5% of sparkle with a tiny amount of saturation. I leave the input and output Saturators all the way down, because I usually don't do ultra-distorted vocals. But the EQ saturation is something else. There's a switch for each band that enables saturation for that band, and a "global"

Saturation slider for the three bands. What works for me is applying saturation only to the highest band and turning up the Saturation fader until the little tube icon barely glows on peaks. The extra sheen can be a subtle but audible enhancement.

Doubling and Delay

Now that the vocal sounds solid, let's put on the audio equivalent of makeup.

If you like to double your vocals, you'll love the Doubler. The Doubler is a stereo effect, so if the vocal track was recorded in mono, click on the track's Interleave button (visible only in Console view) and select Stereo if you plan to use the Doubler. The Presence control mixes in the doubled line, while Stereo changes the doubling's stereo width. You can reinforce your voice without necessarily having it sound "doubled" by turning Stereo fully counterclockwise and then bringing up Presence just enough to add fullness. On the other hand, if you want to sound like a trio of voices, turn Stereo fully clockwise and add a lot of presence.

The Delay is fairly standard—Delay, Feedback, and Level controls, with Delay synchable to tempo. A very cool feature is that you can filter the echo with a morphable filter (from low-pass, to band-pass, to high-pass, with variable cutoff frequency). High-pass is excellent for adding an ethereal quality, while a midrange band-pass filter sounds more like an old tape echo. I haven't found much use for echoing only the bass, but someone will probably figure out some amazing application for it and end up getting a hit record.

Effects Order

Like the ProChannel, you can change the order of effects just by dragging around their little icons in the lower right. Try the DeEsser in various locations to determine which does the best job. (Usually it's the first slot, but experiment.) Also, try EQ both before and after compression; generally, I get the best results by placing the Doubler and Delay last.

Finally, remember to re-tweak if needed, and when you hear something you like, save it as a preset. You just may need the same effect again—in fact, you probably will!

PX-64 Percussion Strip

The PX-64 (see Figure 23.8) is called a "percussion strip," but bass can be pretty percussive—and the PX-64 makes a very interesting bass processor. It can also create useful effects with either clean or pre-distortion single-note guitar lines, but we'll restrict ourselves to bass. To open the documentation, click on the PX-64 GUI (but not the header; you need to click within the interface) and then type F1. The documentation file PX-64_Percussion_Strip.chm is in the Percussion Strip folder in your Vstplugins folder.

Although you can create similar functionality on an *à la carte* basis by adding plug-ins and creating a track preset that includes them, the PX-64 adds a few twists of its own and offers the convenience of bundling multiple functions into a single plug-in.

Let's suppose you have a bass part that you want to make larger than life. Here's how you'd go about the tweaking process with the PX-64.

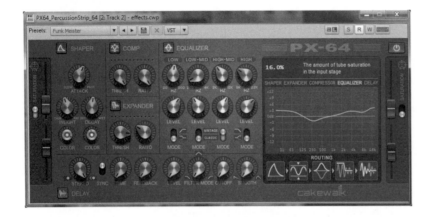

Figure 23.8

Although intended for drums and percussion, the PX-64 can be useful with a variety of percussive sounds—including bass.

Adding Saturation

There are saturation options (the brown fader controls and associated bypass switches to the extreme left and right of the GUI) for the input and output. If you want to use saturation, it's best to add it early on in the editing process, as EQ and dynamics will probably need to be changed if you alter the signal's distortion level.

To add some growl, turn on input Saturation, and turn up the Saturation fader. The Saturation and Input level controls interact, so you can set the amount of "crunch" with the Input level control. If you really want to pile on the distortion, dial in some output Saturation, too (see Figure 23.9).

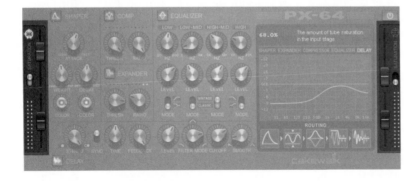

Figure 23.9

The highlighted areas are the input and output saturation sections. The graphic of a triode tube above the input Saturation switch it lit, which indicates that the saturation algorithm is processing the signal.

Equalizer Settings

I've always had the best luck with processing when nailing the tone first—after that, everything falls into place much more easily.

Of course, EQ is great for bass—but note that you can change its position in the signal chain. If we use EQ to really boost the bass and then place it before the compressor, there's more bass range compression. This can give a rounder, fuller sound. But post-compressor, there's less compression and more dynamics, and the added bass acts more like a tone control.

One common tweak for bass is to add a slight midrange or upper-midrange boost to bring out the pick's attack sound. This also gives the perception of the bass "cutting" better on systems that have questionable low-frequency response. Here, the Low-Mid band comes into play; try boosting by a couple dB in the 800 Hz to 2 kHz range and listen to whether that gives the bass a more percussive feel.

One limitation with the PX-64 is you don't have a band-pass option for anything below 200 Hz. So, you can't bring out individual ranges of notes in the lowest two octaves; your only option is a shelving response. If you want a bit more body, try adding a dB or two with the Frequency parameter set around 100 to 150 Hz.

To accentuate the high and low ends even further, you can cut response a bit around 200 to 300 kHz. This keeps the lowest notes and pick noises intact, while taking out a bit of the midrange buildup that may interfere a bit with other instruments (see Figure 23.10).

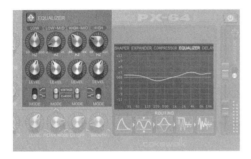

Figure 23.10

The EQ set as described in the text. Note how the graph toward the right shows the equalizer's frequency response.

The Vintage/Classic switch for the two midrange controls adds a different sort of character. I find Vintage a little more aggressive and Classic a bit more neutral—but it's a subtle difference.

The Shaper

Now let's check out the Shaper, which can make radical bass attack changes. This is a prime example of "just because you have it doesn't mean you have to use it," as the Shaper can produce effects anywhere along the scale of gimmicky to magical. I find it most useful for making muddy bass parts sound better, but it can also increase definition for well-recorded parts and add unusual special effects. Note that placing the Shaper before or after compression creates very different sounds.

As to how the Shaper works, like other dynamics processors, it analyzes the input signal and applies gain changes to alter the signal's characteristics. However, it applies these gain changes to the initial transient (and in some cases, the signal immediately following the transient) rather than the signal as a whole.

Here's how the controls affect bass. Turn the Attack control counterclockwise for a softer attack or clockwise for a sharper, harder one. Regarding how the "hardening" works, consider a signal with a slight attack. The Transient Shaper adds significant amounts of gain during the attack time, thus giving the illusion of shortening the attack time—but what's really happening is that the lower levels of the attack are made much louder. Because of that, be aware that increasing the Attack percentage can also increase the output, thus causing clipping. Monitor the level setting carefully to make sure that any additional percussiveness comes from the Transient Shaper, not from overloading the output.

However, also note that Attack settings that are even slightly over 100% can make a big difference—with some guitar tracks I cut using Roger Linn's AdrenaLinn and the PX-64, a setting of 104% added an obvious percussive effect.

Turning the Weight and Decay controls clockwise gives the bass more girth, while turning them counterclockwise thins the sound. As an analogy, increasing Weight above 100% is the equivalent of increasing the hold time on a synthesizer envelope—the initial attack and subsequent decay stay louder, longer. Settings below 100% "thin" out the sound. You can think of this as similar to compression that occurs only immediately after a transient.

The Decay control increases gain during the end of a sound's decay. Compared to compression, turning up Decay would be like having a compressor that affects only signals below about –12 dB. Like the Attack and Weight controls, Decay extends from 25% to 400%, with settings below 100% acting more like an expander and settings over 100% bringing up the signal as it decays.

The Weight and Decay parameters both have associated Color controls, which provide tonal contours to the initial attack and the decay. This is different compared to EQ, which changes tonality over the sound as a whole.

Weight Color adds multiband compression-type thinking, because it splits the signal into three bands (low, mid, and high) using linear-phase filtering. Turning the Weight Timbre control determines which band will get the most weight (for example, with the Low setting, the low band gets more weight than the mid and high bands), but note that there is a continuous morphing from low to mid to high. So, "in between" settings allow Weight to apply to more than one band at a time. The Decay Color control acts similarly but applies the multiband concept to the frequency ranges subject to the Decay control.

If that's too techy, here's the executive summary: The Weight Color control changes the transient's tone, from bassier and rounder (counterclockwise) to thinner and brighter (clockwise), while the Decay Color control does the same for the bass's transient decay. With bass, the two Color controls seem to be most effective when they move more or less together and track each other (see Figure 23.11).

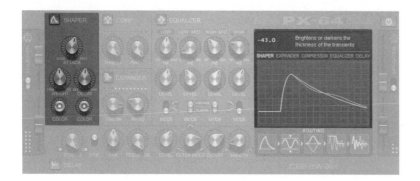

Figure 23.11
The Attack has been made a bit faster, but also, the Color controls are very much involved in this sound: The Attack Color control is thickening the sound of the transient (indicated by the red line being above the transient), while the Decay Color is thinning out the transient's decay.

The key is to start by adjusting the Attack, as this determines whether the bass notes are going to sound sharp (fast) or mushy (slow). Although it may seem counterintuitive to want mushy bass, this can actually work well if you want the bass to sit farther back in the mix. For example, you can "mush" it when vocals and other parts are happening and then sharpen the sound when the guitar solo kicks in. And while ultra-fast attacks can sound annoying if overdone, they can help the bass punch through a mix better, even at low levels.

Here are some typical PX-64 settings I like to use with bass.

▷ **Attack:** 119.7% gives a little extra definition.

▷ **Weight:** 290% is a good amount of weight to add to the mids.

▷ **Weight Timbre:** Set this around 7. Adding weight in the mids gives the sound more meat.

▷ **Decay:** 194.5% extends the decay tail.

▷ **Decay Timbre:** Setting this to full low (–100) adds a deep, round low end.

We've spent a lot of time on transient shaping, but it can be a wonderful effect if it's not overused. At least in my experience, transient shaping works best with sounds that need to punch and stand out more but that don't benefit from traditional dynamics processing or EQ. For example, with bass, you can always boost the treble to bring out the existing transient more, but the Transient Shaper actually changes the shape of the transient itself. This can let you make an organic bass timbre sound more electronic.

Automating parameters can also be very important, because "all attack all the time" can get rather tedious. Automating the various controls, particularly Attack and Decay, allows an entirely different type of dynamics compared to compression—one that, for better or for worse, is well suited to today's heavy-handed mastering techniques that pretty much obliterate dynamics based on level changes. By having dynamic changes based on timbre, it's possible to convey some sense of dynamics even with really squashed recordings.

Dynamics

The PX-64 has both a Compressor and an Expander. The Compressor can soften attacks and increase sustain, and the complement of controls is mercifully simple: There are controls for Threshold, Ratio, and Bypass...period. Due to the fast release time, decays may click or distort with certain Threshold and Ratio combinations; to minimize potential distortion, set a high threshold (for example, –6 dB) and use the Ratio control to set the attack and sustain.

Don't overlook that you can turn the Compressor into a limiter by setting the Ratio control to Inf to 1. In this case, I strongly suggest keeping the threshold high, so the limiter catches only the highest peaks. Percussiveness lost at this stage will almost certainly not be regained.

To tighten up a bass note's decay and make it more percussive, enable the Expander. There's the same complement of controls as for the Compressor, but instead of compressing above a threshold, this expands below a threshold. The Ratio control might as well have been called a "naturalness" control, because higher ratios give a more gated effect. (In fact, one way to get gated effects and nuke the last part of a bass note's decay is simply to set a high ratio.) Like the Compressor, the Expander has a fast release time, so follow the same guidelines—start with a high Threshold and then set the decay with the Ratio control.

Delay Options

Granted, not a lot of bassists use delay—Pink Floyd being a notable exception—but part of that may be because bass is a rhythmic instrument, and with hardware effects, it's difficult to sync bass to the beat. However, the PX-64 delay can sync to tempo, thus ensuring that delays are always "in the pocket." Furthermore, there's a novel variation compared to typical delays: A filter, with a variable cutoff frequency and response that can morph smoothly from low-pass to band-pass to high-pass, alters the delay's timbre. You can even approximate some 20th-century tape delay sounds by emphasizing the midrange with the band-pass response.

Effects Routing

The lower right shows the routing for the five modules; just drag and drop to change their order. My standard order is Shaper, Compressor, EQ, Expander, and Delay. However, here are some other useful combinations.

> ▷ **Delay/Shaper.** If you're a badass psychedelic bassist who uses delay with a lot of feedback, this lets the Shaper alter the transients of individual echoes. Although having Shaper before Delay gives a similar effect because you're delaying the shaped sound, if the delayed signal itself incorporates filtering, that can negate some of the Shaper's effect. If the Shaper is after the delay, it processes the transients regardless of how they've been filtered.

▷ **EQ/Compressor.** If you're using EQ to cut response in order to solve a problem (for example, muddiness), putting a compressor after it will bring up the level of the section you cut, thus reducing the effectiveness of the cut. On the other hand, if you've used EQ to boost a range of frequencies, compressing after EQ may be needed to prevent overloads on resonant peaks. Experiment—that's the advantage of having an interface where you can move sections around.

Vintage Channel VC-64

The VC-64 is a multifunction audio processor that is reasonably kind to your CPU. Its roster of effects includes a noise gate, de-esser, two compressors, and two equalizers. Each of the four equalizer stages has five possible filter responses (parametric, low-shelving, high-shelving, low-pass, and high-pass)—see Figure 23.12.

Figure 23.12
The VC-64 is a multifunction processor that works well with various instruments, including guitar and bass.

Although designed as a general-purpose processor, given how often guitarists use compression, the VC-64 is different from the norm in that it has multiple signal-routing presets. For example, compressors can be "patched" in series or parallel, and sidechaining (see Chapter 28, "Novel Rhythmic Effects with Sidechaining") is also possible within the channel strip to allow for frequency-selective compression. If you think this all adds up to something considerably more versatile than the average effect, you're right.

We'll cover the highlights; for more details, call up the manual by clicking on the Manual label just above the VC-64's Gain control in the lower left. However, as of this writing, the part called Main section—which describes how the inter-module routing works, as well as the main controls—is missing from the contents page. To find it, click on the manual's Index tab and then double-click on Routings. Scroll upward to see the rest of the manual's documentation on the Main section.

Let's give a brief rundown of each section and then get into the applications made possible by the different routings.

Noise Gate

This is one of the simplest modules, consisting solely of a power button, Threshold control, Decay Time control, and meter (see Figure 23.13). As a result of the simplicity, you can't set a particular amount of gate attenuation (the only choice is off or on), nor can you set an attack time for "attack delay" effects.

Figure 23.13
The Noise Gate is very simple, but it's possible to tweak it to obtain some non-traditional effects.

However, in addition to gating noise, the processor does offer another useful effect: "tightening up" single-note lines. Set a relatively high Threshold and short Decay, and as you play, leave a space between notes; the note decay will sound short and damped. It's almost like the effect you get from muting strings, but with the standard string tone.

DeEsser

The DeEsser is basically a frequency-selective compressor (see Figure 23.14). The Frequency control sets the frequency above which compression occurs, while the Threshold control sets the level needed to trigger compression.

Figure 23.14
Like the Noise Gate, this is a simple processor that has uses other than its intended one.

Aside from de-essing vocals, I've found this useful to bring down the "buzziness" of distorted guitar signals with lots of highs.

The VC-64 Dual Compressors

How compressors work is explained in Chapter 21 in the section on the Sonitus:fx Compressor, so I'll forego the standard features and instead jump ahead into what makes the VC-64 different.

First of all, there are two compressors, which opens up a bunch of applications that we'll cover shortly. Each can be bypassed individually.

Second, there are some non-standard controls. One button gives optical or VCA compression characteristics (these produce different compression curves—try them both and see what you prefer), and a clean (smooth)/ warm switch for different characters. There's also an auto attack/release button that when enabled, sets attack and release times automatically; this feature isn't unusual, but it's given an unusual name (PDE) so you may not recognize it. Also note that the compressors can be thrown out of phase if desired.

The VC-64 Dual Equalizers

The dual equalizers take advantage of various routings that put them in series, in parallel, in the path of EQs to perform frequency-selective compression, and so on. The equalizers work as expected but include a few uncommon features.

▷ **Selector Switch and Power Switch.** There are selection buttons for Equalizer 1 and Equalizer 2, which enable a common set of controls for one equalizer or the other. The power button is available for both EQs, so you can turn one off and one on, both on, or both off.

▷ **Constant-Q button.** In a nutshell, a filter with a constant-Q response has sharp notches and broad peaks, whereas one without constant-Q has equally broad (or narrow) notches and peaks. Turn on constant-Q if you need to make deep, narrow notches to get rid of unwanted frequency anomalies yet allow for relatively broad boosts, or turn it off for a more natural sound.

▷ **Range buttons.** These have no effect on the sound but alter the range of the graph by setting the vertical axis to ±5, ±10, or ±20 dB. As you generally want to use the minimum amount of EQ possible, I recommend setting this value to 5, as it makes subtle equalization settings easier to see. Wide ranges (as found on most EQs) can induce people to boost or cut more than they really should so they can "see the curve."

VC-64 Routings

This is where it gets really interesting, as the VC-64 allows various series, parallel, and sidechaining options. Clicking on the routing window steps through the various options, but you can also right-click on it and select one of the ten options from a pop-up menu (see Figure 23.15).

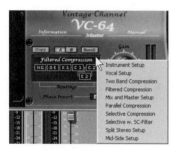

Figure 23.15
Click on the routing window to cycle through the various options, or right-click to choose the desired routing from a menu.

Parallel Routing

Let's look at the Parallel Compression routing first, which patches all effects in series except that the output splits through two compressors in parallel. As discussed with the ProChannel, parallel compression is handy for when you want to do a fair amount of signal squashing, but you still need a sense of dynamics. I'll assume you're doing some guitar compression where you still want to retain percussive attacks.

Use one of the paralleled compressors for the "squashing." Typical settings for guitar would be Threshold −20 dB, Attack 0.1ms, Release 100ms, and Ratio 10:1. Then, set up the second compressor for very light compression. Try Threshold −6 dB, Attack 10ms, Release 150ms, Ratio 1.5:1. Use each compressor's Gain Out control to adjust the blend between the super-squashed and lightly squashed sounds (see Figure 23.16).

Figure 23.16
Two sets of compressor settings are shown side by side. The one on the left provides heavy squashing, while the one on the right adds in a lightly compressed signal.

A variation on this theme is to use the Two Band Compression routing. This is similar to the Parallel Compression routing, except that each compressor is preceded by an equalizer. Thus, you can tailor the frequency response of what gets compressed. For example, with guitar, you might want to notch the midrange on one of the channels and apply significant compression to bring up the pick noise transients, as well as the boom from an acoustic guitar's body. Or, you could compress the upper midrange to bring up the melody—you get the idea.

Of course, you can also use this routing as a primitive multiband compressor. However, as SONAR already includes the Sonitus:fx Multiband compressor, which can do "real" multiband compression with up to five bands, as well as the linear-phase LP64 Multiband, I find the VC-64 most useful for creating effects.

One of my favorite applications for this routing is to create a cool wah-wah effect by throwing one of the equalizers out of phase. Chapter 30, "How to Emulate Vintage Effects," describes how to create a similar effect with the ProChannel, but this requires duplicating tracks; using the VC-64 simplifies the process somewhat. Here's the procedure.

1. Bypass all stages on one of the EQs so that its response is flat. (The Bypass button is the straight line in among the buttons showing the various possible curves.)

2. Also on this EQ, turn on the phase switch.

3. Use the Two-Band Compression routing, but make sure the compressors are off.

4. On the second EQ, select a band-pass response.

5. Set Gain to about +8 dB and Q to about 8.

6. Sweep the second equalizer's Frequency control.

Series Routing

The Mix and Master routing option patches the equalizers and compressors in series. With the equalizers, this means you essentially have eight stages of EQ. One application would be having eight band-pass/notch filters to deal with weird resonances, while another would be employing multiple high-pass filters to create a steep rolloff for cutting out low frequencies. Again, though, the ProChannel and Sonitus equalizers are excellent for dealing with this type of straightforward EQ, so the VC-64 once more comes into play for more effects-oriented settings.

My favorite application for this routing is to put two compressors in series, each one set for an extremely light amount of compression (see Figure 23.17).

Figure 23.17
Two compressors set in series, with very light amounts of compression, can provide a useful lift to a signal without making it sound compressed.

Figure 23.17 shows typical settings. If you used these settings with only one compressor, you wouldn't hear much of a difference. But put two in series, and the effect seems to multiply. For example, I used these settings for compression on a fairly dry jazz guitar sound. Like classical music, you really don't want to do a lot of dynamics processing with jazz, but the subtle compression helped make the guitar sound more live and present. In this case, I also used the Optical and PDE settings.

Of course, as with other compressors, you can trim the compression by varying the Gain In parameter. (Turning it up causes more of the incoming signal to exceed the threshold, which is equivalent to turning down the threshold.)

Split Stereo Setup

Ever wish you could equalize and compress the two sides of a stereo signal separately in SONAR? Well, you can, if you separate them into two mono tracks and then process them individually. But the VC-64's Split Stereo routing lets you do this with an existing stereo track.

With this routing, the Noise Gate and DeEsser affect both sides of the track equally. However, past these two modules, the signal splits to an EQ/compressor pair: The E1 equalizer and C1 compressor affect the left channel, while E2 and C2 process the right channel. This can be extremely handy when restoring old stereo tracks, including stereo program material, particularly because you can automate the control settings. For example, if an instrument is too prominent in the left channel and unbalances the stereo mix, you can bring in compression (or EQ, or both, depending on what does the job best) to tame that instrument only while it's playing.

Filtered Compression

This is another name for sidechain compression, which causes frequency-selective compression. In this routing, equalizer E2 taps the signal after compressor C1, and its output serves as the control for compressor C2. In other words, instead of compressor C2 listening to its output to determine when to initiate compression, it listens to the filter. Thus, if the filter passes only high frequencies, then only high frequencies will be compressed.

However, remember that unlike compressor sidechains, which typically have a high-pass filter to do de-essing, there are many more filter options in the VC-64. For example, suppose you're applying sidechain compression to drums. If you set up a high-shelf boost, then the high end will be compressed. But if you use another band of the VC-64's equalizer to add a low-shelf cut, then the low frequencies will sound expanded compared to the rest of the drums.

Sidechaining with the VC-64 EQ is more complex than with compression, as the results depend on which EQ you have set to Key and the routing. The following isn't mentioned anywhere that I could find in the documentation—and so that you don't get frustrated looking for this information, here's the way sidechaining works for the various VC-64 effect routing options. (You select these by clicking on the block diagram in the VC-64's lower-left corner.) This is pretty advanced material, so if your eyes start glazing over, skip ahead so that you don't fall asleep.

▷ **Instrument Setup.** Sidechain replaces the input signal if EQ1 and/or EQ2 is set to Key.

▷ **Vocal Setup.** Sidechain replaces the input signal if EQ1 or both EQs are set to Key, or mixes with the input signal if EQ2 is set to Key.

▷ **Two Band Compression.** Sidechain replaces the input if both EQs are set to Key or mixes with the input if one EQ is set to Key.

▷ **Filtered Compression.** With EQ2 set to Key, the sidechain signal goes to EQ2 on the way to controlling the compressor. With EQ1 set to Key, the sidechain signal replaces the input signal.

▷ **Mix and Master Setup.** Setting EQ1 and/or EQ2 to Key replaces the input signal with the sidechain signal.

▷ **Parallel Compression.** Same as Mix and Master Setup.

▷ **Selective Compression.** With EQ1 (or EQ1 and EQ2) set to Key, the sidechain signal replaces the input signal. With only EQ2 set to Key, the sidechain signal gets mixed in after going through EQ2.

▷ **Selective with Sidechain Filter.** Setting EQ1 to Key does nothing. Setting only EQ2 to Key can produce some really interesting compression-meets-gating effects, depending on how you adjust the C2 compressor settings. As far as I'm concerned, this setup is the most convincing argument for giving the VC-64 a sidechain. Setting EQ1 and EQ2 to Key mixes the sidechain and input signals, with the sidechain going through EQ2.

▷ **Split Stereo Setup.** With EQ1 set to Key and EQ2 off, the sidechain signal comes out of the left channel and the input signal comes out of the right. With the opposite EQ Key settings, the sidechain comes out of the right, and the input signal out of the left. With both EQ1 and EQ2 on, the sidechain signal replaces the input signal.

▷ **Mid-Side Setup.** This does various combinations of mixing and stereo effects—it will take less time for you to check it out and hear for yourself than for me to try to explain it!

The Secret Sound of the Psychedelic '60s

Okay, this has nothing to do with guitar—but it makes such a cool sound with drums that it's worth including. It's based on the fact that the Parallel Compressor routing allows for a lot of special effects if you set one compressor for an out-of-phase response (see Figure 23.18).

Figure 23.18
The Parallel Compressor's routing allows for some pretty wild effects if you throw one of the compressors out of phase.

The settings are pretty crucial here. With compressor C2, set the following parameter values:

▷ Attack = 10ms

▷ Release = 224ms

▷ Threshold = 0 dB

▷ Ratio = 1:1

▷ Gain Out = 0 dB

▷ Phase = Out of phase (lit)

▷ Gain In = Start at −10 dB

With compressor C1, use the following values:

> Attack = 10ms   > Gain Out = 0 dB

> Release = 224ms   > Phase = In phase (not lit)

> Threshold = −20 dB or so   > Gain In = 0 dB

> Ratio = 2:1

In other words, C1 is quite compressed, and C2 is not really compressed at all.

Now adjust C2's Gain In control. When fully counterclockwise, you'll hear that "super-squashed" drum sound used by the Beatles, Traffic, and others—the effect that sounds as if the cymbals are being sucked into a vacuum. Turn the Gain In control more clockwise, and as it approaches 0 dB Gain In, the sound will come closer to resembling expansion. Continuing to turn the control clockwise reduces the "special effect" element, and the track will sound more normal.

Saving and Comparing

The VC-64 comes with a bunch of very useful presets you can choose from the Presets field. But if you're going to come up with great patches, you're going to want to save them—so to save a preset, use the VST drop-down menu and choose Save Preset.

However, also note that a preset can have an A and B set of parameters. This is what you use for doing comparisons; use the Copy button to copy the values from the current set of parameters to the other. (For example, if you're using A, clicking Copy will copy the parameters to B.)

Saving a preset will save both sets of parameters, but closing the host (or the plug-in) will cause the preset to "remember" the currently selected parameters only. When recalled, these will be placed in A, regardless of which set you were using when you closed the host or VC-64.

Finally, the Recall button recalls the original preset parameters, regardless of how much editing you've done.

And that's about it for the VC-64. One last comment: For those into bus compression, this is an excellent alternative to the ProChannel, as it can provide both subtlety and character—the VC-64 is not just for track inserts.

SONAR's Miscellaneous FX

ALTHOUGH LESS COMMONLY USED than bread-and-butter effects, such as EQ, dynamics, delay, reverb, and so on, SONAR's miscellaneous effects can sometimes be just the spice you need to make a track really stand out.

Alias Factor

This adds intentional low-fidelity effects via three main functions: filtering, sample rate reduction, and bit rate reduction (see Figure 24.1). One possible result is creating "aliasing," additional frequency components not part of the original input signal. The help file, accessed by clicking on the GUI and pressing F1, gives a good explanation of what aliasing is, how it's produced, and why Alias Factor often has a more musical sound than some other lo-fi effects.

Figure 24.1
The Alias Factor effect creates lo-fi, sci-fi type sounds. It's not for the faint of heart.

▷ **Filtering.** With Cutoff Mode set to Free, the Filter Cutoff and Resonance controls edit low-pass filter settings. This emulates some older pieces of gear that were deficient in high-frequency response, and it works like standard low-pass filtering. However, there are also three other cutoff modes. When set to Under, aliasing effects sound smoother. The At setting produces a somewhat rougher aliasing quality, while the Over setting produces the rudest aliasing sounds—particularly if you turn up the filter Resonance.

▷ **Sampling Frequency.** With digital audio, the sampling frequency determines the upper frequency response limit. If the sampling frequency is lower than the frequencies being reproduced, they interfere with each other and create atonal, metallic-type effects. The lower the sampling frequency and the higher the frequencies in the audio material, the more pronounced the interference. The sampling frequency is editable from 100 Hz to 32 kHz.

▷ **Bit Depth.** CDs have a bit depth of 16 bits, which is adequate for high fidelity. Some older samplers and early digital synthesizers used 12- or even 8-bit depth; some toys use 4 bits. Lower bit depths add noise and a sort of roughness to the signal; the effect of bit reduction is most pronounced with lower-level signals and less so with high-level ones.

▷ **Mix.** Here's where you adjust the blend of messed-up sound with the dry, unprocessed sound.

FX2 Amp Sim

This emulates the sound of a guitar amp. Although the Guitar Rig 4 LE amp sim (included with SONAR X1 Producer Edition) is more sophisticated, each amp simulator plug-in has its own "personality"—just like real guitar amps—and therefore may be the right sound for a particular application (see Figure 24.2).

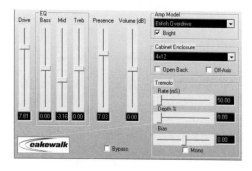

Figure 24.2
The Amp Sim provides a variety of guitar amp effects.

Note that distortion is useful for more than guitar and bass. For example, clone a drum track so that there are two drum tracks in parallel, process one with the Amp Sim, and mix the distorted sound in the background. This can produce a wonderfully trashy drum sound. Also, distortion can sound good on individual drums, such as kick, to add an edge.

▷ **Amp Model.** This is the most basic shaper of the Amp Sim's character, so you usually decide which model you want first.

▷ **Cabinet Enclosure.** The bigger the speakers and the more there are, the broader the response. Checking Open Back reduces bass and emphasizes treble because with an open-back cabinet, the waves coming from the front and back cancel somewhat, which diminishes bass response. Checking Off-Axis emulates miking the amp cabinet off to one side, which gives a thinner, less full sound.

▷ **Drive.** This control dials in the desired amount of "crunch" or overdrive. It interacts with other controls, such as tone and volume, but it is the main determinant of the amount of crunch.

▷ **EQ.** These three controls work like the standard tone stack of bass, middle, and treble controls you'd find on a typical guitar amp.

▷ **Presence.** Turn this up for a bit of a high-end boost.

▷ **Volume.** This acts like an amp's master volume control.

▷ **Bias.** The effect this has on the distortion characteristics is subtle but noticeable.

▷ **Tremolo.** Rate determines the speed of this pulsing-amplitude effect, while Depth determines the difference between the maximum and minimum levels of the pulsing. Note that the Rate decreases as you move the slider to the right, which is somewhat counterintuitive.

▷ **Mono.** This converts stereo signals to mono, as most guitar amp setups are mono as well.

FX2 Tape Sim

Analog tape isn't just a recording medium; it's a signal processor, and quite a few people like the kind of warmth and saturation effects it adds. Many engineers prefer to record drums to tape because of the way tape affects the drum sound; they'll then transfer the drums over to a digital recording medium, such as SONAR.

While the Tape Sim processor can add a bit of punch to signals, as with the Amp Sim, don't think of the Tape Sim solely as a device to do what the name says—it's useful for adding certain sonic qualities to a variety of sound sources. Due to the limited number of parameters, in a lot of cases it's most convenient to try out different presets and find out what works best for a particular sound. For example, the Medium Saturation 30 ips preset (see Figure 24.3) can sound very good on drums.

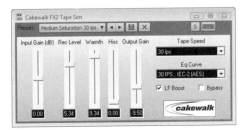

Figure 24.3
This preset adds a bit of punch to drums, but without creating any obvious distortion.

The Tape Speed and EQ Curve parameters determine the sound's character. Checking LF Boost gives the bass increase associated with a phenomenon known as *head bump*, where the physics of the tape head add a low-frequency boost. Hiss adds tape hiss (which, of course, everyone wanted to get rid of back when tape ruled the recording world).

Keep the Output Gain low as you tweak your sound. The key control is Rec Level, which sets the initial level and hardness. The Warmth control adds the crunch. For a really crunchy sound, set Rec Level and Warmth to maximum and pull back Input Gain until the degree of nastiness is just right. Finally, adjust the Output Gain to avoid clipping the track.

If you're really overloading the sound to generate mega distortion, you might not be able to lower the Output Gain sufficiently. In this case, you'll need to use the track's output control to trim the overall level.

One of my favorite uses of the Tape Sim is with a kick drum track, and the LF Boost switch is Cakewalk's gift to dance music kick drums. Dial up the right amount of distortion and then add LF Boost. The end result is a kick drum that can move mountains.

Click the Bypass switch from time to time to get a dose of reality—you might be shocked at how much you can raise the overall level without hearing objectionable levels of clipping. Finally, note that the parameters are not automatable, nor can the FX2 Tape Sim be used with the ACT protocol covered in Chapter 18.

Analyst

This is a plug-in, but it's a diagnostic tool (called a spectrum analyzer) rather than a signal processor—although it can also do some interesting envelope tricks, as described in Chapter 33, "SONAR's Multiband Envelope Follower." We needn't get too deep into spectrum analysis here, as the help file (click on the GUI and press F1) is quite complete. In a nutshell, the Analyst monitors the signal for the track where it's plugged in and shows the frequency response in real time (see Figure 24.4).

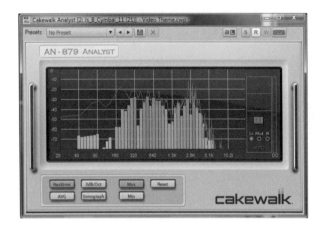

Figure 24.4
The Analyst is showing the frequency spectrum for a guitar track.

There are several ways to tailor the display—for example, you can trade off accuracy for response speed, track average as well as peak levels, hold peak levels, and more.

Pitch Shifter

If you want to shift pitch, the non-real-time, DSP-based stretching options described in Chapter 34, "Transposing in SONAR X1," do a better job in terms of fidelity. However, this processor can produce some really bizarre and interesting effects you can't obtain any other way (with the possible exception of some really old pitch-shifting effects, such the ADA Harmony Synthesizer or MXR Pitch Transposer). I'll cover each parameter (see Figure 24.5), but note that no parameters are automatable.

  ▷ **Pitch Shift.** This is the main control, and it lets you shift pitch up or down up to 12 semitones. The bigger the shift, the lower the sound quality (or if you like bizarre sounds, the more interesting the sound quality).

  ▷ **Dry Mix.** This sets the amount of unprocessed signal in the overall output.

  ▷ **Wet Mix.** This determines the amount of pitch-shifted signal in the overall output.

Figure 24.5
The Pitch Shifter can create some amazingly bizarre effects.

▷ **Feedback Mix and Delay Time.** These work together to produce an echo unit–type effect, but with a twist: Because the pitch-shifted output signal can be sent back to the input, each time it feeds back the pitch changes. For example, if the pitch shift is set for one semitone up, then each time it feeds back, the pitch will increase by another semitone. The Delay Time parameter sets the delay between each successive repeat.

▷ **Mod Depth.** This seems to produce a more natural sound when increased, but it's the kind of control where you just play around with it until you get the sound you want—or at least get *closer* to the sound you want.

Although most people think of using pitch shifts for transposition, small amounts of shift can provide interesting thickening and doubling effects to guitar but also to vocals. Here's how to set up pitch transposition.

1. Select the track you want to thicken.

2. Go to the Tracks Edit menu and select Clone Track(s). Check everything under Clone Tracks except Link to Original Clip (unless you also *don't* want to clone any effects that are used or any sends; in that case, uncheck these as well). The clone needs to be independently editable.

3. Click on the Clone function OK button, and you now have two tracks.

4. Insert the Pitch Shifter in the cloned track's FX Bin (for example, via drag and drop from the Browser).

5. After cloning the track and inserting the Pitch Shifter, set its parameters as follows:
    *   Pitch Shift = –0.24
    *   Dry Mix = 0
    *   Wet Mix = 100
    *   Feedback Mix = 0
    *   Delay Time = 2.61
    *   Mod Depth = 12.16

These are just suggested settings; adjust for the best effect with your guitar or vocals.

For the thickest, smoothest sound, pan the two tracks to center. If you pan one track full right and one full left, you'll hear two individual tracks instead of a rich composite track. Panning to opposite channels works very well for processing material such as a background vocal chorus, as the individual parts should be thick enough by themselves; shifting pitch widens the stereo spread.

Also try panning lead vocals slightly left and right (for example, left channel at 10 o'clock, right channel at 2 o'clock). This gives a somewhat fuller sound and a slightly wider stereo spread, which can also be useful under some circumstances.

Part V

MIDI and Guitar

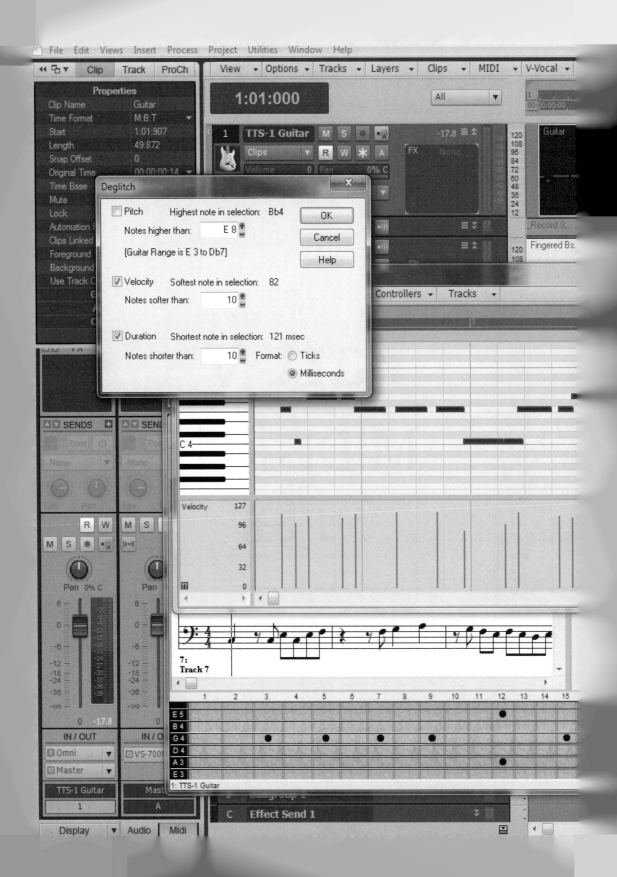

Guitar Tablature with SONAR

ALTHOUGH SONAR HAS A STAFF VIEW that's ideal for keyboard players, guitarists who can't read conventional notation needn't feel left out: SONAR can generate tablature (called "tab" for short) from MIDI data. As opposed to notation, tablature shows the fingerings that would be used on a guitar neck. This is useful not only for SONAR-savvy guitar players, but also for musicians and arrangers who write parts intended for a guitarist.

Generating Tablature

To generate tablature, select a MIDI track so it has the focus and then open the Staff view (press Alt+6). This shows the track's notes as standard notation. While working with tablature, you might find it helpful to see the "virtual guitar neck" by clicking on the staff editor's View button and selecting Show/Hide Fret Pane.

Next, choose Edit > Layout. Choose the clef (Bass, Treble, Alto, Tenor, and so on) and then check the Display Tablature box. Choose a preset string layout, such as six-string guitar or four-string bass, but note that you can also create a new layout by clicking on the Define button if, for example, you use alternate tunings or an unconventional number of strings (see Figure 25.1).

For simplicity's sake, choose the Guitar - Standard 6 String preset for now and then click on Close (see Figure 25.2).

The tablature appears underneath the standard notation view. However, we're not done yet, because the fingering may or may not actually be possible with guitar. Fortunately, the Regenerate Tab option can turn this into a part playable by humans.

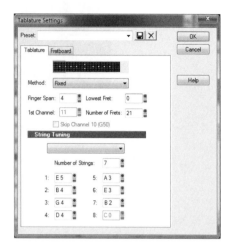

Figure 25.1

It's possible to show a tab for other than a standard four-string bass or six-string guitar, as you can define your own guitar with up to eight strings.

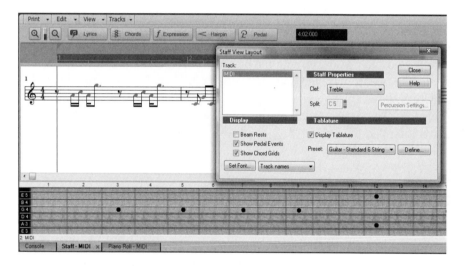

Figure 25.2

The Staff View Layout dialog box has been set up to generate and display tablature along with conventional notation.

Regenerating Tablature

To regenerate tab, select any notes (in other words, draw a marquee around them) that have obviously unplayable tab settings; if you're in a hurry, just select all the notes in the track by pressing Ctrl+A. Then choose Edit > Regenerate Tab.

A dialog box will appear where you have three tab regeneration choices (Fixed, Floating, or MIDI Channel) for choosing where on the neck the notes will be played. Fixed is usually best, as it lets you define the range of frets into which the notes should fall by offering two parameters—Finger Span (the total number of frets your fingers may need to stretch; the default is 4) and Lowest Fret. The latter is generally 0 if you're playing on the lower part of the neck, but if you want to create voicings that are higher on the neck, you could set this to 5, 9, 12 or whatever you want the lowest note to be. For example, if you choose a Finger Span of 4 and a Lowest Fret of 5, then all notes will fall in the range of the 5th through 8th frets; a small red box in the dialog box's neck graphic will show the selected range graphically.

Floating analyzes all events in a track and makes an attempt to optimize tablature with respect to the open position.

The MIDI Channel option analyzes the event's MIDI channel to determine the string on which the note should be displayed. This mode is particularly useful for MIDI guitar players who record in Mono mode, where each string transmits on a different MIDI channel. With this option, you need to select the series of six consecutive channels on which SONAR receives MIDI data, with the number you select representing the lowest-numbered channel. For example, if SONAR is receiving data on Channels 1–6, select 1. If it's receiving over Channels 11–16, then select 11.

After choosing the desired mode, click on OK, and all the notes should end up with playable, realistic fret assignments (see Figure 25.3).

Figure 25.3

The Regenerate Tab option converts "raw" tab into a more human-friendly format that can be played more easily.

If the fret assignments aren't playable, then check for doubled notes in the sequence—because guitars allow only one note per string, SONAR will interpret this as playing one note on one string and the same note on a different string.

ASCII Tab

If you choose Edit > Export ASCII Tab, SONAR will export the tab as an ASCII text file format (see Figure 25.4), suitable for sending in an email, posting in a forum message, or printing out.

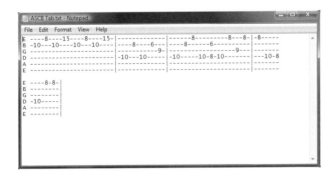

Figure 25.4

Tab saved as an ASCII text file can be sent as an email or posted as text on an Internet forum.

MIDI Guitar with SONAR

BACK IN THE '80S, MIDI GUITAR WAS SUPPOSED to be the next big thing: What guitar player wouldn't want to be able to play anything from pianos to trumpets to ambient pads from that familiar six-string fretboard?

Unfortunately, the question that *wasn't* asked was, "What guitar player wants to give up the expressiveness of a guitar and modify his technique in order to hear sounds with delays and glitching?" The answer was, "Not as many as the industry hoped, by a long shot." However, lots of guitarists did embrace the options MIDI gave them; and while MIDI guitar never broke through on a huge level, over the years Roland has introduced their GR series of products that made continuous, incremental improvements in tracking, sound quality, and flexibility. Quite a few studio musicians also took advantage of MIDI to extend their sonic palette.

A MIDI guitar needs a special divided pickup (also called a *hex pickup*) that provides a separate output for each string. This then feeds a special module to translate the hex data into notes that can drive a synthesizer, whether internal to the module or external. Roland has collaborated with other companies to produce "Roland-ready" guitars that work with Roland's electronics, and it's also possible for the somewhat adventurous to retrofit an existing guitar for MIDI.

Overall, I feel MIDI guitar isn't about replacing guitar, but supplementing it with new choices. Although getting heavily into MIDI guitar is beyond the scope of this book—among other topics, we'd have to spend a lot of time on synthesizer basics—there is an alternative for those who are curious about the possibilities of MIDI guitar and want to get started. The G2M from Sonuus, a small company out of the UK, is quite inexpensive but provides true guitar-to-MIDI conversion.

But, there's a major limitation compared to Roland's approach: As of this writing, Sonuus's technology is monophonic, not polyphonic, so you play only single-note lines and not chords. On the plus side, no special pickup or cable is needed; it works with a standard guitar output. Besides, many players would argue that where guitar excels as a MIDI controller is with single-note lines anyway. Trying to play piano from a guitar can be awkward; playing synth lead sounds makes a lot more sense.

Just remember that MIDI is constantly butting up against the laws of physics. Keyboards are controlled by switches, and a guitar string is anything but a switch—trying to convince it to be one is not easy. You have to play notes cleanly, and you'll have to modify your technique to a greater or lesser degree (although there are MIDI guitarists who say that working with MIDI guitar has made them more accurate guitar players in general). But no matter how carefully you play, MIDI will not be able to reproduce your performance perfectly, and you will need to do some editing to clean up your part. Fortunately, SONAR has some features that can streamline the editing process for MIDI guitar.

For now, we'll stick with monophonic playing and reference the G2M, but if you end up feeling comfortable with MIDI guitar on a basic level, you might want to move up to the next step and go for polyphonic, GR-series MIDI guitar.

Sonuus G2M Basics

The input patches to your guitar with a standard, 1/4-inch phone jack (see Figure 26.1), and the unit is battery-powered. The rear panel has a 5-pin MIDI out connector, along with a 1/4-inch thru phone jack that carries the guitar's audio signal.

Figure 26.1
The G2M is pretty minimalist: input jack, MIDI and audio output jacks, and several indicator LEDs.

The thru option is helpful, as one of the common uses for MIDI guitar is to layer standard guitar sounds with synthesized sounds. This offers two advantages: You can get a "bigger" sound, but also, the "real" guitar signal can help mask any glitching that may be in the MIDI synth sound. However, to optimize MIDI tracking you may need to reduce the guitar's level and pull back on the tone control, which limits the thru's usefulness.

The MIDI out can drive standard synthesizers and any interface with a 5-pin MIDI jack input, but note that some interfaces no longer have physical MIDI input jacks, as they assume you'll hook up USB-based MIDI devices. (For guitar players in this situation, Sonuus makes the i2M, a guitar-to-computer interface that replaces the MIDI connector with a USB port.)

SONAR Track Setup for MIDI Guitar

Let's go through a typical MIDI guitar setup. I'll use Cakewalk's TTS-1 synthesizer not because it's the latest and greatest virtual instrument, but because it's easy to use and has some useful features for MIDI guitar.

I'll assume you're using the Sonuus G2M, but other converters work similarly.

1. Plug your guitar into the guitar-to-MIDI converter and patch the converter's MIDI out to your interface's MIDI in.

2. Choose Edit > Preferences. Under MIDI Devices, make sure your interface's MIDI input is enabled.

3. Choose Insert > Soft Synth > Cakewalk TTS-1.

4. When the Insert Soft Synth Options dialog box appears, let's keep things simple for now—simply check Simple Instrument Track and Synth Property Page.

5. Expand the instrument track's height and select All Widgets so you can see the track's I/O, Mic, and so on. You'll see something similar to Figure 26.2.

Figure 26.2
SONAR's simple instrument track combines an instrument's MIDI input with its audio output. The instrument's user interface opens when you insert the instrument if Synth Property Page is checked in the Insert Soft Synth Options dialog box.

6. Thanks to the miracle of default settings, if you play your guitar, the TTS-1 will probably make some noises. They may be ugly, but we're on our way.

7. Let's look at the track I/O fields. Use the I (Input) field drop-down menu to select your interface's MIDI input.

8. The O (Output) field selects the synth's audio output, which will typically be the Master bus.

9. The C field selects the channel that will carry the MIDI data. The TTS-1 can play back up to 16 different instrument sounds, each assigned to its own channel. For example, if Channel 1 is set to Piano and Channel 2 to Bass, if you select 2 in the C field, you'll trigger the bass. If you select 1, you'll trigger the piano. An instrument that can play back different sounds on different MIDI channels is called a *multi-timbral* instrument.

10. You can ignore the B field for now.

11. The P field selects the sound for the current channel. For example, if the C parameter is set to 12 and you use the P field to choose Marimba, Channel 12 will play a Marimba sound. You can also change sounds by clicking on the sound's name in the TTS-1's virtual mixer and then selecting a sound from the Preset menu.

Optimizing the TTS-1 for MIDI Guitar

Assuming that you're successfully triggering the TTS-1, you're hearing an audio output, and you have selected a suitable instrument, there are edits you can do with the TTS-1 to improve tracking with MIDI guitar.

Suppose you've selected a Sax sound for Channel 1. Click on the Edit button at the top of the channel strip to open the sound editor. Click on the Mono button so that its label turns from Poly to Mono. This allows the instrument to play only one note at a time, making it a better match for the G2M.

Also, set the Bend Range to 2. Most guitar synths expect to see a plus/minus two-semitone bend range, which optimizes the response with string bending. See Figure 26.3, where all these parameters are circled for clarity.

Figure 26.3
Editing a sound for a mono response and a pitch range of 2 improves tracking with the G2M converter.

Other Optimizations

▷ Tune your guitar as accurately as possible. As we're dealing with pitch-to-MIDI, you want the pitch to be spot on. You can use the tuner in Guitar Rig 4 LE (bundled with SONAR Producer Edition), the one in the G2M, or of course, the tuner app in your smartphone!

▷ Try using the neck pickup instead of the bridge pickup for more consistent triggering. Pulling back on the tone control might help, too.

▷ Play with a relatively light, consistent touch. The more you play MIDI guitar, the more you'll develop a picking style that produces the most consistent results.

▷ Light compression patched between the guitar and G2M input can contribute to more consistent tracking.

▷ The G2M has a front-panel Chromatic switch. This turns off bend messages so that the notes you play are quantized precisely to the nearest chromatic pitch. With sounds like piano, this can produce better tracking.

▷ Be careful that you're not standing too close to transformers and other sources of interference that can get into your pickups, as this can confuse the tracking—even if you don't use the audio thru out, use it to audition the guitar sound and make sure all is well.

▷ Some synthesizer patches work better than others for MIDI guitar. It's almost impossible to get pads to screw up, but highly percussive patches are quite sensitive to little glitches.

▷ Resting the heel of your hand against the bridge to deaden the strings somewhat can lead to a dramatic improvement in tracking.

▷ If you're an advanced user, there's an advantage to not selecting a simple instrument track, but instead selecting MIDI Source Track and First Synth Audio Output (or All Synth Audio Outputs) from the Insert Soft Synth Options screen. MIDI tracks can accept MIDI plug-ins, and SONAR provides several (Arpeggiator, Chord Analyzer, Echo Delay, MIDI Event Filter, Quantize, Transpose, and Velocity). These can process the MIDI data coming from your guitar. For example, Transpose is fun for doing bass parts as you can transpose down an octave as you play in real time, and the Velocity plug-in (see Figure 26.4) lets you set a maximum and minimum velocity range. This is helpful because guitars can generate wide dynamics, and you might want to tame them somewhat.

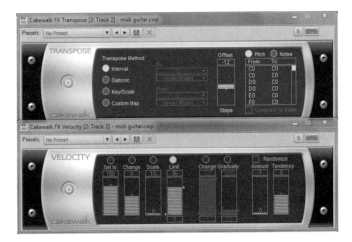

Figure 26.4
The Transpose plug-in is transposing down an octave, while the Velocity plug-in has limited the maximum velocity to 96.

Editing MIDI Guitar Parts

If there's one thing I've learned about MIDI guitar over the years, it's that you better get ready to do some MIDI editing. Frankly, today's devices track far better than they used to, but still, a little cleaning up never hurt a part.

To do editing, you'll need to learn how to use SONAR's Piano Roll view. Given the thrust of this book, getting into the intricacies of MIDI and MIDI editing would require a major detour, and there's no guarantee the average guitar player will find it all that useful. Fortunately, with SONAR's online help, it's not too difficult to figure out how to edit MIDI data: Your main edits will use the Smart tool to move and delete notes, change velocities (dynamics), lengthen or shorten notes, and sometimes quantize notes so they fall exactly on the beat.

Compensating for Delay

The conversion process to MIDI is not instantaneous; see Figure 26.5.

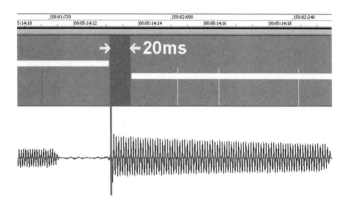

Figure 26.5

The delay between playing a note (the waveform) and when the note appears (the white block above it) is about 20ms.

Figure 26.5 shows the delay between playing the guitar into a track and the MIDI note it produces. The latency with the G2M is about 20ms, which is actually pretty good and relatively constant over the guitar's range. Although some guitar players compensate for any delay unconsciously by playing slightly ahead of the beat, if needed you can select all notes in the Piano Roll view and then shift them ahead a little bit to compensate.

Cleaning Up Glitches

To illustrate a real-world situation, I tried to play cleanly but not ridiculously so. See Figure 26.6 for the results; most of the part is relatively error-free.

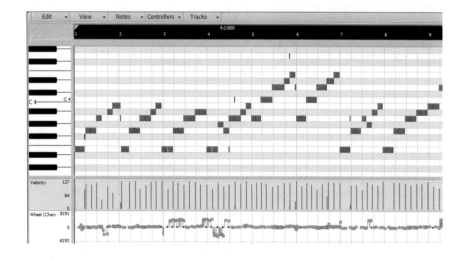

Figure 26.6

This screenshot shows the original solo as played, without any editing.

The thin, vertical lines in the main piano roll represent glitches. If you look at the Velocity strip below the notes, where the vertical lines represent velocity, you can see that the glitches are considerably lower in amplitude than the "real" notes. There are a few other issues, such as a missed note or two, or a note that was bent enough to register as a different note, but overall this is quite clean. The strip on the bottom shows pitch bend.

Fortunately, SONAR has a Deglitch editing option (see Figure 26.7) where you can specify that notes below a particular velocity, shorter than a specified duration, or out of a particular pitch range should be deleted.

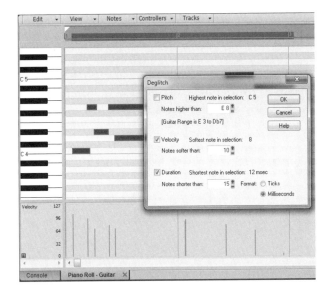

Figure 26.7
The Deglitch dialog box can help clean up MIDI guitar parts by removing notes with unusually short velocities or durations.

To make the editing process easier, the dialog box shows the softest and shortest notes in the selection of MIDI notes, as well as the one with the highest pitch. In this example, there's a note with a velocity of 8, which was surely not intended, and a note that's 12ms long—again, this hardly seems intentional. So, the Deglitch menu specifies that all notes softer than a velocity of 10 or shorter than 15ms will be deleted.

I didn't want to go overboard to the point of "perfection," but Figure 26.8 shows the result of spending a minute or two editing the part. You'll note it's cleaner because Deglitch removed the glitches; I also shifted the timing of a few notes manually for a better feel. Most importantly, I didn't have to edit it all that much.

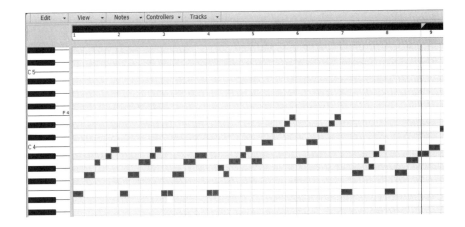

Figure 26.8
Here's what the musical passage in Figure 26.6 looked like after editing.

Final Thoughts about MIDI Guitar

I don't want to paint a rosier picture than is justified; every MIDI guitar I've played takes some effort to get good results. If you expect to just pick up a guitar and start sounding like a concert pianist, you're going to be disappointed. In fact, a product like the G2M can be a bit more demanding than a typical Roland GR-series device due to being monophonic. You need to play carefully and deliberately; there will likely be some mis-tracking, and if you try to do some fast shredding, the G2M probably won't be able to keep up.

On the other hand, there's a lot to be said about opening up the synth world, and sometimes the results can be wonderful. I generally prefer playing synthesizer sounds to trying to imitate acoustic instruments, because unless you're really good at both playing and editing, the acoustic instruments will always have a tendency to sound fake. On the other hand, a synth lead or pad can stand as its own sound and is a good candidate for triggering with MIDI guitar.

As long as you don't expect to play with the same level of abandon as a standard guitar, you'll be fine. Best of all, you'll be able to add textures to your music that would normally require having keyboard technique.

The "Virtual" MIDI Guitar

COMPARED TO KEYBOARDS, ONE OF THE GREAT ASPECTS of guitar is those wide-open voicings that use a mix of open and fretted strings. If you're a guitar player who dabbles at keyboards, odds are you can play the basic majors, minors, and so forth. But what about those wonderful jazz voicings that you're only comfortable with when playing guitar? And what if you're a keyboard player who knows a little guitar but has a hard time fingering some of the more challenging guitar chord shapes?

MIDI guitar is a possible, although pricey, solution. Fortunately, SONAR has a workaround for getting guitar voicings in a keyboard world. This means that as a guitarist, you can enter the kind of chord shapes and note patterns you're used to playing, but trigger all kinds of sounds other than guitar. This process also allows you to create "perfect" guitar parts that might be difficult or impossible to play otherwise.

To start off with something familiar, I'll show how to use this technique to create a "pseudo-MIDI guitar" track; you can move on into other sounds after you get a feel for how this works.

Start by inserting a virtual instrument with some suitable guitar sounds. Dimension Pro has lots of great guitar patches, so that's a good place to start; you can insert it using the Simple Instrument Track option. In the Instrument track, use the Input field's drop-down menu to select your MIDI controller.

Give the focus to the Instrument track by selecting it and then choose View > Staff (keyboard shortcut: Alt+6). Choose View > Show/Hide Fret Pane to display a guitar neck with 21 frets (see Figure 27.1).

Note that you can right-click on the fretboard to show a rosewood, ebony, or maple look—cute, eh? (No, you can't choose between a Les Paul or Strat scale length.) You also have the option to "mirror" the fretboard, so it appears as if you're looking at it from the position of facing a guitar player.

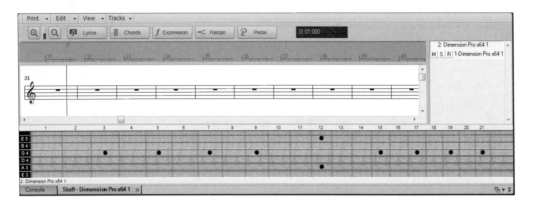

Figure 27.1

Staff view is showing the Fret view, which displays a 21-fret guitar neck. In a tribute to all the Telecaster fans reading this book, the maple neck option is selected.

Entering notes on the fretboard is a step-entry process, so start by choosing the desired note length from the Event Draw Duration pop-up (see Figure 27.2). Of course, you can change this value at any time while entering your part.

Figure 27.2

Specify note duration from the Event Draw Duration pop-up menu.

Click within the measure indicator timeline (above the staff) where you want to enter the chord. Then click on the desired fingerboard notes or on an open string (in other words, below the first fret). Like a real guitar, you're allowed one note per string. As you enter each note with the Pencil tool, it will show up as notation on the staff (see Figure 27.3).

As with any other kind of notation-screen entry, you can cut, copy, paste, and so on individual notes or groups of notes.

Notes within a region show up as blue; if you start playback, notes on the staff will light in red as they sound. Otherwise, notes are black. Also during playback, the fretboard notes are black instead of showing the pitches against a green background. Note that you can jump to the next note or chord by hitting the Tab key or go in reverse by using Shift+Tab.

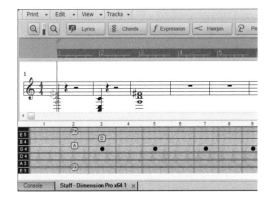

Figure 27.3

Here, a guitar's D major chord (with the 5th as the root) is being shown in the staff's Fret view. The D chord is followed by a C major chord and then another D chord.

Strumming Time

Now for the *pièce de résistance* to make this sound truly guitar-like: Open the Piano Roll view (the keyboard shortcut is Alt+3), so you can edit the chord notes to create a strum effect. To do this, first turn off Snap (keyboard shortcut F12 toggles between snap on and off), as you'll want to make subtle timing adjustments. Then, spread the note attacks so that the lowest note starts a bit ahead of the beat, the highest note starts a bit behind the beat, and the other note attacks follow an even gradient between the highest and lowest notes (see Figure 27.4).

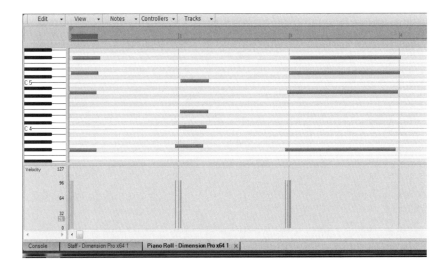

Figure 27.4

The chord notes have been offset slightly to give a "strumming" effect that makes this part sound much more like a guitar.

You can also try moving the whole chord, including offsets, so that the highest note hits right on the beat. This provides a different kind of phrasing; see what works best for a given song.

If you're in a hurry to get a strum effect, and you don't want to deal with editing individual notes, here's a shortcut. Select the notes you want to "strum" and then choose Process > Run CAL > Random Time.cal and click on Open. Specify around 100 ticks of variance. This isn't as good as adjusting notes individually, but at least it prevents simultaneous attacks (see Figure 27.5), which sound very unlike a guitar.

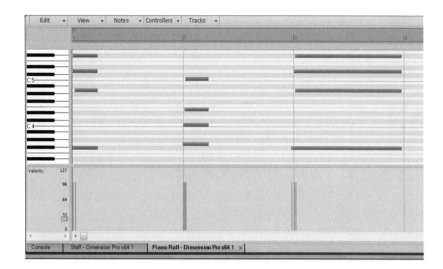

Figure 27.5

Here are the same notes as shown in the previous screenshot, but instead of modifying the start times manually, they've been run through the Random Time.cal process.

If the offset isn't too drastic, SONAR will retain note placements in the Staff view, rather than try to figure out "what's the notational symbol for 'a few MIDI clocks ahead or behind the beat'?" This makes for much better-looking notation.

Part VI

Advanced Techniques

Novel Rhythmic Effects with Sidechaining

*S*IDECHAINING **IS A TERM FROM THE DAYS OF ANALOG,** when effects would include a sidechain jack (or jacks) to access particular portions of the signal path. An effect with sidechaining includes a standard audio input but also has a *second* input that allows a signal other than the one at the audio input to control some aspect of the effect's sound.

The classic example of sidechaining involves compression. Normally, the amount of compression depends on a detector monitoring the input signal; the detector causes gain reduction when the input signal goes over a certain threshold. A sidechain jack provides a connection to the detector so that it can accept *any* signal, rather than always being tied to the input.

A common real-world use for this is *de-essing*, a technique used with vocals to remove excessive sibilants (*S* sounds). You do this by splitting a vocal into two paths; one goes directly to the compressor input, while the other goes through an EQ to the compressor's sidechain input. If you boost the EQ's treble, then higher frequencies will exceed the compressor's threshold more readily than lower-frequency ones, thus compressing the highs and reducing sibilants.

Of course, there are plenty of ways to use the sidechain input for special effects—such as using a drum track to chop a rhythm guitar part so that its level follows drum hits, or locking bass and guitar together by having bass notes trigger changes in guitar level. We'll get into these types of applications shortly, when we cover SONAR's sidechain implementation.

Some devices, such as noise gates, have "key" inputs, which are basically the same as sidechain inputs—remember, there's no language police in the audio industry! You can think of "key input" and "sidechain input" as essentially interchangeable, given that they both access the insides of a signal processor and allow triggering it from an external source. Like compressors, noise gates have a detector that monitors the input signal to decide whether to open the gate for high-level signals or close it to mute low-level signals, such as hiss. This noise gate's key input provides access to the gate's detector, allowing you to gate one signal with a different signal altogether.

How SONAR's Sidechain Function Works

SONAR includes four effects that offer sidechain inputs: Sonitus:fx Gate, Sonitus:fx Compressor, Vintage Channel VC-64, and (in the Producer Edition) the ProChannel's 4K bus compressor. As soon as you insert one of these effects into a track's FX Bin, the sidechain input becomes available as any track or bus's output destination. However, as a track (or bus) output can have only one destination, if you send it to a sidechain input, it will no longer be available for monitoring over a master audio bus. In some cases, this is beneficial: It's easy to create an audio track that's designed specifically to drive the sidechain input, but you don't have to hear it.

It's likely, though, that you'll want to hear the track providing the sidechain input, and this is where busses come into play. For an example of how to set up a "utilitarian" kind of sidechain, let's solve a potential problem involving bass.

Suppose you have a drum part and a bass part, and the bass part's peaks tend to "step on" the drums. So, you do the obvious and insert a compressor in the bass track's FX Bin to tame the peaks. But then you find that while you've solved one problem, you've introduced another: Now the bass part lacks dynamics and sounds flat compared to the original sound.

This is an excellent candidate for sidechaining, where you can use the drums to compress the bass. That way, if a drum hit exceeds the compressor's threshold, the bass is compressed to get out of the drum's way. But if the drums stay below the threshold, the bass part retains its original dynamics (see Figure 28.1).

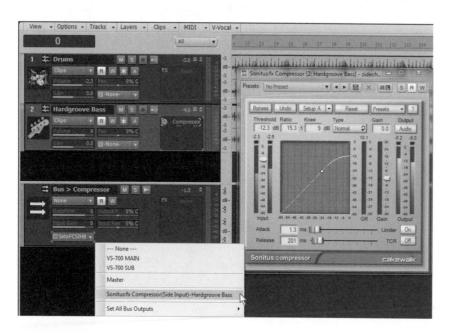

Figure 28.1

Track 1 is drums, while Track 2 is bass and has a Sonitus:fx Compressor inserted. The key element here is the bus, called Bus > Compressor, whose output goes to the compressor's sidechain input. The drum track has a send that feeds this bus, allowing the drum signal to control the sidechain input.

You can use this setup to evaluate sidechaining's effect on the sound. If you set the Bus > Compressor bus output to None instead of Sonitus:fx Compressor (Side Input) – [track name], then the bass will be compressed normally (in other words, the detector will listen to the bass only).

If you really want to hear the difference between this and using the sidechain signal for compression, bounce the two tracks to one track with sidechain active and a second track with sidechain inactive. Then, reverse the phase on one of the tracks so you can hear any differences more clearly. In this particular example, you should hear lots of peaky bass notes—this will indicate how much louder the bass peaks sound on the track where the compression is controlled by the drums.

Sidechaining Applications

Sidechaining is a valuable technique that can solve problems or add novel special effects, depending on how you use it. Given the title of the book, we'll concentrate on applications for guitar—but note that sidechaining is also used with narration, to give special effects with drums on dance mixes, and for lots more.

Frequency-Selective Compression

Sometimes with compression, it seems that a guitar part lacks sparkle if the stronger lower frequencies that trigger compression affect the lower-level high frequencies as well. In this case, you can use sidechaining to compress only the guitar's lower frequencies, while leaving the higher frequencies uncompressed. (You can do this with multiband compression as well, but sometimes you might prefer the sidechaining approach if you need more flexibility in controlling frequencies than the multiband compressor allows.)

Note, however, that when you're trying to modify a track by itself, you can't use a bus, because SONAR prevents you from setting up a bus that could feed back. So, here's another way to accomplish what we want (see Figure 28.2).

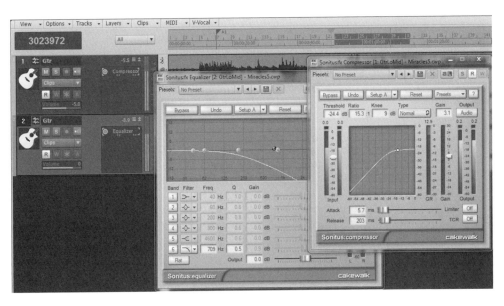

Figure 28.2
The equalizer restricts the highs going to the compressor's sidechain input, thus causing compression only on lower frequencies—sort of the opposite of de-essing.

1. Clone the track with the guitar part so you have two tracks playing the same part.

2. Insert a Sonitus:fx Compressor in the main guitar track.

3. Insert an equalizer in the second guitar track and then change its track output to Sonitus:fx Compressor (Side Input) – [track name].

4. Click on the compressor's Output button so it reads Sidech. (This button toggles between the regular compressor output and the sidechain input.)

5. Using the EQ's low-pass filter, tweak the EQ to tune out the high frequencies.

6. Click on the compressor's Output button to change it back to Audio and then adjust the compressor for the desired amount of low-frequency compression.

Being able to monitor the sidechain signal is very important when doing frequency-selective compression. With hardware units, there's usually a monitor button of some kind; the Sonitus:fx Gate, like the Sonitus:fx Compressor, also has an Output button that selects between Audio and Sidech. The VC-64 has a Listen button that lets you listen to the sidechain signal.

Ducking

This is another technique made possible by sidechaining. A typical application involves a singer/songwriter playing guitar, where you want the guitar to "duck" down a bit when the singer sings. This is easy to do: Insert the Sonitus:fx Gate in the guitar track and use the vocal to provide the sidechain signal (either by sending it to a bus and sending the bus output to the guitar gate's sidechain input, or by cloning the vocal track and sending its output directly to the gate's sidechain input). You'll probably want to set Depth conservatively so that the guitar isn't reduced too much and choose a relatively long gate attack and release time so that the gating action isn't too "choppy" as it follows the vocals.

Chopping and Gating

On the other hand, there are some applications where chopping can add a great special effect.

The Sonitus:fx Gate's sidechain capabilities allow interesting chopping and rhythmic effects. For example, suppose you'd like to make a sustained power chord more rhythmic. Just insert the Sonitus:fx Gate into the guitar track's FX Bin, send the drum track to a bus, and then assign the bus output to Sonitus:fx Gate (Side Input) - [track name] (see Figure 28.3).

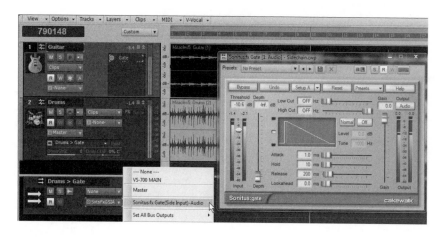

Figure 28.3

A drum part is triggering the gate via the Drums > Gate bus; the gate chops the guitar track into a rhythm that corresponds to what the drums are playing.

One particularly useful gate feature is that you can change the attack and release times to mold the chopped sound into being more percussive or more flowing. Also, once you've "percussified" a sound, try putting a delay plug-in after the gate to give it even more motion—dotted values (such as dotted half-notes) work well.

Sidechaining with the VC-64

The VC-64 channel strip also has a sidechain input, and the two compressors as well as the EQs can be set at the VC-64 to listen to the sidechain signal. The instrument routings that use compression work like the examples I gave for the Sonitus:fx Compressor and are useful for the same types of effects. However, with the VC-64 you can "double" the effect. For example, you could use a VC-64 patch with two series compressors (like its Instrument Setup preset) and make any effect even more radical by keying both of them to the sidechain. For more information, refer to Chapter 23, which includes information on the VC-64.

Tuning Out Mic/Direct Differences

IN CHAPTER 5, I MENTIONED HOW RECORDING A DIRECT sound and a miked sound could result in a time difference between the two. The reason this matters is because combining the two signals could result in cancellations that weaken the overall sound (or it might produce a sound you like—but you should at least know how to compensate for time differences in case there's a problem). Bass players are also likely to record direct and miked sounds, and time differences can have an even more deleterious effect due to the low frequencies that are involved. In any event, if there are cancellations, lining up the peaks and valleys of the two signals allows them to reinforce each other.

One solution to tuning out these timing differences is SONAR's Nudge feature. To use this, first zoom in horizontally on both the direct and the miked signal, as you'll be dealing with very small timing increments. You might want to zoom in vertically as well, so you can easily see the peaks of low-level signals. The goal is to line up these two signals with respect to time, which will require moving the miked signal earlier. However, unlike the example shown in Chapter 5—where the miked and direct tracks were relatively similar—you'll often encounter situations where the waveforms are very different, making it harder to line them up (see Figure 29.1).

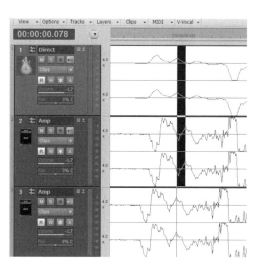

Figure 29.1

The top track is the direct guitar. The second track down is the miked guitar signal; the black band indicates the time difference between a peak in the top signal and the same peak in the signal below it. The lowest track shows the second track moved forward in time, so that it lines up with the direct track. Note the peak that was used as a reference to line them up; it's one of the less ambiguous matches between the two signals.

As a result, you'll need to use a combination of your eyes and your ears to line these up properly. First, measure the distance between the mic and speaker. Because sound takes about 1ms to move 1 foot, you can do the math and move the miked track forward by an equal amount—for example, if the mic is 18 inches away from the speaker, move the miked track 1.5ms earlier with respect to time, and you'll be at least somewhat more closely matched to the direct signal.

Now it's time for fine-tuning; there are three main ways to line up these signals.

▷ Click on the miked clip, and with Snap to Grid turned off, drag it forward until the waveforms line up visually.

▷ Use the Nudge feature. Choose Process > Nudge > Settings, and for the three nudge groups, select the desired amount of nudge (see Figure 29.2).

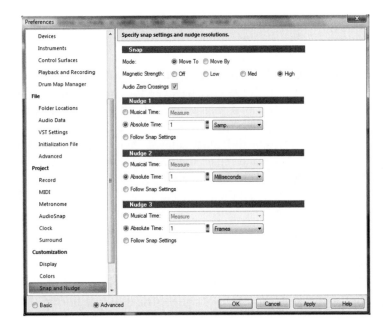

Figure 29.2

Nudge resolutions have been set up for "fine-tuning" clip positions, with nudge choices of 1 sample, 1 millisecond, and 1 frame.

For example, if you choose 1 sample with Nudge Group 1, you can then move the clip earlier or later in one-sample increments using (for Group 1) the 1 and 3 numeric keypad keys, respectively (the default key bindings).

You can "nudge" tracks forward or backward in time based on a user-selectable number of seconds, milliseconds, frames, samples, or ticks if you choose Absolute Time, and by various note values if you choose Musical Time.

▷ Invoke Process > Slide (see Figure 29.3). This has two disadvantages compared to the previous methods: You can't enter amounts in samples or milliseconds, and unlike Nudge, there are no "native" keyboard shortcuts. The advantage is that because you can enter values in ticks (which usually gives sufficient resolution), if you record with a consistent mic position, once you figure out the right amount of slide, you can just enter the amount in ticks, and you're done. Negative values slide earlier; positive values slide later.

Figure 29.3

The Slide function is designed to move a track
by a fixed, consistent amount.

When nudging, it can help to switch one track out of phase, which you can do in the Console view (see Figure 29.4).

Figure 29.4

In Console view, clicking on the Phase button switches a channel's phase.

As you nudge one track compared to the other, the thinner the sound, the closer they are to being matched. Nudge one sample at a time until you reach maximum cancellation and then go back to the in-phase position. You might also find it helpful to switch both tracks to mono (the button to the left of the phase switch chooses between mono and stereo interleave) to make any cancellation more obvious.

How to Emulate Vintage Effects

INTERESTINGLY ENOUGH, THE THOROUGHLY MODERN SONAR X1 can emulate vintage effects pedals if you're willing to do a little tweaking. For example, the Pro Channel EQ is a natural for automated phase-shifting effects. After all, phase shifting places several deep notches in the frequency spectrum and moves their frequencies up and down in unison. We can do this in SONAR by linking multiple EQ bands, setting them all to create deep notches, and then using grouping and automation so that they all track together. SONAR X1 Studio owners needn't feel left out; the Sonitus:fx Equalizer can give the same general results as the Pro Channel when inserted in a track's FX Bin.

You can not only create standard phase-shifter effects, but also interesting phasers variations, resonators (like you find in some delay units), and best of all, vintage wah effects. We'll also cover how to control these effects with a footpedal.

Vintage Phase Shifter Emulation

If you have SONAR X1 Producer, open the Inspector so you can see the Pro Channel. With the Studio edition, insert the Sonitus:fx Equalizer in the FX Bin of the track you want to process. The following instructions relate to the Pro Channel, but it's easy to adapt them to the Sonitus:fx Equalizer.

1. Enable the Equalizer and then enable the two middle bands.

2. Turn up the Q control to around 16 for both bands.

3. Now turn the associated Level controls all the way down, creating steep notches.

4. Next, adjust the filter frequencies so they're about two octaves apart. For example, if the low mid (LMF) band is set to 500 Hz, set the high mid (HMF) band to 2 kHz (see Figure 30.1).

Figure 30.1

Creating two steep notches is the foundation for a classic phase-shifter emulation.

5. As we want the filters to track together, we'll assign the Frequency parameters to a group. Right-click on each Frequency control and choose Group > [select a group, such as X].

6. After the two controls are grouped, right-click on one of the controls and select Group Manager. Absolute (toward the right) should be checked.

7. Now when you sweep one Frequency control, the other will follow and create the classic "notch filter" phase-shifter effect.

Automating Phase-Shifter Moves

To automate these control moves, right-click on each Frequency knob and select Automation Write Enable. Start playback and then tweak one of the Frequency knobs as desired. (Remember, they're grouped together, so you need to vary only one of them.) You'll hear the sound of the phase shifter, and SONAR will write the automation data.

As long as the controls have Automation Read Enable selected, they'll play back the automation and re-create your phase-shifter effect moves.

Additional Options

▷ Experiment with different EQ types. (I generally like the Vintage setting for phase shifting, but try Pure and Modern as well.)

▷ For a more intense effect, use the same principle with four bands to create four notch filters that all sweep together. Set each band approximately an octave apart.

▷ In the Group Manager, also try checking Relative instead of Absolute. This gives a different effect, as all frequencies move relative to each other and therefore remain spaced one octave apart as they move, rather than being offset by a constant amount.

Emulating Phasers with Positive Feedback

Some phase shifters, such as Electro-Harmonix's Polyphase, used positive feedback so that they swept sharp peaks instead of notches. The Pro Channel has the ideal type of response to create this effect.

Use the same basic setup as the phaser, with all Q controls set to maximum, but this time enable all four bands. Set the initial frequencies an octave apart—200 Hz, 400 Hz, 800 Hz, 1600 Hz. Unlike the phaser we covered previously, turn up the level controls to maximum (see Figure 30.2). Also as we did before, group the controls so they all move together—and now you have yet another vintage effect sound.

Figure 30.2

This variation produces another type of vintage phase-shifter effect.

Resonator Emulation

A resonator effect produces a series of harmonically related peaks that impart a sense of pitch to the material being processed. You can use delay lines with feedback or equalizers to create resonator effects. In this example, we'll use the Sonitus:fx Equalizer instead of the Pro Channel because the Sonitus has six bands instead of four and allows Q settings up to 24. (The Pro Channel maximum is 16—the sharper the Q, the more resonant the sound.)

The filter type for all six bands should be Peak/Dip. We want an exact octave spacing between the peaks, so it's a good idea to type the optimum frequencies into each Freq field (remember to hit Return after entering each one): 100, 200, 400, 800, 1600, 3200. Set the Q for all bands to 24 and the gain to maximum (+18.0 dB) —see Figure 30.3.

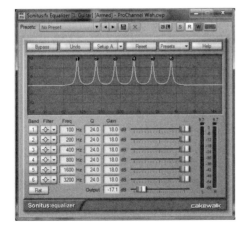

Figure 30.3

By adding lots of gain instead of creating notches, the basic phaser configuration can turn into a resonator.

Be careful; with all those peaks, you'll have to pull the output control way down to avoid distortion. To automate your moves, as you can't group the Sonitus frequency parameters the same way as with the Pro Channel, draw a marquee (in other words, a rectangle) around each of the frequency markers (1, 2, 3, 4, 5, 6) in the graphic to select them all. They'll turn from yellow to black to indicate that they're selected.

Click the Write Automation Enable button, and now when you move one filter frequency, they'll all move together in unison. If your moves aren't recorded properly, right-click on Equalizer in the FX Bin, select the Write Enable parameter, and make sure Freq 1 through Freq 6 are checked.

As you spent all that time typing in frequencies, why not save this as a preset? You can do this in two ways:

1. Double-click in the Sonitus:fx Equalizer presets field at the top.
2. Type in Resonator.
3. Click on the Save (floppy disk) button.
4. Resonator is now added to the drop-down menu.

The other option is to use the Sonitus:fx Preset Manager.

1. In the toolbar just above the graph, click on Presets and select Add Preset from the drop-down menu.
2. Enter the preset name.
3. Specify the bank (from the Add to Bank drop-down menu) where you want to store the preset, or enter a new bank's name.

Now you can retrieve the preset easily. As to why you would use one option compared to the other, the Preset Manager allows more sophisticated preset management options, while the VST presets option is a good way to build up a single, easily accessible list of favorites.

Combining Phaser and Resonator

Before leaving the world of phasers and resonators, let's touch on one more response that gives some very interesting sounds: a combination phase shifter/resonator ("phasenator," perhaps?) that includes both peaks and notches—see Figure 30.4. This works well with either the Pro Channel or the Sonitus:fx Equalizer; the main difference is that the Sonitus:fx option offers more bands.

By now, you should be pretty familiar with the whole concept of grouping controls, moving them together, and writing automation, so I'll forego describing that process. However, note that because of the sharp peaks, you'll need to pull back on the track input gain to avoid distortion.

Figure 30.4
Yet another phase-shifter variation produces yet another timbre-warping effect.

Vintage Wah Pedal Emulation

This produces a surprisingly realistic emulation of a vintage wah effect. Of course, you can try to create a wah sound with the Pro Channel or Sonitus:fx Equalizer by setting a parametric stage to a sharp peak and sweeping it, but it just doesn't sound the same as a true classic wah. That's because vintage wahs had steep high- and low-frequency rolloffs that emphasized the midrange; fortunately, there's a way we can simulate that.

1. In the Track view, start by right-clicking on the track number for the track you want to process and then select Clone Track. This creates a copy in a separate track.

2. Switch to Console view and, if needed, widen the strips by going to the Console view Strips menu and selecting Strips > Widen All Strips, or simply by right-clicking on the two guitar strips and unchecking Narrow Strip.

3. Reverse the cloned track's phase by clicking on the cloned track's Phase (Ø) button. If you play both tracks together, they should cancel, and you'll hear no sound.

4. Enable the first track's Pro Channel EQ and enable one of the bands. Turn its Q up to about 4 and its level to 12 dB.

5. Sweep the frequency, and you'll hear that vintage wah sound. The Pure and Vintage EQ options seem particularly applicable to this effect. The reason why this sounds so realistic is because all frequencies other than the midrange cancel each other out (see Figure 30.5).

Figure 30.5
The guitar track is cloned. The main track goes through a parametric EQ, while the other has its phase inverted so that any frequencies not swept by the EQ are canceled.

Controlling the Wah with a Footpedal

Of course, we can automate our control movements, as we did with the phaser. But what's a wah without a footpedal? You'll need either a MIDI footpedal or a synthesizer with a MIDI output and footpedal input. I use the BOSS FV-500H footpedal not because I'm being politically correct (Roland and Cakewalk are partners, and BOSS is a division of Roland), but because it's built like a tank and has connections that let it serve as a standard volume pedal or expression pedal—see Figure 30.6.

Figure 30.6
The two jacks toward the left of the FV-500H act like a standard volume pedal, while the jack on the right is a stereo jack designed to work with synthesizers and other devices having an expression-pedal input.

The following might get a little deep, but just follow the steps carefully, and you'll be rewarded with a truly funky wah effect. We'll use the Roland A-300PRO keyboard to illustrate how this works, but other keyboards work similarly. And of course, you can apply this technique to effects other than wah.

Note that what complicates this procedure is that you probably won't want the wah to cover the full frequency range from 20 Hz to 20 kHz—a real wah covers a much more restricted range. Fortunately, there's a workaround that allows you to do this.

1. Under Preferences, make sure your keyboard is enabled as a MIDI input device (see Figure 30.7). If there are multiple MIDI input options, and you're not sure which one to use, you can check them all without adverse effects.

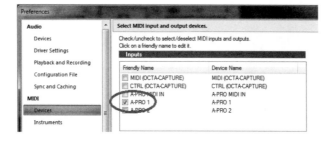

Figure 30.7
Make sure SONAR's corresponding MIDI input is enabled for the device you want to use as a controller.

2. Plug an expression pedal into the keyboard's Expression Pedal input. Virtually all keyboards will require a stereo cable (also called *tip-ring-sleeve* or *TRS*) to make this connection; see Figure 30.8.

Figure 30.8
A stereo cable looks like a standard guitar cable but has an additional "ring" connection between the tip and ground.

3. Let's assume the LMF band is controlling the wah, and no other bands are enabled. Right-click on the Freq knob for any band *other than the LMF band* (for example, right-click on the LF band—the instructions that follow presume this is the band you'll be using) and then select Remote Control.

4. Move the pedal and then click on Learn. The Controller button should turn on, and the field next to it should show the controller number. (You needn't concern yourself with what this number is; SONAR does the "housekeeping" for you.)

5. Click on OK to close the Remote Control dialog box.

6. Move the pedal, and the LF Freq knob should change, but the LMF Freq knob—the one you actually want to control—should not change, at least for now.

7. Assign both the LF and LMF knobs to a group.

8. Right-click on either knob and click on Group Manager. When the Group Manager opens, click on Custom.

9. The top line should show a Start Value of 0 and an End Value of 127. If not, click on the line to select it and then edit the values in the Start Value and End Value fields. This is the range covered by the LF band.

10. Now click on the bottom line and set the Start Value and End Value. These will determine the range covered by the LMF channel in response to the pedal motion. I've found that a Start Value of 45 and End Value of 85 sound pretty authentic (see Figure 30.9).

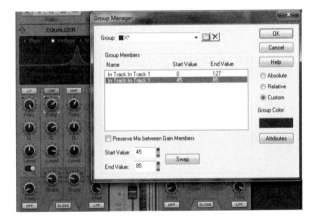

Figure 30.9
The LMF control is grouped with the LF control, which covers the full frequency range. However, we've restricted the LMF's highest and lowest frequency limits to cover a more wah-like range. Note that the LF control is all the way up in the Pro Channel, but the LMF is up only about 2/3 of the way.

11. Click on OK. Now when you move the pedal over its full range, the LF band will cover its full range, but the LMF band will cover a restricted range.

Multiband Processing

MULTIBAND COMPRESSION, WHETHER IN HARDWARE or plug-in form, is a familiar studio processor for processing dynamic range. However, the concept can be taken much further and applied to other types of processing—such as distortion for guitar.

I first discovered the joys of non-compression-based multiband processing with the Quadrafuzz, a distortion box I designed many years ago that split the guitar into four non-overlapping frequency bands and distorted each band individually. By reducing intermodulation distortion caused by the highs and lows being distorted through the same processor, there's much greater clarity and a fuller sound—for example, power chords have a lot more "focus." When translating this concept to the studio, there were additional possibilities (for example, panning the bands to create a stereo image, or doing additional processing, such as multiband chorusing).

There are commercially available ways to split signals by frequency, from the crossover module in Native Instruments' Guitar Rig 4 LE (it's under the Tools section) that's included with SONAR X1 Producer Edition, to programs such as iZotope's Trash. But the ideal solution is a method that can be applied to *any* signal, and this requires an accurate multiband crossover. Fortunately, SONAR has just such a module—but it's hidden in plain sight.

The Sonitus Solution

SONAR includes two multiband compressors: the LP-64 linear phase multiband and the venerable Sonitus Multiband compressor. The latter is ideally suited for our purposes because it's very CPU-friendly, so you can insert multiple instances in multiple bands, even with a relatively modest computer. The LP-64 will also work, although practically speaking, I don't hear much difference when using one compared to the other. Regardless, in either case we'll be using the processor's filters to create a series of frequency crossovers.

There are two basic strategies to implementing multiband processing:

▷ Clone a track so the number of tracks equals the number of bands you want to process. In this case, you insert an instance of the Sonitus Multiband in each track, followed by the processing you want to use.

▷ Create as many busses as bands you want to process, and again, insert a Sonitus Multiband and processor in each bus. These then get mixed back together into a bus, typically the Master bus.

I prefer the first option, as the tracks and effects are readily visible in Track view, and you can create a track folder and collapse the tracks down to a single slot in Track view. It's also easy to group track parameters together, which is convenient for making universal adjustments for all tracks. However, if you want to apply multiband processing to different instruments—for example, three layered rhythm-guitar tracks—then bussing uses less CPU power, and sending each instrument to the same bus guarantees that you'll be applying the same effect to the various instruments.

Setting Up

Let's run through using multiband processing to get a great distortion sound for power chords and rhythm guitar.

Set up one track the way you want it, so that cloning it will create the additional tracks exactly as desired. For example, suppose you're using the version of Guitar Rig 4 LE bundled with SONAR X1 Producer Edition as your amp sim. Insert the Sonitus Multiband Compressor, followed by GR 4 LE, in your original rhythm-guitar track (see Figure 31.1).

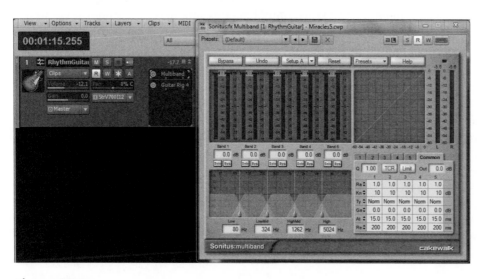

Figure 31.1
This is the basic rhythm-guitar track we'll use to generate the additional tracks for multiband processing. The Sonitus Multiband has been reset so that it doesn't apply any compression and has fine, evenly spaced frequency bands; it's followed by Guitar Rig 4 LE.

For the Sonitus Multiband, click on the Reset button. This results in no compression, which is what we want. Then, go to the Common tab and turn off the Limiter (unless you want to use the Sonitus Multiband as a maximizer for a particular track—see later).

Now tweak GR4 LE for the distortion sound you want; for example, drag in the Jump amplifier component and call up the Distorted preset. (With this preset, I usually turn down the amp Treble control a bit.) Spend some time to get an amp sound that satisfies you, because once you've cloned multiple tracks, it's inconvenient to have to go back and tweak each instance individually.

Before cloning the tracks, get a feel for how the Sonitus Multiband affects the guitar. Note that each band has a Solo button and that these are additive, so you can solo more than one band at a time. While monitoring the track, solo each band in turn and listen. I found that the top band didn't really do much for the sound; in fact, it seemed somewhat harsh. So, I decided I didn't really need five bands of distortion, because four would do the job.

Also listen to band pairs. For example, soloing the two lowest bands (the Solo buttons are located just above the frequency band range graph at the bottom) gives a chunky, fat sound, while soloing the middle and upper-middle bands gives more definition and midrange prominence. Based on this, you might decide that you really only need two tracks of distortion (one for each band pair). However, let's assume you want to go ahead with four discrete tracks, with four bands.

Right-click on the track number in the track header and then select Clone Track (see Figure 31.2). A dialog box will open where you can specify the number of cloned tracks. Specify three cloned tracks, starting with the next higher track number compared to your "base" track, so they'll be grouped together as consecutive tracks.

Figure 31.2

This dialog box makes it easy to create multiple versions of the same track—ideal for multiband processing. In this screenshot, the track is being cloned three times, starting with Track 2.

The Multibands

After cloning the tracks, now it's time to edit the multibands.

Figure 31.3 shows all four multiband compressors. Each has one band soloed; note that the dynamics graph in the upper right indicates that no compression is being applied. As you can see from the output meters toward the right, the lowest band has the least output, and the midrange band (lower-left window) has the highest output. This gives a natural sound, and while you can adjust the output to even out any variations, you probably won't want to.

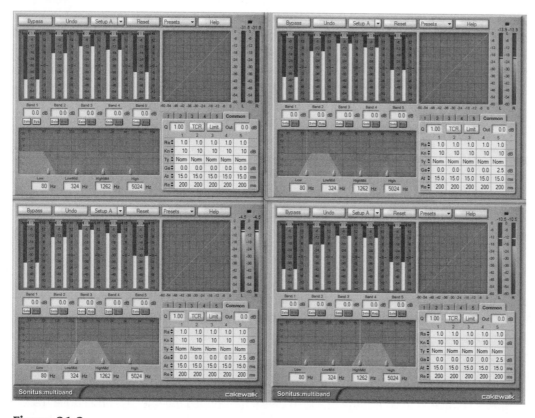

Figure 31.3
The Sonitus Multiband Compressor settings for the four cloned guitar tracks.

To get the big picture, check out Figure 31.4. The four cloned, consecutive guitar tracks are placed with the lowest band in Track 1 and the highest band in Track 4.

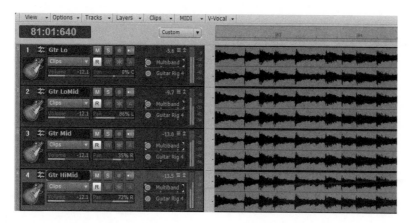

Figure 31.4
How the cloned tracks and effects appear in the Track view.

Note the pan controls: The lowest frequency band, which is very bassy, is panned toward center. (Sometimes when listening to these tracks, it almost sounds as if a bass is playing along with the guitar.) The low mid is panned toward the left, the midrange (the loudest of the three bands) is panned slightly to the right to keep the image mostly in the center, while the highest band is panned far right to increase the left-right spread from low to high frequencies.

Going Further

These are the basic techniques, but there are many opportunities to take this concept further. In addition to panning and adding more processing, here are some additional tips.

▷ You can vary the crossover frequencies for the various bands by moving the small triangular points in the lower-left pane. You can also type specific frequencies in the related numeric fields so that multiple multiband processors have matched frequency bands.

▷ The low band has a low-pass response, and the high band has a high-pass response. To create a two-band crossover that simply splits the signal into lows and highs, drag their frequency markers until they meet in the middle.

▷ You can vary the level of each band. To the left of the Common tab, click on the numbered tab that's associated with a particular band—you'll see a Gain slider.

▷ If you click on the Limiter button, the Multiband becomes a multiband limiter, which gives similar results to "maximizer" processors (see Chapter 21). When the signal is being limited, the red clipping indicator lights above the output meter, but the output is clamped to 0.1 dB. If you push the level too much, you'll hear distortion, but you can usually get away with an extra 4–6 dB of boost with no audible degradation.

Multiband processing sounds great with signals that are rich in harmonics, but experiment—you might be surprised by the many ways this technique can augment your sound.

Create a Looper in SONAR

LOOPERS ARE LONG DELAYS, TYPICALLY USING DELAY TIMES of four or more seconds, with feedback set to maximum so anything you play into them repeats and repeats and repeats and...you get the idea. Loopers are popular for making atmospheric, ambient effects but can also serve to set up a groove where you can keep playing as the loop repeats in the background—think of it as live overdubbing.

You can use the Sonitus Delay as a looper with up to four seconds of delay by turning the feedback way up so you get a continuing series of repeats. However, that's kind of a minimum for looping, so this chapter explains not only how to obtain delays longer than four seconds, but also various techniques you can do that are unique to looping within SONAR's environment.

This technique requires a spare set of stereo outputs and inputs on your audio interface (although you can get by with mono if you'd like). For example, suppose you have a 6-in/6-out interface, and you use Inputs 1 and 2 for recording stereo signals and Outputs 1 and 2 for monitoring SONAR's stereo output. That means you can dedicate Inputs 3/4 (or 5/6) and Outputs 3/4 (or 5/6) to implementing the looper. You'll also need two patch cords so you can patch the outputs back to the inputs. In this example, we'll assume you're using Inputs and Outputs 5 and 6, so patch Output 5 to Input 5, and Output 6 to Input 6.

Looper Routing

The signal path is a little complicated, so before we get into the details of implementing the SONAR looper, let's check out the signal flow (see Figure 32.1).

The audio input comes into an audio track, which we'll call the *Source track*. The output goes to the Master bus so you can hear your original audio signal. (You of course have the option to insert effects into the Source track's FX Bin.)

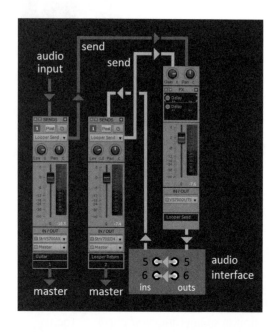

Figure 32.1

Understanding the signal flow makes it easier
to implement a looper in SONAR.

Meanwhile, the Source track has a send that feeds what we'll call the *Looper Send bus*. The Looper Send bus inserts delays in series to lengthen the delay time. For example, if you want 16 seconds of delay, you would put four Sonitus:fx Delays in series. The Looper Send bus output with the delayed signal is assigned to the spare audio interface outputs—in this case, Outputs 5 and 6.

Another audio channel has its input set to interface Inputs 5 and 6. This is basically a Looper Return track that picks up the delayed signal and then feeds it to the Master bus so we can hear the delay.

But the key element that turns this setup into a looper is inserting a send into the Looper Return audio track and assigning the send output to the Looper Send bus. This creates a feedback path so you can have delays that repeat for pretty much as long as desired, because delayed audio appearing at the Looper Send bus output can feed back to its input.

Implementing the Looper in SONAR

Let's translate this to a SONAR project. Insert a source audio track for your guitar or other signal source and then insert a bus that we'll call the *Looper Send bus*. Assign the output in its output field to the spare audio interface outputs (see Figure 32.2).

Now insert the desired number of delays in the Looper Send bus FX Bin. For starters, set each delay's right and left Feedback and Crossfeed to zero, and Mix to 100% (delay only). For the longest possible delay that syncs to the host tempo, choose a delay time factor of 8 (see Figure 32.3). You may find it more convenient to link the two delay lines so that you have to move only one fader to affect both lines simultaneously.

If you prefer not to have the delay follow the host, click on the Tempo Sync button until it shows Off and then use the Delay Time slider to set the delay time. Set all delays you've inserted into the FX Bin identically.

Figure 32.2

The Looper Send bus is being assigned to two spare audio interface outputs.

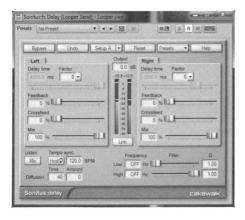

Figure 32.3

Make sure the delay Mix is set to 100%, and for now, set Feedback and Crossfeed to 0%.

Next, insert a send in the Source track. It's probably easiest to right-click on the track header's track number and choose Insert Send > Insert Send Assistant. When the Send Assistant appears, choose Send to Existing Bus and specify the Looper Send bus. Check the Pre Fader box.

Now insert another audio track, which we'll call *Looper Return*. Set the input field to the spare audio interface inputs (for example, 5 and 6 in this case) and the output field to master so you can hear this track's output. Insert a send into the Loop Return track and, again using the Send Assistant, assign it to the Looper Send bus using the pre-fader position (as you did for the send in the Source audio track). Your looper is now complete (see Figure 32.4).

Note that if you inserted an effect in the Source track, then you'll be looping the processed sound, not the dry sound.

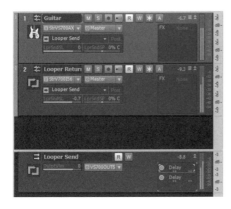

Figure 32.4

Here's the complete looper, with Source track, Looper Send bus, and Looper Return audio track.

Tweaking the Looper

This setup is ripe for tweaking. Set the looper's feedback with the Looper Return track's Send control. To prevent uncontrolled feedback (in other words, the feedback loop's output is higher than the input), be careful not to set the Send control too high; the optimum setting will also depend on the input level settings for Inputs 5 and 6. Usually, the easiest way to set this is to temporarily specify a short delay time for the delays in the Looper Send bus so you don't have to wait forever to hear the results of any changes you make. Then, adjust the feedback just below the point of uncontrolled feedback, or lower if you want the loop not to last as long. Another option to help control feedback is to insert a limiter, such as Boost Eleven, in the Looper Return track's FX Bin.

One trick that you can't do with other loopers is access the parameters "inside" the delay, because you can tweak the Sontius:fx Delay controls. For example, you can set different delay times in the two delay lines for polyrhythmic, stereo effects (for example, a factor of 8 coupled with a factor of 6). What's more, you can add internal feedback and crossfeed for each delay within the overall feedback. However, be careful when adjusting the internal feedback, as introducing this can make the setup less stable—you'll likely have to adjust the Looper Return track's Send control carefully to make sure the feedback doesn't get out of hand. You can even tailor the internal feedback's frequency response with the two Filter sliders in the Sonitus:fx Delay's lower right (one slider cuts highs, the other cuts lows).

Finally, a tip about recording: Record-enable the source and Looper Return tracks so that you record both the source audio input and the echoes.

242

33

SONAR's Multiband Envelope Follower

IF YOU'RE NOT FAMILIAR WITH HOW ENVELOPE followers work, consider the classic Mu-Tron III "envelope filter" effect—the envelope follower is the part that follows the dynamics of your playing and uses that to control the filter frequency to give an automated wah effect. The Cakewalk Modfilter effect (see Chapter 22) has an envelope follower that works like conventional envelope filter guitar effects.

But now that we know how automation works, we can take advantage of a super-sophisticated envelope follower that's one of SONAR's secret weapons. The Analyst plug-in can analyze a track and generate envelopes that represent the levels in four specific frequency bands, as well as another envelope that represents the overall level.

Recording (and Time-Aligning) Analyst Envelopes

Suppose you'd like to use the envelope from a percussion track to modulate a wah effect on a guitar track. Here's how.

1. Insert the Analyst plug-in into the percussion track's FX Bin.
2. Select Lo resolution for now, click on Auto to enable automation output, and then click on the automation Write Enable button.
3. Start playback to write the automation (see Figure 33.1).
4. After hitting Stop, go back to the beginning. Note that the Analyst envelope starts a little late (about 20 milliseconds), as evidenced by the dashed line leading up to the first nodes (see Figure 33.2). We want to line up the first nodes with the track beginning.

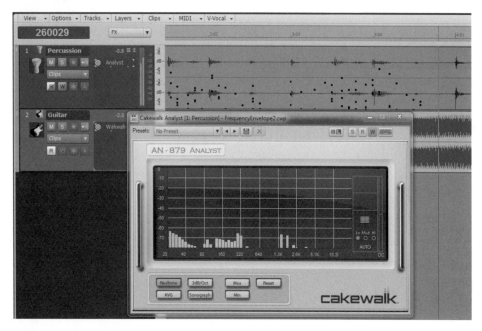

Figure 33.1

The Analyst envelopes—five bands total—are all being recorded as automation. The dots superimposed on the audio track are the automation nodes created by the envelopes.

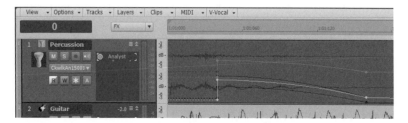

Figure 33.2

The Analyst envelopes don't start right at the beginning, but we can fix this.

5. Go to the Edit view Options menu and disable Select Track Envelopes with Clips.

6. Set the track's Edit Filter to Clips and turn off Snap. Then, move the clip so the left edge lines up with the leftmost envelope node.

7. Go back to the Edit view Options menu, re-enable Select Track Envelope with Clips, and move the clip back to its original position. The envelopes will move with it.

Note that you can also move individual envelopes using the Process > Nudge command. Use the Edit Filter to select the envelope you want to move and then select all the envelope nodes by using the Smart tool or Select tool to draw a rectangle around the nodes. You can now slide these right or left with the Nudge command.

Using One Track's Envelope to Modulate Another Track's Processor

Now that we have our envelopes, let's have them do something useful—such as apply one of the envelopes to a wah effect processing a guitar power chord.

1. Insert the Sonitus:fx Wahwah in the guitar track.

2. Select the track with the recorded Analyst envelopes and choose Edit > Copy.

3. Check the Track/Bus Automation box and leave everything else unchecked.

4. Select the guitar track and choose Edit > Paste. The envelopes will now be superimposed on the guitar track.

5. However, as you've copied Analyst envelopes, you won't be able to see them in the guitar track's Edit Filter unless the track has an Analyst plug-in. So, insert one in the guitar track's FX Bin.

6. We'll apply the Analyst's overall envelope. Use the guitar track's Edit Filter to go to Automation > Analyst > Analyst Full. Now you can see the envelope, so let's assign it to the wah.

7. Right-click on the envelope, choose Assign Envelope, and select Wahwah. In the dialog box that appears, click on the Wah parameter and then click on OK (see Figure 33.3).

8. Start playback, and you'll hear the envelope affect the Wahwah.

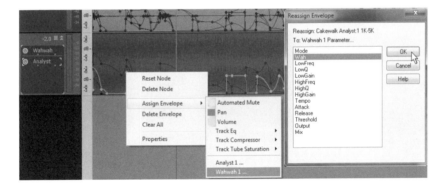

Figure 33.3
Reassigning an envelope is a two-step process. Assign the envelope to the target processor and then to the appropriate processor parameter.

If you want to alter the frequency range covered by the wah, there are two ways to do this.

▷ On the Sonitus:fx Wahwah, adjust the High and Low frequency sliders to cover the desired range.

▷ Use the Smart tool or Select tool to draw a rectangle around all the envelope nodes. You can now click on any of the nodes and then drag to move the entire envelope. Note that you can't use the Shift key as a modifier to constrain vertical movement, so if you want to make sure the envelope doesn't get out of rhythm, here's a tip: Zoom way in, place the now time over the node you're going to grab, and use the now time as a guide when you move the node up or down.

Transposing in SONAR X1

Transposing digital audio is never easy—to raise pitch, you have to remove data to increase the frequency, and to lower pitch, you need to insert data where none existed to make for longer waveforms. Yet sometimes pitch transposition is necessary, and SONAR X1 offers several different options.

Note that this chapter doesn't cover the MPEX pitch transposition option found in previous versions of SONAR, as it's not supported in 64-bit SONAR, and the Radius DSP stretching algorithms licensed from iZotope—included in both 32- and 64-bit versions—are equal or better anyway.

Real-Time Transposition with the Pitch Shifter Plug-In

We'll start with the lowest quality option, the Cakewalk Pitch Shifter plug-in (see Figure 34.1). It reminds me a lot of the ancient (circa 1979) and very rare ADA Harmony Synthesizer, an analog pitch transposer that used bucket-bridge delay line chips. It had this kind of horrible wobbling quality that the Pitch Shifter can, for better or worse, emulate.

As with most pitch shifters, the less the amount of shift, the better the fidelity. If nothing else, this plug-in is useful for checking out a "draft" of what a harmony will sound like. However, I would be remiss if I didn't mention that you can also get some really strange and radical effects by using the "wrong" settings. Here are some of my favorites.

Pitch Shift amounts between −0.1 and +0.1 can give some wonderful chorusing and doubling effects. Adjust the amount of chorused sound with the Wet Mix and Dry Mix controls (typically set for equal amounts). Set Feedback to 0 and adjust the Delay Time to add a time difference between the two signals if desired.

Figure 34.1
The Pitch Shifter is a real-time pitch transposer plug-in. These settings drop the pitch down by an octave to produce a pseudo-bass sound from guitar.

The Mod Depth control modulates the delay time; its effect varies tremendously depending on the amount of Pitch Shift, Delay, and Feedback. It's basically a "mystery control" with unpredictable results, so just play with it until you get as close as possible to the kind of sound you want. One of its talents is to add ring modulator–type effects if you set the Pitch Shift to +12, Feedback to 0%, and Delay Time to 0 and then vary mod depth between about 13ms and 20ms.

Another pitch transposer application is to create pseudo-bass parts from guitar, using settings as shown in Figure 34.1. Although you probably wouldn't use it for a final mix, it's good enough to serve as a placeholder, and if you mix in some of the dry signal, you'll get a pretty cool 8-string bass. The Mod Depth control makes a huge difference to the sound quality and is pretty critical. You should experiment with it, although I found that settings around 30ms seem to work best.

Pitch Transposition with Acidized Files

This is an effective technique for transposing down to about 8 semitones or up to 3 semitones (or sometimes even more). However, this does require some setup, so let's explain how that works.

You'll simplify matters if you use Acidization solely for pitch-shifting and not time-stretching, so record the part to be transposed after you've established the tempo; then do the following to transpose using Acidization.

1. Record the part. If necessary, slip-edit the beginning and end to measure boundaries, and then with the clip selected, in the Track view Edit menu, choose Clips > Apply Trimming to discard any audio beyond the slip-edited boundaries. Note that you'll need to know the part's exact length in beats.

2. Choose Project > Set Default Groove Clip Pitch and set it to the song's key.

3. Double-click on the clip to open the Loop Construction window.

4. Click on the Loop Construction window's Loop button and then enter the number of beats in the Beats field if it isn't already entered correctly. (It probably will be.)

5. Although you're not time-stretching, you still need to make sure that transient markers are in the right places, particularly as you stretch farther from the base pitch. For example, you may be able to get decent stretching to 3 semitones, but with better transient marker editing, increase that to 4 semitones. We've covered this process in previous columns, but in a nutshell, you want a marker at the beginning of each transient and at the end of a note that's followed by silence. You can add a marker by clicking in the timeline above the waveform, and you can move it back and forth by grabbing the "stem" that appears over the waveform. I generally specify "No Slice" in the drop-down menu to the right of the Loop button and then add slices manually as needed.

6. To transpose, use the two rightmost fields in the Loop Construction window toolbar, for semitones and fine tuning (see Figure 34.2).

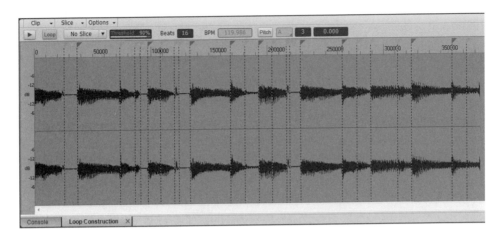

Figure 34.2
The loop has had its transient markers edited in the Loop Construction window; the ones with the lighter "handles" were added manually. The clip is 16 beats long and is being transposed up 3 semitones.

Transposition will reveal any problems with the Acidization. Missed transients are pretty obvious as a sort of echo; a flutter in a sustained note can sometimes be fixed by placing an additional marker partway through the note. It's really a matter of experimentation, so experiment! If you put a marker in the wrong place, you can remove it with the Eraser tool.

There's one really great sound you can get with rhythm guitar parts if you're combining MIDI and audio tracks, as MIDI tracks can be transposed so easily. Here's the scenario: Suppose you're recording in E and have recorded a rhythm guitar part. Mute the audio tracks and then transpose the MIDI tracks down two semitones to D. Now record a doubled guitar part while playing in the key of D.

When you're finished, transpose the MIDI parts back to E and unmute the audio tracks. Now use the Acidization technique described a moment ago to transpose the guitar part you just recorded up two semitones, from D to E. It will have a brighter tone that will add another dimension to the original rhythm guitar part. The more you transpose up, the more the guitar will start to sound like a variant on Nashville tuning.

Similarly, recording a guitar part at a higher pitch and transposing down gives a "heavier" sound—metal fans, take note.

Offline Transposition with DSP

This yields the best possible fidelity over the widest possible range, but the reason why is because it's an offline process. You can play through the Pitch Shifter plug-in in real time, and once a clip is recorded and Acidized properly, you can adjust its pitch in real time during playback. With offline DSP transposition, you need to apply the transposition to a recorded file and then invoke the DSP and wait for SONAR to crunch some numbers to do the transposition.

To transpose, click on the clip to select it and then choose Process > Transpose. When the Transpose dialog box appears, check the Transpose Audio box, enter the transposition Amount, and then choose the transposition Type (see Figure 34.3).

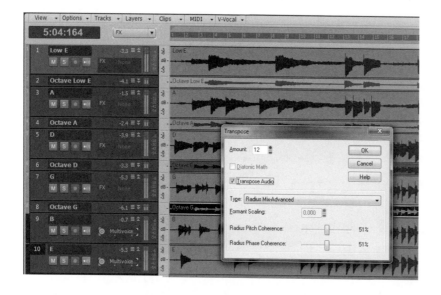

Figure 34.3

The Transposition dialog box is set to transpose up one octave, using the Mix-Advanced algorithm. The end result will be a 12-string emulation, as described later.

There are five pitch-transposition algorithms: Solo, Bass, Vocal, Radius Mix, and Radius Mix-Advanced. Solo, Bass, and Vocal are designed for monophonic lines, while Radius Mix and Radius Mix-Advanced are optimized for polyphonic material. However, I've found that even with solo guitar notes from a hex pickup, the Mix algorithms sound the best. (The tradeoff is that they take longer to crunch numbers than the Solo algorithms.)

If you choose the Mix-Advanced algorithm, you'll see two additional parameters—Pitch Coherence and Phase Coherence. The latter is important mostly for surround, so we can safely ignore it. (Really, how many of you are recording in surround?) I've experimented with Pitch Coherence and haven't yet found source material where it makes a huge difference in sound quality.

The DSP fidelity is so good that I've been able to create a really cool and extremely authentic-sounding 12-string emulation. I used the hex outputs from a Gibson Firebird X, although any guitar with hex audio outs will work. I recorded each string in its own channel, ending up with six channels of recorded sound. I then copied the lower four strings (low E–G) to create additional "octave" tracks and used the Mix-Advanced algorithm to transpose these up 12 semitones. I was pretty amazed by the sound quality, even when transposed that high.

Even better, I could delay or advance the octave string clips in time to emulate different 12-strings. With Rickenbackers, a down strum hits the octave string first and then the standard tuning string. With a Fender 12-string, it's the other way around. Adding about a 25ms differential between the octave and standard strings emulates the time difference between hitting these strings. (For the high E and B channels, I cheated and used a chorus to create the "doubled-string" sound.)

So why not just record a 12-string? Several reasons. The Firebird X has a piezo-based acoustic sound that's quite wonderful, and I don't have an acoustic 12-string. Furthermore, it's easy to do alternate tunings; you can do tricks such as Nashville tuning electronically or drop some strings down an octave while bringing others up—or do both and get something like an 18-string guitar. The sound is huge!

Create Drum Backing Tracks with Session Drummer 3

THERE'S MORE TO LIFE THAN GUITARS (REALLY!), and it's very helpful to be able to practice against a backing drum track instead of just a metronome, or to create drum tracks to kick-start the songwriting process. Fortunately, SONAR includes the Session Drummer 3 virtual instrument (SD3 for short), which offers multiple ways to put together a drum track—from a quickie glorified metronome for tech newbies to a sophisticated tone module for experts.

SD3 offers 12 individual drum channels and a master output channel (see Figure 35.1). It can open kits (sounds only), patterns that trigger kit sounds if you want to treat SD3 more like a drum machine, or programs, which combine a kit with a specific set of eight patterns.

Because I like to create custom drum kits, one of my favorite features is that you can drag just about anything onto an SD3 pad—AIF, WAV, FLAC, or OGG files, at any sample rate, with bit depths from 8 to 32 bits, mono or stereo. Each pad can also load SFZ files for multi-sampled sounds. Getting too deep into making custom kits is beyond the scope of this book, but the bottom line is that SD3 is an instrument that can grow with you.

Incidentally, the Drumkit page takes up a lot of screen real estate, because it's the same size as the mixer page. Here's where SONAR's X-Ray feature is really welcome—when you want to see the drum track, just enable X-Ray by pressing Shift+X to make SD3 less opaque (see Figure 35.2). You can adjust the X-Ray opacity and fade-in/fade-out times under Customization > Display.

Figure 35.1

SD3's mixer lets you edit level, panning, width, tuning, and drum output. In this example, multiple audio output channels are available; drums are assigned to different audio tracks so different drums can have different processing.

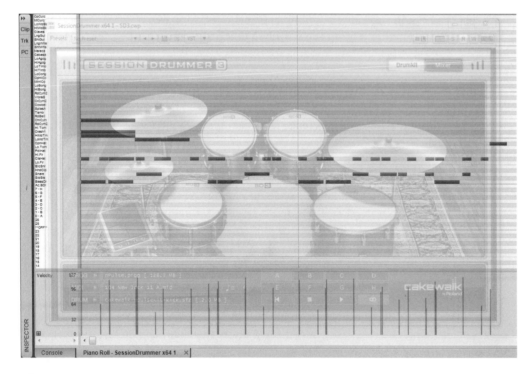

Figure 35.2

SONAR's X-Ray feature has made the SD3 Drumkit page less opaque, so you can easily see the MIDI track driving it.

For more info on SD3, locate your Vstplugins folder, open the Session Drummer 3 folder, and look in the Documentation folder. You'll also find a Resources folder in the main SD3 folder with BMP files for SD3's graphic elements, which you can edit if you want to re-skin the look.

Easy Drum Tracks: The Glorified Metronome

This way of using SD3 gets you up and running as quickly as possible. Insert SD3 into your project by choosing Insert > Soft Synth > Session Drummer 3. When the Insert Soft Synth Options screen appears, the simplest option is to check Simple Instrument Track and Synth Property Page (this opens up the instrument's interface) and not concern yourself with the other choices.

When SD3 appears, the drum kit is semitransparent to indicate that a kit or program hasn't been loaded yet. SD3 won't do anything until you load some sounds into it, so:

1. Right-click in the Prog field. (It should currently say New Program.) A browser will open for kit selection.

2. Open the appropriate category and double-click on a program to select it.

3. Close the browser window, and now the drums will be "solid" to indicate that a drum kit has been loaded. (Note: An alternative way to select a kit is to click on the Prog button in the lower left, select Load Program, and navigate to the program you want to load.)

4. On the Drumkit page, click on one of the lettered patterns (A–H) to serve as a metronome. In general, the first few letters are more "basic" patterns, and the last few letters are fills.

5. Click on Play (>) to hear the pattern.

6. If you like the pattern and want it to repeat indefinitely, click on the Loop Pattern button (the infinity-sign button to the right of Play). You can do this while the pattern is playing or before you click on Play. You can also select other lettered patterns; a newly selected pattern will play as soon as the current pattern stops playing, which makes for a seamless transition.

7. SD3 can operate without having to be recorded—it will play along with SONAR, starting and stopping based on SONAR's Transport and auto-locating based on the now time.

If you find a universally applicable "point of departure" pattern, you could save a template project with SD3 inserted and the desired program/kit selected. Then when you call up the project, everything will be ready to go.

Tweaking the Pattern

Suppose you like the "glorified metronome" pattern, but you want to use it with a couple of slight variations. Click on the Note button (to the right of the MIDI pattern name field) and then drag and drop the note into the SD3 instrument track (see Figure 35.3; if you're using a separate MIDI track, drag the note into that track instead). This will copy the MIDI file to the track.

You can now edit this track, but also note that these patterns are what SONAR calls a *MIDI groove clip*. If you hover over the clip's right edge with the Smart tool, a blue line will appear. Click and drag to the right, and you can "roll out" this clip to be as long as you like.

Figure 35.3

Dragging the note symbol to a MIDI track copies the currently selected MIDI pattern to the track.

If you've rolled out the clip a bunch of times and want to add some slight variations, no problem: Double-click on the clip to open the MIDI Piano Roll view and edit away. (See Appendix A, "MIDI Basics.")

Real-Time Beat Machine

For a more improvisational feel, here's an alternate approach. Each pattern (not just individual drum sounds) responds to MIDI notes: MIDI note #27 triggers Pattern A, MIDI note #28 triggers Pattern B, MIDI note #29 triggers Pattern C, and so on, consecutively for eight notes total. Note #24 stops whatever is playing. You can retrigger patterns, or if you turn on looping (by clicking on the SD3 Transport's infinity button), whatever pattern you trigger will continue playing until you trigger the next pattern. So, with a keyboard or MIDI pad controller, you can improvise and play patterns in real time to create a part.

Note that when you insert SD3 as a virtual instrument, SONAR will load a "drum map" that labels the pattern-triggering notes with the pattern letter. (Of course, there are also names for the various drum sounds.) To see this, double-click on the clip to open the Piano Roll view; the note names are along the left side (see Figure 35.4).

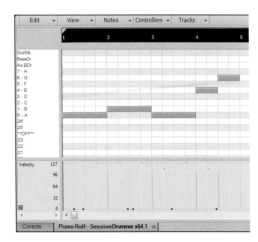

Figure 35.4

The Piano Roll view's drum map shows that notes were played to trigger Patterns A, B, E, and G. If you want to augment the patterns with additional hits, you can still play individual notes on top of the patterns while they play.

If you want to create a backing drum track, turn on SD3's Loop button, record-enable the Session Drum track, and start recording in SONAR. Play the keys (or hit the pad controller pads) that correspond to the patterns you want to hear, and on playback, the patterns will play back as you triggered them. This is really handy if you already have all the patterns you need to create an arrangement, as you can simply string them together, drum machine–style, to create the desired overall part.

Using the Browser to Audition Other Patterns

The patterns that load with a program are intended to be appropriate for the kit, but you might not agree with the choices. You can choose different patterns within SD3's Drumkit page by clicking on the MIDI field in the lower left (or the MIDI Pattern Name field to the right of the MIDI button), selecting Load Pattern, and navigating to a pattern. But you can also use the Browser (see Figure 35.5); here's how to set it up for fast auditioning.

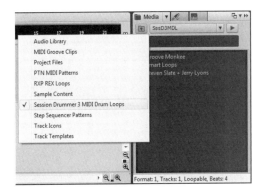

Figure 35.5

The Media Browser makes it easy to audition all MIDI patterns for SD3—not just the ones within SD3 itself. Here, Session Drummer 3 files are being called up from the Content Locations field, but you can open up other folders with drum-friendly MIDI files.

1. Press B to open the Browser if it isn't already open.

2. Click on the Media drop-down button, and for the Synth Preview Output, choose Session Drummer. Also check Auto-Preview (otherwise, you'll need to click on the Browser's Play button to preview the various patterns). You're now finished with the Media drop-down menu.

3. Click in the Content Location field (the large field just below the Browser's top tabs) and then select Session Drummer 3 MIDI Drum Loops from the drop-down menu. (Note: The drum loops are located in your Vstplugins folder under Session Drummer 3/Contents/Patterns.)

4. You'll see folders of loops from Groove Monkee, Smart Loops, and Steven Slate + Jerry Lyons.

5. Double-click on the folder you want to audition. Keep drilling down through folders, if needed, until the pane fills with patterns.

6. You're set up and ready to audition. Click on a pattern to play it. You can click on different patterns or use the QWERTY keyboard up and down arrow keys to step through the patterns. (If there are multiple columns of patterns, you can also use the left and right arrow buttons to jump from one column to another.) As soon as you land on a pattern, it will load immediately in sync with the beat and will begin playing.

7. To stop a pattern from playing, click on the Browser's Stop button.

It can be very inspiring to call up the "wrong" pattern with the "wrong" kit. For example, try loading Drum 'n' Bass patterns into one of Steven Slate's rock kits, at a tempo around 120 BPM instead of the typical Drum 'n' Bass tempo of about 175 BPM; you might be surprised (and pleased!) by the results.

Even better, you're not limited to the patterns included in SD3. The browser offers a separate category for MIDI groove clips, and you'll find drum patterns in the Drums, Groove Monkee, and SmartLoops folders. Another category, PTN MIDI Patterns, includes a Drums folder of (not surprisingly!) additional drum patterns. And if you really want to "roll your own," you can ignore all the included patterns and create your own patterns in MIDI tracks that drive SD3.

Inserting Browser Patterns into the Project

While you're in the Browser, if you like a pattern, then double-click on it to insert it into SD3's MIDI track, at the now time. Or, click on the pattern name or icon and drag it into the track.

But here's a really useful feature: If you have simple patterns (just hi-hat, just kick drum, and so on), this process makes it easy to build up a drum part from these patterns. For example, suppose you find a kick-drum pattern you like; double-click on it to insert. Then let's say you find a perfect hi-hat pattern. If you double-click on it without changing the now time or track, it will layer in the same track, on top of the kick pattern, in a separate layer.

If the patterns aren't the same length, no problem. Turn on the track's Track Layers to see each pattern in its own "lane" within the track (see Figure 35.6). Note that you may need to go to the View Edit menu's Layers tab and select Rebuild Layers to position each MIDI clip in its own track.

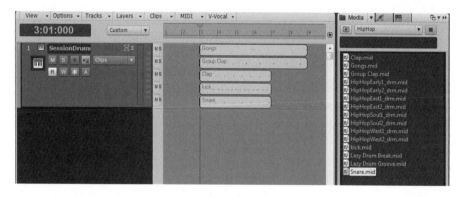

Figure 35.6
With Track Layers turned on, note how five patterns that were all loaded on the same track at Measure 3 are now visible as separate, layered patterns.

Here you can lengthen or shorten particular patterns. (They're groove clips, so you can roll them out as you would loops.) For example, if the kick pattern is one measure long but the hi-hat pattern is four measures long, you can roll out the kick pattern so that it's four measures long as well. If you want to keep separate lanes for separate patterns, fine; that allows for the most editing flexibility. But if you want to bounce them all into a single MIDI track (possibly for easier manipulation on a clip level, because all the patterns end up as one clip), select all of them and, from the Clips tab just above the Track view, select Bounce to Clip(s). Turn off Track Layers, and now you have a single clip that incorporates the parts from all layers.

Overall, SD3 is much more than a glorified metronome—although it's convenient to use it as one when you want to get a part down quickly.

Backing Up

I T'S TIME FOR A LECTURE. Yes, backing up is not guitar-specific information, but I cannot tell you how many times people have come to me and asked in desperation, "My hard drive failed, and I lost all my data! What can I do?" Of course, the answer is, "Just copy everything over from your backup." Unfortunately, you'd be shocked by how many people don't have an organized way to back up their files or even save their projects. So, think of this as the "eat your vegetables" section of the book.

Remember, the most important item in your computer isn't the CPU or motherboard; it's the data. You never know when you might want to revisit some project you did years ago, nor do you know when the project you're working on today will be sabotaged by a crash or hardware failure. If you consider yourself even remotely professional, it's not enough just to save your work; you also need to make sure you'll be able to access it in the future.

I'll first cover the different ways to do backups in SONAR and then branch out into archiving projects. So that we're clear on definitions, I'll consider backups as saving your work from day to day, while archiving is something you "put on the shelf" when you're done—which requires longevity as well as security.

Along the way, I'll also mention how to back up all the SONAR customizations you've made—track templates, custom track icons, Plug-In Manager layouts, and the like.

Backing Up SONAR Projects

It's important to know what you're backing up. Cakewalk's primary file format, the .CWP project file, contains no audio, as it's a "roadmap" for the project—paths to audio clips, where clips sit on the timeline, MIDI data, which plug-ins are inserted, and the like. So, although saving this file is vital, you also need to save the audio to which it points. Furthermore, samples used by virtual instruments aren't saved as part of the file.

As long as the instrument and effects plug-ins are installed on your computer and SONAR knows where to find them, loading the .CWP file will load the appropriate plug-ins and sounds. If SONAR can't find these, you're in trouble—but we'll cover possible solutions later in this chapter.

Backing Up Audio Files

SONAR has three main ways to deal with the audio-file part of the puzzle.

▷ **The global Audio Data folder.** When hard disks were expensive and had limited memory, Cakewalk introduced the concept of a global Audio Data folder where all audio for .CWP project files lived. (The default location is C:\Cakewalk Projects\Audio Data, but you can change this location under Preferences > File > Audio Data.) Then, you could just back up that folder and know all your audio files were safe. However, with the low cost of hard drives, optical media, and even USB sticks, the Audio Data folder concept is much less relevant. So, SONAR includes a configuration option that allows you to store audio data in the folders for individual projects.

▷ **The Bundle file.** When you choose Save As for a project file, in the Save as Type drop-down menu you have the option to choose the Cakewalk Bundle (.CWB) format. This single file incorporates everything stored in a normal project file, as well as all audio (but not video) used in the project. Although convenient and portable—and a great way to transfer works in progress to collaborators—if the bundle file becomes corrupted, you lose the entire project (another good reason to back up your work).

▷ **Per-project audio folders.** With per-project audio folders, you can save all audio, along with the project file using that audio, in a dedicated folder—back up the folder, and you back up the entire project (with the exception of plug-in sample library data, as mentioned earlier). Unlike a bundle file, if one of the per-project files becomes corrupted, you can still use the remaining ones. I use and recommend the per-project approach, so let's investigate it further.

Per-Project Audio Folders Setup

We'll begin with some prep work. Choose Preferences > File and then click on Audio Data. Check Always Copy Imported Audio Files. This is useful if, for example, you load a loop from a CD-ROM; SONAR copies that loop and makes it part of the project audio, so the audio is available even if the source CD-ROM isn't in the drive. Also check Use Per-Project Audio Folders, as that automatically sets up the file structure we want: a folder for the project containing the .CWP project file and an Audio subfolder that holds the audio used in the project (see Figure 36.1).

Figure 36.1
Check these two options to simplify saving and backup.

Now when you save, all audio goes into the audio folder, and when you call up the .CWP file, it knows to look in that folder for its audio. Note, however, that we still haven't taken care of what happens if a virtual instrument or plug-in used in this project is uninstalled or becomes incompatible prior to calling up the file in the future. I'll describe how to deal with this later.

You can easily verify that the project file setup is working properly and storing the right information. Choose Project > Audio Files to open a window that displays the file path for the project folder, the project file, and the audio folder. It also shows all files that are used in the project, along with their individual file path, bit depth, file size, and status (see Figure 36.2).

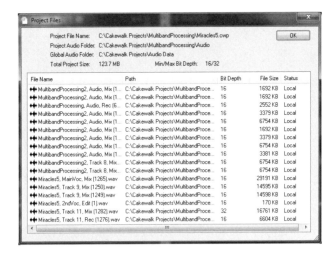

Figure 36.2
You can keep track of all the files in your project via the Project Files window.

All status entries should read "Local" because any audio from an external source should have been copied to the hard drive. If an entry doesn't show "Local," then you need to make sure Always Copy Imported Audio Files is checked, as described previously.

Backing Up Data from External MIDI Gear

When the MIDI specification was invented, although the intention was to create a "universal language" so all MIDI gear could communicate, it was also recognized that some gear would have unique features (such as particular patch formats) not covered by the general specification. So, the spec's designers created a "system exclusive" data type (also called SysEx or Sysx) with a header that identified the manufacturer. Thus, Roland gear knew to ignore messages intended for, say, Yamaha gear, but to pay attention to messages intended for Roland equipment.

One of the main uses of system exclusive data is to take a "snapshot" of the parameter values in an effect, instrument, or other MIDI gear. This could be of an individual preset, a complete bank of presets, or all parameters. Saving this data in some kind of memory and then sending it back into the device restores the selected parameter values.

If you're using external MIDI gear—multi-effects, controllers, or whatever—you'll want to save any of the presets you're using as part of your project. Fortunately, you can save Sysx data within a SONAR .CWP project file. This is extremely convenient, as you can then consolidate associated MIDI data with the rest of the project.

To get started, patch the MIDI device's MIDI out connector to your interface's MIDI in connector. This allows MIDI data to flow from the MIDI device into SONAR. Then, choose Preferences > MIDI. Click on Devices and make sure the appropriate MIDI interface input is enabled (checked). Also, click on Playback and Recording and, under Record, check System Exclusive (see Figure 36.3).

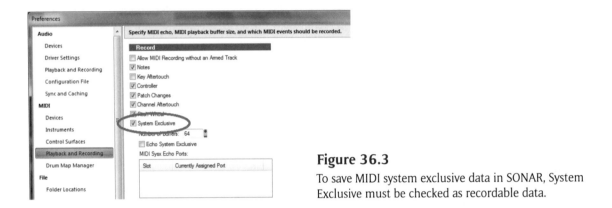

Figure 36.3

To save MIDI system exclusive data in SONAR, System Exclusive must be checked as recordable data.

Next, choose Views > Sysx, which brings up a window that shows 8,192 banks of Sysx. (That should be enough!) A bank could be anything from one program to a multi-effect's complete internal memory. To store Sysx data, choose File > Receive; a window will appear with a list of supported MIDI gear. If you see the device you want to back up, select it and click on OK to initiate the Sysx recording procedure. If the device isn't listed, select <You Start Dump on Instrument> and then click on OK (see Figure 36.4).

Figure 36.4

This composite illustration shows the Sysx recording process. Clicking OK in the Receive System Exclusive window opens up a Sysx Receive window (the lower, smaller window). When the Sysx dump is complete, this window's counter shows the number of bytes that were transferred. At the top, Auto Send On/Off has been checked so that whenever you open this project, it sends Sysx data to your MIDI gear.

If you don't know how to send Sysx data from your MIDI gear, you'll need to consult the manual. However, in some gear this is pretty intuitive—for example in the Alesis SR-16 drum machine, if you hit the Backup button, the Send Out MIDI (Press Play)? option appears. So if you press Play, the SR-16 transmits its backup data over the MIDI out connector. Initiating a dump (if needed) on the external MIDI device also initiates Sysx recording. A counter increments as SONAR receives the data; when it stops, the process is done.

After you click on Done, you'll probably want to name the Sysx bank. Highlight the bank and choose Edit > Name. Enter a name for the Sysx bank and then click on OK. If you're a truly advanced MIDI geek, you can even edit the Sysx data by highlighting the bank and, in the Sysx view Options menu, choosing Edit > Edit Data.

This Sysx data is saved with the project and available when you load it; however, you can choose File > Save and save the file independently. Although you can send a bank to a device manually by highlighting it and selecting File > Send (or Send All if you want to send all Sysx banks in a project), you can also set up automatic bank sending when you load the project—go to Settings and select Auto Send On/Off. You can direct this data to a particular MIDI port by choosing Settings > Output. However, if your interface has only one MIDI out connector, you needn't concern yourself with this, as SONAR will choose the right port automatically.

Auto-Save

SONAR can automatically back up .CWP files throughout the course of a project. To access this, go to Preferences (you'll need the Advanced Preferences pages, so if needed, click on the Advanced button in the Preferences window's lower left) and then go to the File heading and click on Advanced (see Figure 36.5).

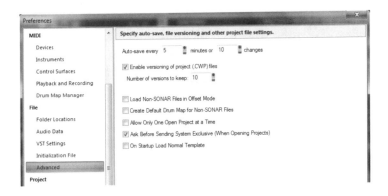

Figure 36.5

Auto-saving is very convenient if you're the kind of person who gets so involved in your work that you forget to save periodically.

You can specify auto-saving after a certain number of minutes have elapsed or after a certain number of changes have been made, but it's a good idea to do *versioning*—where SONAR saves successive versions of the project—as well. This is crucial so that if you make a change you didn't want to make, and SONAR saves that version, you can revert to a previous version. Because .CWP files aren't very large (typically a few megabytes for medium-sized projects), feel free to pile on the versions.

Backup Strategies

I'm frequently asked how often to back up. The answer is simple: whenever you have something you don't want to lose.

You need to be at least somewhat disciplined about backup. The first week of every month, I send a tweet reminding people to back up their data because that's when I do a major backup of my data. I've found that if you have a regular backup schedule, you're more likely to do it. Depending on how much data you generate, you might want to back up every couple of weeks, every week, or even every day.

Given the relatively low cost of mass storage, it's not expensive to buy a big external USB or FireWire drive and do a mass copy of what's on your music hard drive. (You do have a dedicated hard drive for your music projects, right? You don't want to keep everything on your system drive.) If you have lots of data, this can take several hours, so start the backup before watching a movie, eating dinner, going grocery shopping, and so on. When you return, your files will be backed up.

However, be aware that a hardware failure can happen at any time, not only right after backing up your data. (You should be so lucky!) So, buy a high-capacity (8 or 16 GB) USB thumb drive and leave it plugged into your music computer. At the end of the day, copy whatever you did that day to the USB drive. This will hold you over between the more complete, regularly scheduled backups.

Saving SONAR Customizations

If you want to retain all the SONAR customizations you've made—custom track icons, plug-in layouts from the Plug-In Manager, track templates, drum maps, and the like—you'll need to back these up. Otherwise, not only can there be a problem if your computer crashes, but reinstalling SONAR will likely return to the default settings.

Frankly, the way all of these are stored is somewhat confusing, mostly because of the way Windows 7 treats user data. To find out where all this data lives, call up Preferences and, under the File heading, click on Folder Locations (see Figure 36.6).

Some content folders are stored under C:\Cakewalk Content\SONAR X1 Producer, while others are stored under C:\Users\[user name]\AppData\Roaming\Cakewalk\SONAR X1 Producer. To make it easier to back up all these customizations, I moved the following folders from C:\Users\[user name]\AppData\Roaming\Cakewalk\SONAR X1 Producer to C:\Cakewalk Content\SONAR X1 Producer:

> ▷ Drum Maps

> ▷ Groove Quantize Files

> ▷ Plug-In Menu Layouts

> ▷ Sysx Files

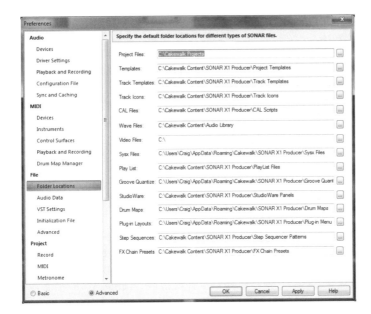

Figure 36.6
Find out where all your customizations are stored in the Folder Locations section of Preferences.

However, you're not finished yet. Return to Preferences and choose File > Folder Locations. (If SONAR mentions that it can't find data from the folders you moved, don't have SONAR browse for the folders—it usually takes less time to enter this data manually.) Click on the small Browse square in the Folder Locations page next to the data type (for example, Sysx Files), browse to C:\Cakewalk Content\SONAR X1 Producer\Sysx Files, and select the folder. SONAR now knows where to look for the Sysx files. Continue the same process for the Groove Quantize Files, Plug-In Menu Layouts, and Drum Maps folders.

Now all you need to do to back up your customizations is save the C:\Cakewalk Content\SONAR X1 Producer folder, which will fit on a CD-ROM or most USB sticks, unless you start loading it up with a huge amount of data.

If you're still using a pre-X1 version of SONAR, you can find the folder locations for various SONAR components by choosing Options > Global > Folders tab. Clicking on the square to the right of the folder field takes you to the folder.

Archiving SONAR Projects

One day you record you neighbor's kid as a favor, and you're surprised by how good he is. And you forget about it until 10 years later, when you see his debut CD has hit number one on the charts. Then you get a call from the Biography TV channel, saying that they're doing a profile on him and that he said you have the first song ever recorded with his band—is there any chance you could clean it up a bit for a special they're doing?

That may sound far-fetched, but the longer you stay in this business, the more you'll find a need to dig up your past. And when you do, you may be in for a rude surprise: plug-ins that don't load because you're using a newer, incompatible version or the old version isn't compatible with your current operating system or hardware—or maybe you used a virtual instrument that you uninstalled years ago and forgot about. Or maybe you archived on a hard drive that no longer spins up, or the project was done on a different platform before you switched to SONAR, and nothing will load it.

Well, there's backing up, but then there's archiving for the future. Here's how.

Virtual Instruments and Audio Files

The first rule of archiving: Render anything that's not audio (mainly virtual instruments) into a standard audio file. Of course, retain the MIDI file driving the instrument, but if for any reason you can't call up the virtual instrument, at least you'll have the audio. Another reason to do this is if your virtual instrument uses a specific library of samples, and for whatever reason that library is missing or in a location the instrument doesn't recognize. Note that if you're using a multi-timbral instrument, you'll need to render each part to its own track.

To render (bounce) a virtual instrument track—or even an external piece of hardware using the External Insert option or a hardware synth used as a plug-in—to audio:

1. Select a range in the timeline that you want to bounce. Start this from the project beginning, *even if nothing plays at the beginning.* Should you reconstruct this project later, you need to know where the audio clip sits in the project. If you *always* render from the beginning, you'll know to place the file at the project's start.

2. Select the instrument's audio track and accompanying MIDI track. To be safe, solo them (but note that soloing isn't sufficient—you need to *select* the tracks.) If the instrument is multi-timbral and has other parts, mute the MIDI tracks for the other parts.

3. For safety's sake, play the track through to make sure the master bus doesn't distort (otherwise, the distortion will be "baked into" the track) and that you're hearing the instrument part you want to bounce.

4. From the Track view Options menu, choose Tracks > Bounce to Track(s). The Transport must be stopped in order to do this. If you see a warning that there's no audio data, check to make sure that the instrument's audio track is selected.

5. When the Bounce to Track(s) window appears, choose the appropriate options. In most cases you'll want to check everything. The one exception is if you're using an external hardware processor or instrument. In that case, uncheck Fast Bounce, as you must bounce in real time.

6. Click on OK, and the audio will bounce to the new track.

Now do some housekeeping. Name the rendered track, including the word "bounced." I also suggest moving this into the instrument's track folder, above the MIDI file from which it was derived. Mute the audio track to remind you that this is a backup and to prevent "doubling" on playback.

Saving All Audio as Separate Tracks

The ultimate archive is to save all tracks as audio files, because no matter what happens in the future, odds are you'll be able to load a standard .WAV file. In this case, treat each track as a separate audio file that starts at the beginning of the song and extends for the duration of where there's audio. Here's the easiest way to do this kind of save.

1. Choose Select All (or press Ctrl+A). Then, from the Track view Options menu, choose Clips > Bounce to Clips. This will consolidate individual clips within a track into a single clip per track. However, note that this will not bounce virtual instruments to clips—you'll need to follow the procedure described earlier.

2. Extend the start of each clip to the beginning of the project by clicking on the edge and dragging to the left (see Figure 36.7).

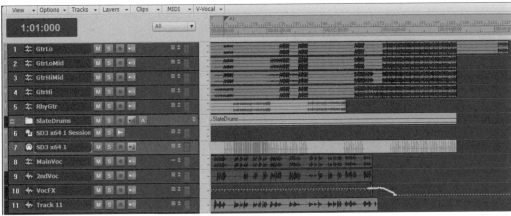

Figure 36.7
The top screen image shows the original project and its collection of clips. The lower image shows the same project after bouncing to clips and extending the start of the clips to the beginning of the project. Note that the Session Drummer 3 virtual instrument has not been bounced to audio.

3. Before doing anything else, name each clip unambiguously. To do this, open the Inspector, click on the Clip tab, and then click on the Track view clip you want to name. Enter a name in the Clip Name field (see Figure 36.8). If you ever need to reconstruct the project, you'll want to know what these clips represent.

Figure 36.8
Name the clips so you don't have to guess what they are someday.

4. As you've hopefully followed my advice about using per-project audio folders, the next step is to choose File > Save As. (Don't use Save, as you don't want to overwrite anything—the intention here is to save an archive of the project.) Check Copy All Audio with Project and also check Create One File per Clip, as the latter will save each track as its own audio file. I'd also recommend updating the .CWP file name, such as [filename]_bounced.cwp. This will save the modified project version along with the audio.

5. The bounced files will be saved in the project's Audio folder along with the original digital audio files. Create a folder for these that says Individual Tracks Archive and place the corresponding _bounced.cwp file in there as well.

If all else fails when you try to recover a project in the future, you can always import the complete tracks, and you'll at least be able to mix and process them.

Saving Processed Audio Files

Note that the aforementioned procedure saves the raw audio but ignores any automation moves or plug-in effects. This is good, because if someday you need to remix the song, you might want to use different automation or effects. However, you may have used some unique effect or particularly effective clip automation moves, and you'd rather have those included than just the raw audio. For this reason, I recommend saving two versions of the track files: one set of raw files and one set with all processing and automation applied. To do this and also apply clip automation, follow these steps:

1. Prior to doing a Save As, select all clips.

2. Choose Process > Apply Effect > Audio Effects.

3. All clip automation envelopes and effects changes will be made to the various tracks. This is a destructive process and may take a little bit if you have lots of tracks and effects.

4. Follow the procedure discussed earlier to save each individual track as an audio file.

If you want to apply envelope automation as well, then you'll need to bounce to track, as described in the "Virtual Instruments and Audio Files" section. In the dialog box that appears, make sure any automation options you want to apply are checked. The bounced track will incorporate these changes.

Cleaning Up Unused Files

Before signing off on a project's archive, it's worth deleting any unused files not just to save space, but also to avoid confusion at some later date. (What's this file called "Skeezix" doing here?) It's easy to build up a bunch of unused files if, for example, you do multiple vocal takes but then decide to get rid of all of them except the keepers. This could also happen if you import lots of loops into a project to compare them to loops that are already loaded, but then you delete most of the candidate loops. Because you imported the files, SONAR will dutifully copy them to the project's audio folder, where they'll stay—unless you use the Clean Audio Folder function. This scans the audio file folder of your choice and then presents a list of unused files you can delete.

To use this, choose Utilities > Clean Audio Folder. A dialog box will open that defaults to selecting the audio folder for the current project, which is probably what you want (see Figure 36.9).

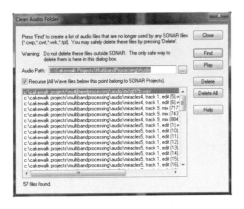

Figure 36.9
After clicking on Find, you'll see all folders that are in the project's audio data folder but not included in the project itself.

If this isn't the audio folder you want (highly unlikely), you can browse for the folder. Check Recurse to include subfolders within the project folder, although I can't envision a common scenario where you'd have these kinds of subfolders. Note that SONAR will ask whether you want to save the project first; you probably should, so that the listing of files is as up to date as possible.

Depending on how much local storage you have, compiling the list of unused files can take a long time because SONAR is considerate enough to check whether these files are used by any other projects. Once the list is compiled, you can delete individual files—or all of them—by clicking on Delete or Delete All, respectively.

Documenting the Archived Version

Now you're covered—you have the original SONAR project, but if all else fails, you have the virtual instrument tracks as audio, the raw audio tracks, and the processed audio tracks. But don't forget one other element: documentation.

Create a text file—preferably MS-DOS text, as almost any word processing program will be able to read it. Save this in the project folder. But while you're at it, copy the text and then choose Project > Info. Paste the text into the large text field and fill in the other info, too. That way you have documentation as text and within the SONAR file itself.

Archival Storage

This could be a whole chapter in itself, but let's avoid the temptation and hit the highlights.

Remember: Digital data isn't real unless it exists in more than one place, and preferably on different media. Big hard drives are so inexpensive that it's easy to archive your files on a drive, but if you do, remember that not only do hard drives fail, but also you need to spin them up to speed occasionally to keep the lubricants and other mechanical parts happy. For safety, also store on optical media (CD-R or DVD-R) and do only one project per disc. That way, if anything happens to the disc, you've lost only one project, not an entire collection. Also, optical media isn't failure-proof; save to two discs, preferably different media from different companies.

Flash USB sticks are also good for archival backup, but they don't last forever either, particularly if you do lots of writes and rewrites. So the lesson is clear: Whatever archival medium you use, periodically test the data to make sure it's readable. If one medium fails, take the alternate media you have and copy that so you still have (at least) two versions. "Refreshing" media is also a good idea. For example, I've taken many of my older CD-R backups and transferred them over to DVD-R but kept the originals. So now I not only have two sets of backups, but in two different formats—just in case.

MIDI Basics

MIDI REPRESENTS A WHOLE OTHER WAY to do recording that was initially adopted by keyboard players. The main difference compared to standard audio recording is that MIDI records and plays back data. When recording, MIDI translates performance gestures from a MIDI controller (which key on a MIDI keyboard is being hit and how hard, which drum pad is being hit with a MIDI drum controller, whether you're bending pitch with a MIDI guitar, which footswitch you hit with a MIDI pedalboard, and so on) into data. Your computer records this data, and on playback, sends the data to a MIDI-compatible sound generator. For example, if the MIDI data recorded that you played middle C on a keyboard, then it tells the sound generator to play middle C.

Chapter 26 describes the basics of MIDI guitar, but it's worth noting that SONAR has extensive MIDI capabilities that can record, edit, and play back MIDI data that's compatible with the included virtual instruments (such as Dimension Pro, TTS-1, Rapture LE, Session Drummer 3, and so on). Even if you're not good at playing keyboards, MIDI allows tricks such as slowing the tempo way down while you record your part and then speeding it back up on playback. MIDI can also quantize your MIDI data to a rhythmic "grid" so that even if your timing is shaky, notes will be placed on a rhythmic value you specify. For example, with a 16th-note grid, if you play a note just a little before or behind the beat, it will be moved to the nearest 16th note.

This appendix is intended to give the basics of how MIDI works, the most important highlights of this protocol, and how it relates to today's recording world. But first of all, don't let the term "Musical Instrument Digital Interface" throw you; just remember that the key word is "interface." MIDI's main purpose is to allow musical machines to communicate musical data to each other; stripped to its basics, you can think of MIDI as a catchall name for the process of sending control messages from one device (for example, a footswitch, keyboard, sequencer, and so on) to another device (in other words, a synthesizer). This can happen over a physical cable or within a computer.

How MIDI Recording Works

MIDI is a special-purpose computer language devoted to music. This language expresses various aspects of a musical performance, such as the notes that are played, their dynamics, and more.

For example, suppose you have a physical keyboard synthesizer that supports MIDI. The first thing it has to do is patch into a MIDI interface that communicates with your computer; otherwise, SONAR won't see the MIDI data. There are two main types of interface. One includes physical MIDI in and out connectors that hook up to hardware MIDI devices, such as keyboards and drum machines—for example, you would send a keyboard's MIDI output that sends MIDI data through a physical cable that patches to an interface's MIDI in, which receives that data (see Figure A.1).

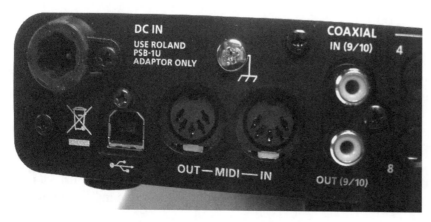

Figure A.1

Roland's Octa-Capture has physical MIDI in and MIDI out jacks. These have been standardized as using the 5-pin DIN format. If you patch a keyboard's MIDI out to the interface's MIDI in, the keyboard data can travel through the interface to your computer.

In addition to MIDI in and out connectors, you'll sometimes see a MIDI thru connector as well. This re-transmits the incoming data at the MIDI in, which you can then feed to another MIDI-compatible device. So for example, a master keyboard can feed one sound generator, and the sound generator's MIDI thru can feed another sound generator's MIDI in. This allows the keyboard to control two sound generators at the same time.

Some devices dispense with physical connectors and hook into your computer via USB (or more rarely, FireWire). MIDI data is sent and received over the USB line, so you don't need a special MIDI interface as long as your computer has a spare USB port. For example, Line 6's KB37 (see Figure A.2) is a combination keyboard/audio interface with a USB port. MIDI data from the keyboard travels over USB into the computer.

The kind of MIDI data a keyboard produces relates to what you play on the keyboard. If you play a C#4 note, then a piece of data will exit the MIDI out that says the computer equivalent of "a C#4 has just been played." When you release the note, another piece of data will say, "C#4 has just been released." If you hit the note really hard or really soft, another piece of data will indicate those dynamics.

Figure A.2
Many companies make MIDI controllers that connect directly to your computer via USB.
The KB37, while an older unit, remains popular because it comprises an audio interface,
keyboard, mic, and instrument inputs, and it bundles Line 6's amp/effects simulation plug-ins.

After recording this string of data into SONAR, if you play this data back into your keyboard synthesizer, it
will reproduce the performance exactly as you performed it. This is very much like a modern version of the
player piano, except instead of punching holes into paper, you're "punching" data into a SONAR MIDI track.

The MIDI protocol is about far more than just notes, though. As described later, there are also commands that
relate to timing, synchronizing, changing sounds, altering effects parameters, and more. In SONAR, MIDI and
audio tracks look similar, but they have very different characteristics because MIDI works with data instead of
audio (see Figure A.3). For example, both tracks offer the option to use plug-ins, but MIDI plug-ins can't be
used in audio tracks and vice versa.

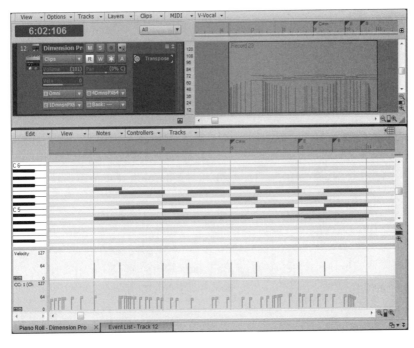

Figure A.3
The Clips pane shows an overview of a MIDI clip, which is shown in more detail in the Multidock Piano Roll view.
The rectangular bars indicate notes, the Velocity lane below shows the dynamics of the notes that were played,
and the CC lane at the bottom displays the controller messages being generated by the mod wheel controller.
Note that a MIDI plug-in, Transpose, is inserted in the MIDI track's FX Bin.

Advantages of Recording MIDI Data Instead of Audio

If you have a synthesizer, why not just record its audio into SONAR? You certainly can, but there are several advantages to recording MIDI data.

The primary advantage is editability. You can change a MIDI note's pitch, dynamics, start time—just about any aspect of the note. This makes it very easy to correct mistakes; if you hit a couple wrong notes, just change the pitch. It's very difficult to do something like change one note inside a chord when dealing with audio, but with MIDI, it's easy. What's more, with SONAR you can do this graphically by just, say, grabbing a note and extending its length or moving it up or down on a grid to change pitch. However, if you want to geek out and edit with a great deal of precision, you can get a numeric list of all data associated with a note and type in new values.

Another advantage is being able to change an instrument's sound, because all you need to do to change the sound is send the MIDI data to a different instrument. And when writing a song, MIDI-driven tracks handle pitch transposition and tempo changes far better than digital audio can, because you're just changing the data being fed to notes—not the timbral quality of the notes themselves. (Granted, DSP-based pitch stretching for audio is getting pretty clean, to the point where with small changes, you might not even notice any difference. But MIDI still handles this sort of task better.)

As a result, using MIDI instruments is great when you're writing a song and it first begins to take shape. You can experiment with different keys and tempos without having to re-record or stretch anything—just invoke the pitch transposition and tempo change options as needed. After the song has settled down, you can then replace the MIDI scratch tracks with digital audio tracks from piano, guitar, and so on. Then again, with virtual instruments sounding so good these days, maybe all you'll really need to do is tweak the MIDI instrument tracks a bit.

The MIDI Language

MIDI groups information in multi-byte "sentences" or "messages" of one or more "words." There are two types of MIDI words:

> ▷ *Status* words, which identify a particular function, such as note-on, note-off, pitch wheel change, and so on.

> ▷ *Data* words, which give data on the function identified by the status word, such as which note is on and how much the pitch wheel has changed.

We don't really need to investigate this further; there are plenty of printed and online references regarding MIDI. Besides, you can use MIDI without knowing the nuts and bolts—just like you can drive a car without knowing how fuel injection works.

However, we do need to cover one more crucial concept: MIDI channels and MIDI modes, because MIDI can send and receive data over 16 different virtual channels. Each channel can carry unique data and drive its own polyphonic MIDI instrument. In the case of SONAR sending data to a physical keyboard over MIDI, you might wonder how MIDI can transmit 16 different channels over a single MIDI cable—after all, to send 16 different audio signals somewhere, you would need 16 different audio cables.

But remember that MIDI transmits information, not audio. Also, it sends this data serially—in other words, each individual piece of information is sent consecutively. If we "tag" each piece of data with a channel identification number (ID), then we can program a particular MIDI instrument to look only for data that has a particular channel ID.

A good analogy would be sorting mail by zip code. Imagine a conveyor belt where each piece of mail goes past a mail sorter, one piece of mail at a time. As each letter goes by, it's scanned for its zip code, and letters are sorted into individual piles according to their zip codes. MIDI works similarly. Each instrument monitors the MIDI data stream (analogous to the mail going past on the conveyor belt), and when an instrument detects data with the same channel ID number as the channel for which the instrument is programmed, it acts on that information. For example, if a note-on message is sent over Channel 1, only those synthesizers tuned to Channel 1 will receive this note-on command; devices tuned to other channels will ignore the data. This situation is also analogous to television, where your TV receiver selects a particular channel for viewing out of the many signals coming down the antenna or cable line.

One of SONAR's great features is that it can load virtual software instruments that react the same way as a physical instrument. As with physical instruments, you can assign these to particular channels and have particular SONAR tracks send data to specific instruments. What's more, some instruments—such as the TTS-1— can receive information relating to more than one channel, known as *multi-timbral* operation. For example, the TTS-1 might have a piano sound loaded in Channel 1, a bass sound in Channel 2, a brass section in Channel 3, and so on. This allows a single instrument to produce a variety of sounds.

Virtual instruments have evolved so much that some musicians don't even buy physical synthesizers anymore; they just get a keyboard controller that produces MIDI data but no sounds and use that to trigger virtual instruments.

In addition to channel data, there are also two main MIDI modes that determine how devices respond to channelized data.

 ▷ Omni mode accepts data coming in over any channel. In other words, regardless of the channel ID, an instrument or track in Omni mode will attempt to act on any incoming data. This is handy if your MIDI keyboard transmits over a specific channel and you want it to trigger a synth, but you can't remember the channel it's transmitting on. Rather than dig into the synth assignments, you can just set the synth to Omni mode, and it will react to whatever the keyboard is transmitting.

 ▷ A receiver in Poly mode will be set to one of the 16 MIDI channels and receive only messages intended for that channel. Thus, two MIDI receivers set to receive different channels could be monitoring the same data stream but be controlled independently of each other. For example, with the TTS-1, Channel 10 might be assigned to drums and Channel 1 to piano. If a SONAR track outputs on Channel 1, its data will trigger piano sounds. But if you change the output to Channel 10, its data will trigger drum sounds.

MIDI Ports

When MIDI was invented, hardware synthesizers were expensive and relatively large, so 16 channels seemed like a reasonable number—those who could afford 16 synthesizers, let alone actually use them, were in a distinct minority. However, it became clear this wasn't enough when multi-timbral synths were introduced, as they could accept data over all 16 channels.

As a result, interfaces were introduced with several MIDI ports, each of which could carry 16 channels. For example, an interface with four ports could deliver data on 4 × 16 = 64 MIDI channels. This became increasingly important as MIDI was expanded to do more than just play synthesizers, such as trigger lighting, change signal processor sounds, and even set off pyrotechnics (really!).

Program Changes

So far we've talked primarily about MIDI note messages, but there are many other types of MIDI data. For example, program changes allow changing an instrument sound (and sometimes multi-effects presets, too) on the fly, even in the middle of a phrase if necessary. This of course assumes the target device responds to program changes. When the MIDI spec was drawn up, provisions were made for 128 MIDI program change messages. This is why many signal processors offer 128 programs. As usual, people wanted more—so an addition to the MIDI spec, Bank Select messages, can select up to 16,384 banks of 128 programs for a grand total of more than 2,000,000 programs. (That should hold you for a while.)

For example, suppose you're adding percussion to a song, and you want tambourine in one section and shaker in another. Instead of inserting two instruments on two tracks, you can just insert one and use program changes to determine when the instrument plays back a tambourine sound and when it plays back a shaker sound.

MIDI Controllers: The Key to Greater Expressiveness

Changing from one program to another is a good start, but sometimes you'd like to vary a particular parameter within an individual program (delay feedback, filter frequency, distortion drive, and so on). A wah-wah sound is a good example of changing a particular parameter (filter frequency) in real time, and thankfully, the powers behind MIDI recognized early on that just playing notes was b-o-r-i-n-g—and thus controller messages became part of the MIDI spec. Think about what happens when you play an acoustic instrument: There's incredible complexity to the sound, whether it's a vibrating string or a blown reed, that changes over time according to performance gestures. Hitting a string or a drum head harder doesn't just make it louder, but it often increases brightness and alters pitch slightly.

The idea of continuous controllers came about because synthesizers have pedals, knobs, levers, and other physical "controllers" that alter some aspect of a synth's sound over a continuous range of values. This is why they're called *continuous* controllers, as opposed to a controller such as an on-off switch, which only selects between two possible values; see Figure A.4. Non-keyboard musicians can use other controllers, such as footpedals or data entered into a sequencer, to alter some aspect of a signal processor's sound.

Unlike a program change, which is a single event, continuous controllers generate a series of events, such as a volume fade-in (each event raises the volume a bit more than the previous event) or a change in some other parameter (for example, increasing chorus depth or altering the wah-wah filter frequency).

Like program changes, continuous controller messages are transmitted over a MIDI output and received by a MIDI input. The transmitter usually digitizes the physical controller motion into 128 discrete values (0 to 127). As one example, consider a footpedal that generates continuous controller messages. Pulling the pedal all the way back typically generates a value of 0. Pushing down on the pedal increases the value until at midpoint, when the pedal generates a value of 64. Continuing to push on the pedal until it's all the way down generates a value of 127 (see Figure A.5).

Figure A.4

Roland's Fantom-G synthesizer has (among other controllers) eight sliders and, above them, four knobs. While these can alter synthesizer parameters, they also generate MIDI continuous controller messages you can record into SONAR and apply to anything you'd like—for example, you might want a slider to control the frequency of a wah-wah effect.

Figure A.5

The rear of the Fantom-G includes not only MIDI connectors (on the left), but also jacks for two control pedals and a hold footswitch.

Note that continuous controller transmitters only send messages reflecting a change; for example, leaving a pedal in one position doesn't transmit any messages until you change the pedal's physical position.

Continuous Controller Numbers

MIDI "tags" each continuous controller message with an ID from 0 to 127. Don't confuse this with channel IDs; each channel can support up to 128 controllers, so something like a Controller 7 message appearing over Channel 2 is independent from a Controller 7 message appearing over Channel 3. Therefore, a signal processor with 100 different parameters could have each assigned to a unique controller number (1 for delay time, 2 for delay feedback, 3 for delay wet/dry mix, and so on).

When controlling a parameter via continuous controllers, the basic idea is to assign a particular parameter (echo mix, filter cutoff, envelope attack, and so on) to a particular continuous controller number. Then all you need is to record continuous controller messages in the track driving the target parameter.

At the receiving end, the parameter being controlled changes in response to incoming message values. For example, if you're controlling wah-wah filter frequency, and it receives a value of 0, the wah-wah filter frequency is at minimum. When it receives a value of 64, the filter might be equivalent to the pedal being halfway up, and upon receiving a value of 127, the filter might be at the setting of having the pedal pushed all the way down. The reason for saying "might be" is that some signal processors let you scale and/or invert the values, as explained later.

Here are some other examples. If a device's level parameter is assigned to Controller 7, and a footpedal can generate Controller 7, hook the pedal's MIDI out to the device's MIDI in, and your pedal will control level (provided that both are set to the same channel, of course). If you assign the chorus depth parameter to Controller 12 and then set the pedal to generate Controller 12 data, the pedal will vary chorus depth.

In many cases, you can assign several parameters to the same controller number so that, for example, a single pedal motion could increase the level and reverberation time and raise the filter cutoff frequency.

Other Control Message Options

In addition to responding to continuous controllers, some synths and effects respond to other MIDI control messages. None of these has a controller number, as each is deemed important enough to be its own distinct class of message.

▷ **Pitch bend.** Most synthesizers have some type of modulation wheel or lever that allows for bending note pitch (the keyboard equivalent of bending a string).

▷ **Velocity.** This indicates the dynamics of playing a keyboard by measuring how long it takes for a key to go from full up to full down. The assumption is that the longer it takes for a key to go down, the more softly it's being played.

▷ **Pressure (also called Aftertouch).** After a keyboard key is down, pressing on the key produces an additional pressure message. A common application is to use this to introduce vibrato to a sound that's being sustained or to change a sound's tone (for example, make it brighter).

How Parameters Handle Controller Value Changes

There are several ways that differing virtual instruments and processors decide how continuous controllers will "take over" from a preprogrammed setting. One approach is to add to (or subtract from) the programmed setting; usually scaling and inversion parameters will be available.

Scaling determines how far the parameter can vary from the programmed setting in response to a given amount of controller change. Inversion sets whether increasing controller values will increase (+ scaling) or decrease (– scaling) the parameter value. Often these are combined into one number, such as +50 (which represents 50% scaling of full value in a positive direction), –37 (37% scaling of full value in a negative direction), and so on.

Figure A.6 shows an example of an input control signal scaled to +100, +50, and –100. Each one covers a different range of the available parameter values. Greater controller amplitudes increase or decrease the programmed parameter value, depending on whether the polarity is positive (+) or inverted (–).

If you encounter a situation where the continuous controller messages don't change a parameter very much, check the programmed value of the parameter being controlled. If its value is close to minimum or maximum, there may not be enough headroom for the controller to make much difference, especially with scaling close to 100%.

Another design approach is to simply have the parameter follow the incoming controller value. An incoming controller value of 0 would set the parameter to its minimum value, and 127 to its maximum. Because the parameter will jump to whatever value the controller is generating, this is called *jump* mode.

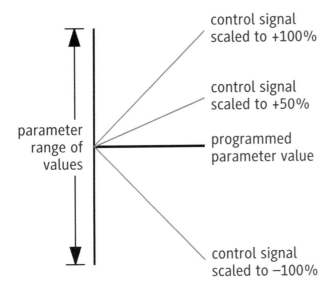

control signal
scaled to +100%

control signal
scaled to +50%

parameter
range of
values

programmed
parameter value

control signal
scaled to −100%

Figure A.6
Controller scaling and inversion affects the
degree to which the receiver responds to
continuous controller messages.

Yet another method will not let parameters respond to continuous controllers until the controller passes
through the preprogrammed value, at which point the parameter follows the controller messages (called
match mode). This is helpful when switching between programs where a controller is programmed to control
different parameters. The parameter will stay as originally programmed until you start using the pedal and go
past the existing setting.

Summary: Assigning Continuous Controllers in a Nutshell

To recap, here's how to assign controllers. We'll use a keyboard's mod wheel as an example of a typical
transmitter, but the same concepts apply to controller data in a SONAR MIDI track or even something like
a footpedal.

1. Set the mod wheel to the same MIDI channel (1–16) as the target parameter you want to control.

2. Assign the parameter you want to control to the desired controller number. The mod wheel
    controller number is fixed as Controller 1, so you'd set the parameter to respond to Controller 1.

3. If you're not using a mod wheel but some other non-standardized hardware controller, you'd need
    to program the hardware controller to the controller number that matches what you programmed
    in the previous step.

4. Adjust the controller amplitude (how much the sound is affected when you move the controller)
    and scaling (whether increasing the controller's position increases or decreases the parameter value).

MIDI Inside the Computer

You may have heard complaints about MIDI being slow or having timing delays. But this is an issue only
when the computer is driving outboard MIDI gear through a MIDI interface, because MIDI is a serial protocol
where a new piece of data gets transmitted every millisecond or so. Furthermore, the instrument or sound
generator takes some time to react to this data. When a computer sends MIDI to an external sound module,
the data has to exit through a port, be scanned by the keyboard, be interpreted, and be turned into a sound.

Fortunately, this is rarely an issue with today's keyboards, which have far more processing power onboard than early MIDI gear.

With virtual instruments, MIDI data flies around inside the computer, and timing is extremely tight. With outboard gear, sending lots of controller data can "choke" the data stream; with native MIDI devices, it takes a lot to bog down a fast processor. Bottom line: If you need tight timing, virtual MIDI instruments are pretty close to perfect.

However, even today's computers have limits, and playing back lots of notes simultaneously puts a lot of demands on your CPU. Therefore, you still want to avoid stressing your computer unnecessarily. If you do start running out of CPU power, SONAR offers a function called *freezing* that records the virtual instrument output as audio and disconnects the instrument itself from the computer so it no longer places a load on the computer's CPU. (Audio tracks stress a computer far less than virtual instruments.) Freezing is reversible if you want to edit your instrument part. For more information on freezing, see SONAR's online help.

Another way to conserve power is to avoiding recording unneeded data. In SONAR, choose Edit > Preferences and under MIDI Playback and Recording, uncheck data you don't want recorded in the Record section (see Figure A.7).

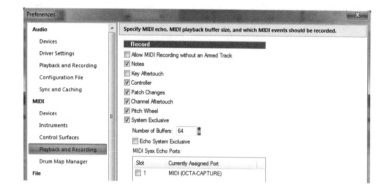

Figure A.7

In SONAR, you can choose the type of MIDI data you want to record.

The most resource-hungry data is Key Aftertouch (note that it's unchecked in the screen shot), which generates a controller whose value depends on how hard you press a key; each key produces its own data. Channel Aftertouch is similar, but the value reflects the highest value of any key that's held down, not each key, so it requires much less data. If you're using a master keyboard with aftertouch to trigger a soft synth sound that responds to aftertouch, by all means, record the aftertouch data. Otherwise, filter it out because it takes up a lot of MIDI bandwidth. Note that if you record any data inadvertently, you can always erase it later regardless.

Index

analog-to-digital converters, 11
architecture (amps), 73
archiving, 263–267
ASCII (exporting tablature), 199
ASIO preferences, 30
assigning ACT effects, 128–129
audio
    MIDI recording comparison, 272
    interfaces
        direct monitoring, 23
        ExpressCard, 20–21
        external, 17–19, 21–22
        FireWire, 22
        guitar processors, 19–20
        laptops, 20–21
        overview, 17
        PCI/PCIe cards, 18–19
        PCMCIA, 20–21
        tips, 23–24
        zero-latency monitoring, 23
        USB, 21–22
    preferences
        amp sims, 29
        ASIO, 30
        devices, 25–27
        drivers, 27–31
        milliseconds, 31
        mixing latency, 29–31
        playback, 27–28
        recording, 27–28
        sample rates, 29
        samples, 31
        streaming data, 31
        troubleshooting, 31
        WDM/KS, 30–31
automation
    mixing
        clips, 114–115
        controls, 108–110
        Edit Filter, 110–111
        envelopes, 110–114
        MIDI controllers, 115–116
        overview, 107–108
        snapshots, 116
    plug-ins (controls), 109
auto-saving, 261

B

background (effects chains), 70
backing drum tracks. *See also*
    percussion
    creating, 253
    editing, 253–254
    looping, 253
    overview, 251–253
    tips, 254–256
backups
    archiving, 263–267
    auto-saving, 261
    creating, 258
    customizing, 262–263
    folders, 258–259
    MIDI hardware, 259–261
    overview, 257–258
    tips, 262
Bins
    effects
        bypassing, 55–56
        Clip FX Bins, 57
        context menu, 56–57
        path delay compensation, 56
        viewing, 55
    overview, 55
Boost 11, 157–158
busses
    creating, 49–51
    effects busses, 48–49
    faders, 52
    levels, 52
    master busses, 47
    MIDI, 52
    multiple, 51–52
    Send Assistant, 51
    solo busses, 52
    subgroup busses, 47–48
buttons (headers), 140
bypassing effects (Bins), 55–56

C

chains (effects), 57
channel strips
    overview, 169
    ProChannel
        compatibility, 175

        compressors, 172–173
        dynamics, 172
        equalizer, 169–171
        overview, 169
        routing, 174–175
        saturation, 173–174
    VC-64
        compressors, 183
        de-esser, 183
        equalizers, 183–184
        gate, 182–183
        overview, 182
        psychedelic sound, 187
        routing, 184–188
        saving, 188
        sidechain compression,
            186–187, 219
        stereo, 186
    VX-64 percussion strip
        compressors, 181
        delay, 181
        dynamics, 181
        equalizer, 178–179
        overview, 177–178
        routing, 181–182
        saturation, 178
        Shaper, 179–181
    VX-64 vocal strip, 175–177
checklists. *See* tips
chopping (sidechaining), 218–219
chorus
    Multivoice Chorus/Flanger, 167
    Sonitus effects (Modulator),
        167–168
Classic Phaser, 165
clean channels (effects chains),
    70–71
cleanup (composite recording), 105
clip effects, 54
Clip FX Bins, 57
clips (mixing), 114–115
cloning (Sonitus effects
    Multiband), 234–235
colors (effects chains), 70
combining physical and virtual
    amps, 37–38
compatibility (ProChannel), 175
composite recording
    advantages, 101–102
    cleanup, 105